UNLEASH THE POWER OF
Adobe® Dreamweaver® CS6

Marek Mularczyk

www.SaiTraining.co.uk

Unleash the Power of Adobe Dreamweaver CS6.

Published by Sai Training

ISBN - 978-0-9571214-5-4 (Paperback)
ISBN - 978-0-9571214-6-1 (PDF)

The author assumes no responsibility or liability for any errors that may appear in the content
of this book.

Adobe, Photoshop, Fireworks, and Dreamweaver are registered trademarks of Adobe Systems
Incorporated in the United States and/or other countries.

THIS PRODUCT IS NOT ENDORSED OR SPONSORED BY ADOBE SYSTEMS
INCORPORATED, PUBLISHER OF DREAMWEAVER.

Windows is a registered trademark of Microsoft Corporation in the United States and/or
other countries.

Mac is a registered trademark of Apple Inc. in the United States and/or other countries.

www.saitraining.co.uk
www.marekmularczyk.com

Table of Contents

Introduction

1 Introducing Dreamweaver CS6

Explore Dreamweaver Interface	19
Dreamweaver's panels	20
Working with Workspaces	23
Welcome screen	30
Working with Documents	32
How websites work	33
Domain Names and Servers	34

2 HTML and CSS Basics

Basic HTML Structure	39
Creating HTML pages in Dreamweaver	43
What is CSS?	50
Formatting pages with CSS	51

3 Quick Start - Set Up a Website

Set Up a new Dreamweaver Site   58

Create your first Web Page   61

Dreamweaver's CSS Starter pages   63

Responsive web design   64

DocType (Document Type declaration)   66

Naming conventions for pages   68

Add Metadata   72

4 Create a Page Layout

Your audience   82

Wireframing   84

Code Navigator   92

Add text based menu   94

Modify the footer with CSS   99

Wrap text around an image   102

5 Working with Text, Tables and CSS

Headings and Paragraphs   106

Fonts on web pages   111

Web fonts   112

Use Web Fonts   113

Add text from other sources   117

Create Ordered/Unordered Lists   119

Add Tables   121

6 Images

Basics of Images on the web	128
Differentiate File Formats	131
Add Images to the web pages	132
Use Assets panel	140
Import images using Adobe Bridge	144
Import images from Photoshop and Fireworks	147
Use Photoshop Smart Objects	149
Edit images with Dreamweaver	154

7 CSS and Navigation

Hyperlinks	162
Create Internal links	165
Create links to external websites	168
Live Google Map with Widget Browser	170
Set up e-mail links	176
Insert drop-down menu using Spry	179
Customise drop-down menu with CSS	183
Pseudoclasses	186

8 Dreamweaver Templates

Dreamweaver templates	190
Create editable regions	192
Create new pages from Template	195
Update Dreamweaver Templates	202

9 Mastering CSS

CSS Refresher 206

Internal or External stylesheet? 206

Customise links with Pseudo-classes 211

CSS Box Model 214

Multiscreen Preview for Mobile Devices 219

10 Sound and Video

Media on web pages 224

Adding Sounds 225

Adding Flash animations 231

Adding Flash Videos 234

Embed videos from YouTube 237

11 Spry

What is Spry? 242

Spry Accordion 243

Customise Spry Accordion with CSS 248

Spry tabbed panels 252

Spry effects 256

12 Forms

Online Forms	262
Text Form elements	265
Process form with PHP	280

13 Publish your website

Define a remote site	286
Uploading your site	291

14 The Future of the Web - CSS 3

CSS3 Borders	299
CSS3 Backgrounds	304
CSS3 Text Effects	306

Introduction

Adobe Dreamweaver has quickly become an industry standard in web authoring. Professional and non-professional web designers harness the power of Dreamweaver in their everyday workflow. One of the reasons for Dreamweaver's popularity is the richness of tools for quick design of web pages. It also offers a number of professional tools for professional web designers as well as enthusiasts.

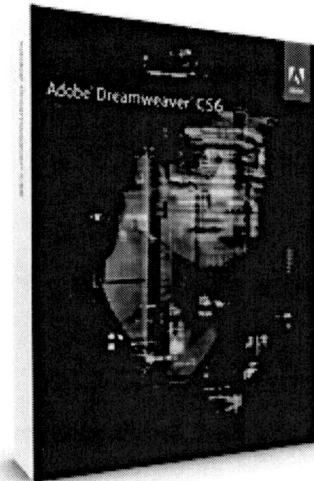

The way this book is created is so that you can follow at your own pace. It is composed of a number of lessons that you can do one at a time or, if you have used Dreamweaver before, you can pick up the book and do the lesson you are interested in. The book was created with beginners as well as existing Dreamweaver users in mind. If you haven't used Dreamweaver before, you will find out how easy it is to use it for creating web pages this is one of many reasons why Dreamweaver became so popular). If you have used Dreamweaver, I hope you will find something interesting for you as well. If you have used previous versions of Dreamweaver, this book will get you quickly up to speed with new features in Dreamweaver CS6.

As mentioned earlier, if you have used Dreamweaver before, you can skip some lessons and jump straight into the lessons you are interested in. If you are new to Dreamweaver, I encourage you to follow the lessons in order starting from Lesson 1. The way the book is structured, each new lesson builds on what you have learnt in previous lessons as well as it introduces new concepts and new techniques.

Before you start

Before you start, here's what you need to know:

- this book doesn't require any knowledge of Dreamweaver

- it does require some knowledge of your operating system

- Dreamweaver works in the same way on both platforms: Windows and Mac OS, so you can use them interchangeably on both platforms

- you need to know how to operate your computer/your operating system

- you need to know how to use menus in Dreamweaver, open/save files

Installing Dreamweaver

Before you start, you need to install Dreamweaver. Dreamweaver can be purchased from Adobe. You can also download a 30-day trial of Dreamweaver CS6, so you can give it a try before you purchase it. For more details go to Adobe website: *http://www.adobe.com*.
As well as purchasing Dreamweaver as a boxed product, you can purchase a subscription to Dreamweaver. More details on Adobe website, just follow the link above.

Dreamweaver comes as a stand-alone application as well as part of Creative Suite, so can be purchased with some of Creative Suite editions.

Working with the lessons

This book comes with exercise files so that you can follow along. The files can be accessed from this website:

http://goo.gl/qgNhz

Download the files, extract them and copy them onto your computer to your preferred location. During the exercises I'm going to keep the files on my desktop as an example.

Keep Dreamweaver updated

Dreamweaver gets updates from time to time and all the updates are free to download and install. Keep your copy of Dreamweaver updated so you don't miss on any exciting new features!

Here's how you can check for any available updates:

In Dreamweaver, choose **Help > Updates** as shown below:

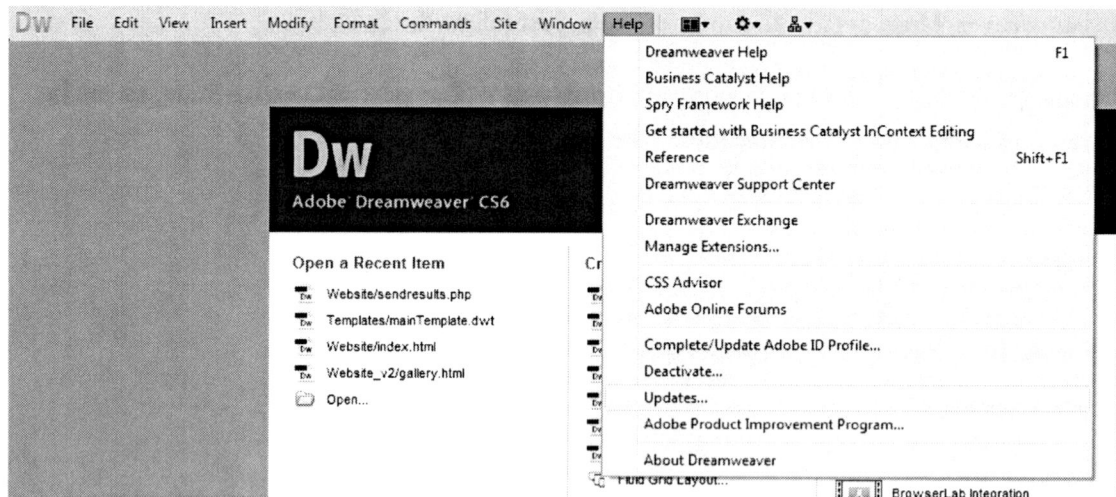

Adobe Updater will open and check if there are any available updates.

If there are any updates you want to install, select them and click Download and Install updates.

This will install the updates for you. The installation process is very easy.

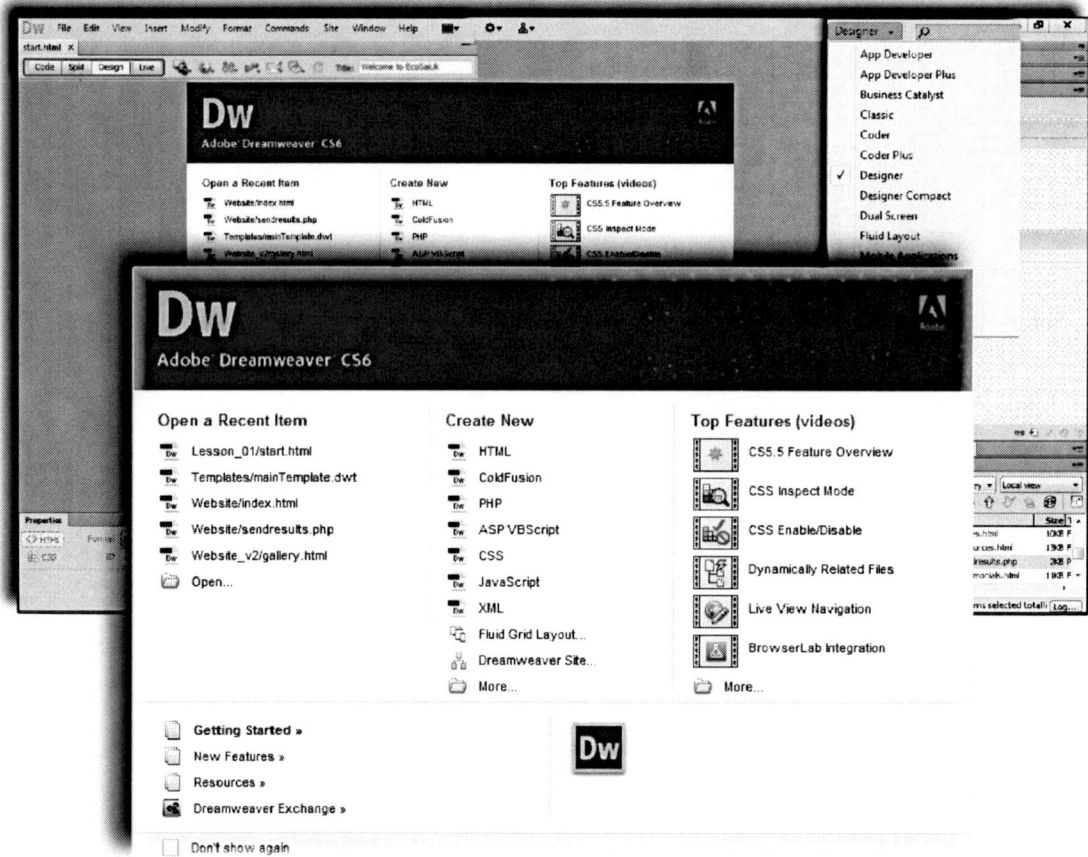

Lesson 1

Introducing Dreamweaver CS6

In this lesson you're going to familiarize yourself with Dreamweaver CS6 and learn how to:

- Explore Dreamweaver interface

- Work with panels

- Use Welcome Screen

- Create, open and save documents

- Learn how websites work

This lesson will take about 45 minutes to complete.

Why Adobe Dreamweaver CS6?

Adobe Dreamweaver CS6 is an industry standard HTML editor (even though it is not just HTML you can work with in Dreamweaver). One of the many reasons behind popularity of Dreamweaver is its incredible set of tools for coders and designers alike. And it's not just a tool for professionals, it's a great tool for beginners as well.

Dreamweaver users could be categorised into two groups:

*   Web designers – they love WYSIWYG functionality (What You See Is What You Get), fantastic for adding content. It saves them many hours that they would spend previewing pages they create in web browsers. It is very easy to use so even beginners (or maybe especially beginners) will appreciate how quick and easy it is to build web pages and add content.

*   Web developers (coders) – they love enhancements built into the Code View in Dreamweaver, with support for PHP, ASP, ColdFusion, and JavaScript.

Another reason why Dreamweaver is so popular and why web designers and developers make it their obvious choice is its simplicity in taking the site from a concept stage to the launch of the website. And all of that is achieved with its built-in FTP functionality used to upload a website to the web server straight from within Dreamweaver! (I use it all the time).

At the same time, Dreamweaver is very easy to use and it has a very intuitive interface. This makes it easy to use by professionals and beginners alike. Beginners are pleasantly surprised when they find out how easy it is to start building web pages with Dreamweaver.

Explore Dreamweaver Interface

Start by exploring Dreamweaver interface. Dreamweaver interface features a number of panels and toolbars that are easy to find and customise. It amazes me that such a powerful and professional application, offering so much within its' interface, provides a number of options to rearrange, minimise, and maximise panels.

1 Start by opening Dreamweaver.

Here's Dreamweaver CS6 interface:

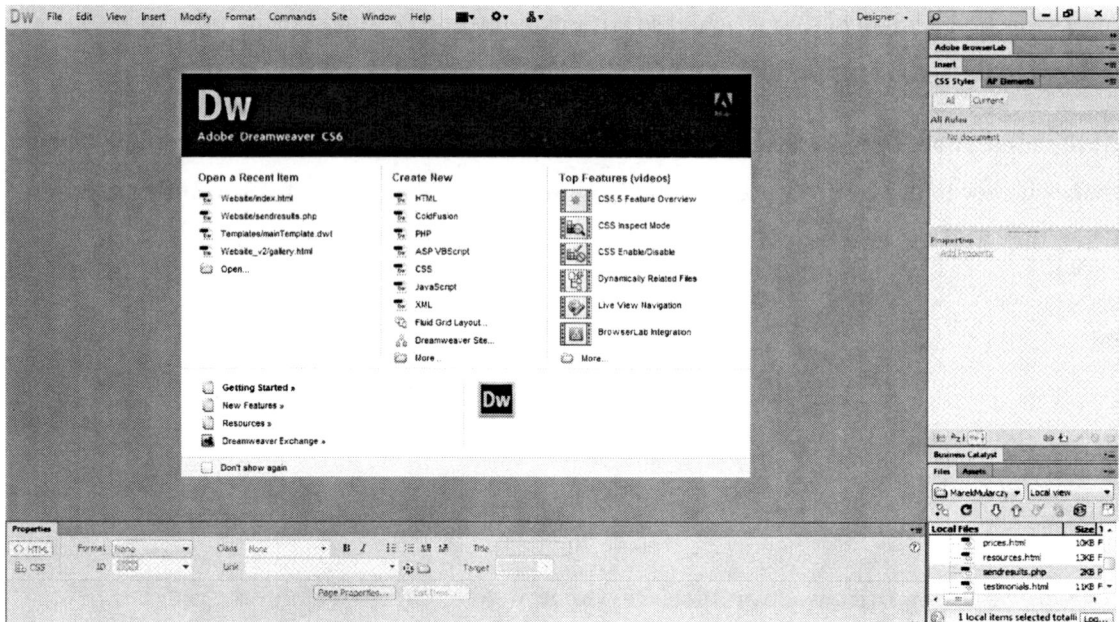

2 When Dreamweaver opens, choose **File > Open** and if you copied the exercise files to your computer, then navigate to the folder Lesson_01 and choose **index.html**. Open it.

Dreamweaver's panels

Dreamweaver's panels are a powerful feature of Dreamweaver (and other Adobe applications). You will be working with the panels all the time, so it will be useful that you get to know the panels, how they work, and how to use them.

As you look on the Dreamweaver's interface, you'll find panels on the right hand side and on the bottom of the application window as shown on the screenshot below (panels circled in red):

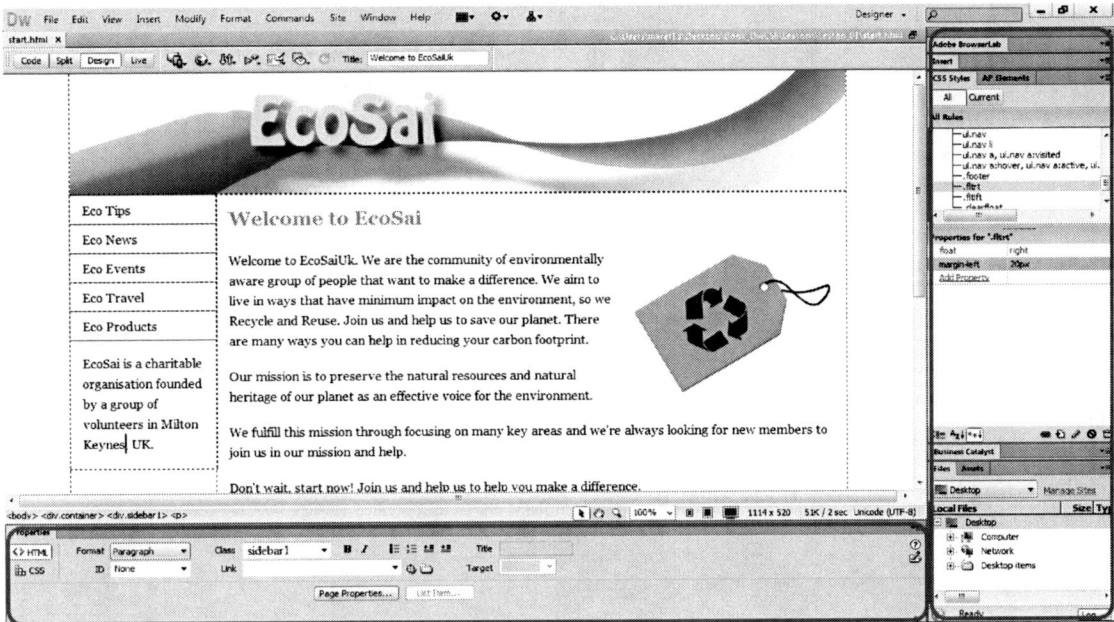

The panels in Dreamweaver make it easy for you to insert content on the web pages and edit pages as well. The Insert panel, as an example, is used for inserting content on the pages and Dreamweaver adds all required code for you. The commands in the Insert panel can also be found in the menu under Insert as shown on the screenshot on the next page.

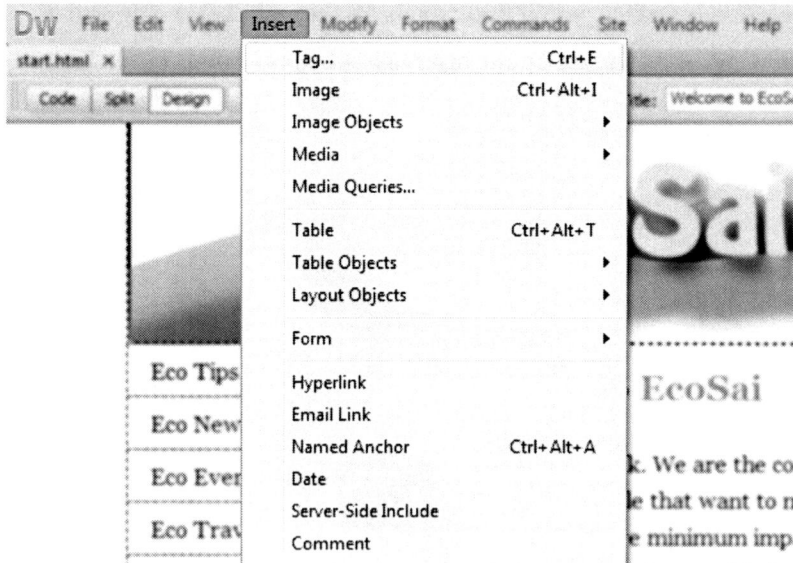

All panels in Dreamweaver can be found under Window menu. If you look under Window, you're going to see a check mark next to every panel that is currently open:

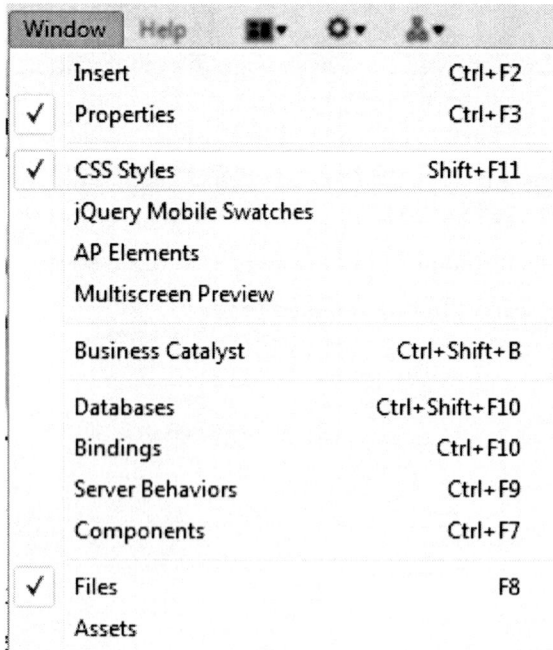

If the panel is open, but it appears behind another panel, it won't have a check mark next to its name. To bring it to front, select the panel from the Window menu.

Each individual panel can easily be resized, minimised and expanded. It's a very useful feature that is often used to assign more screen estate for some panels and less for other panels. To minimise a panel, if it's open, double-click on its name on the tab. Double-click on the name of the panel again to maximise it.

The screenshot below shows an open panel (on the left) and minimised panel (on the right):

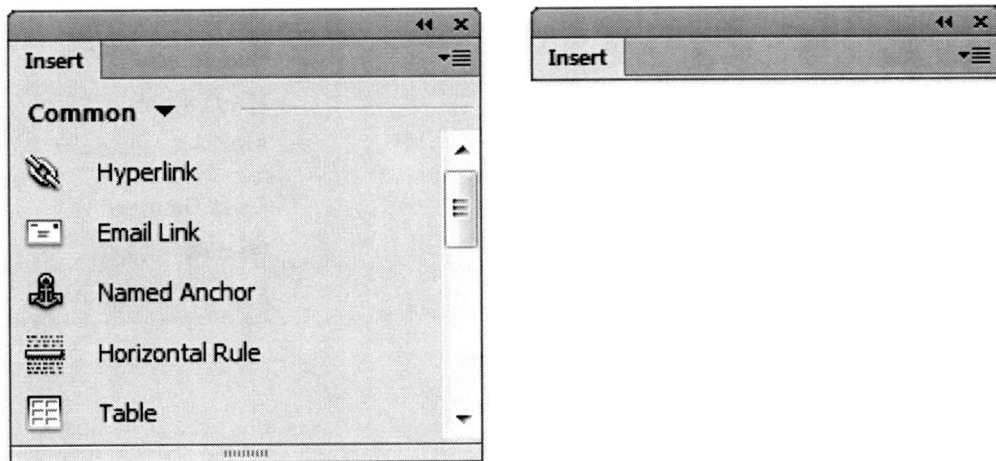

Working with Workspaces

Dreamweaver (like other Adobe applications) comes with a set of workspaces. The workspaces have been created by Adobe experts so you get all necessary tools when you need them.

Here are workspaces that come with Dreamweaver CS6:

- *App Developer*

- *App Developer Plus*

- *Business Catalyst*

- *Classic*

- *Coder*

- *Coder Plus*

- *Designer*

- *Designer Compact*

- *Dual Screen*

- *Fluid Layout*

- *Mobile Applications*

Designer ▾	🔎
App Developer	
App Developer Plus	
Business Catalyst	
Classic	
Coder	
Coder Plus	
✓ Designer	
Designer Compact	
Dual Screen	
Fluid Layout	
Mobile Applications	
Reset 'Designer'	
New Workspace...	
Manage Workspaces...	

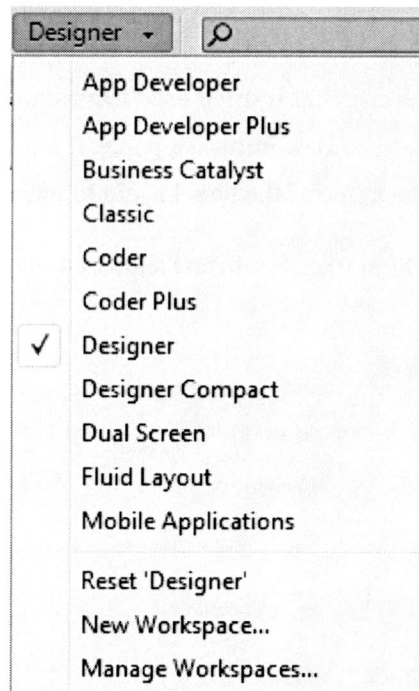

Default workspace in Dreamweaver is Designer and as you can see it's selected on the screenshot above.

To choose one of the workspaces, use either a Workspace Switch:

or Window menu:

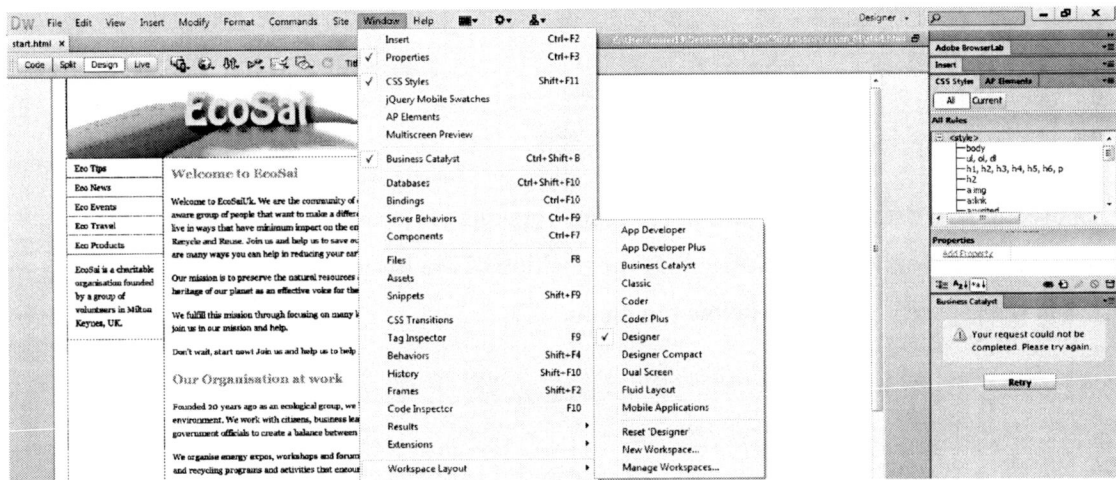

Here are some examples of Workspaces on the next page:

Designer Workspace:

great for designers working visually in Dreamweaver:

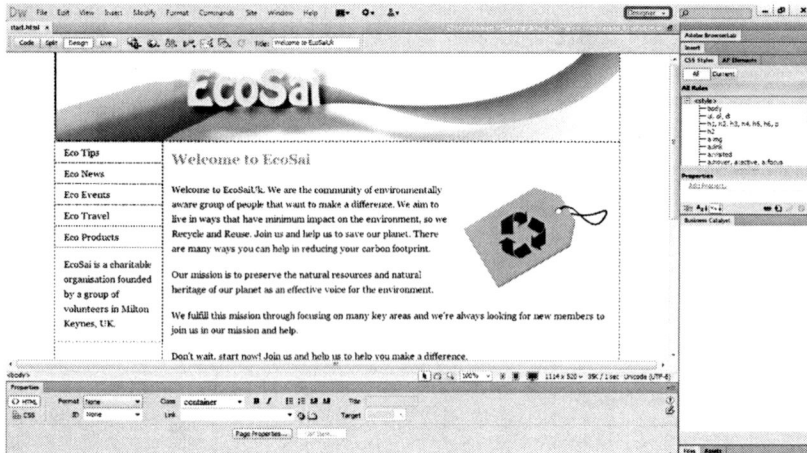

Classic Workspace:

this used to be a default workspace in the older versions of Dreamweaver (back in times of Macromedia Dreamweaver). Notice that the position of the Insert panel changed, in the Classic workspace it's situated below the menu:

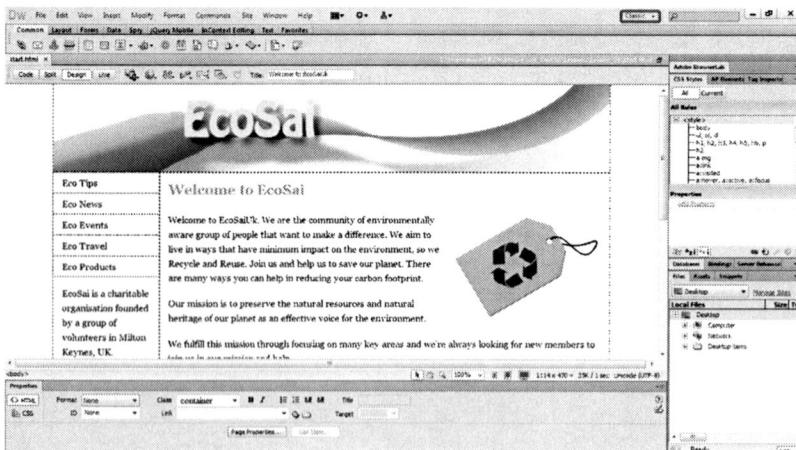

Coder Workspace:

perfect for coding, for web developers who spend all day typing the code:

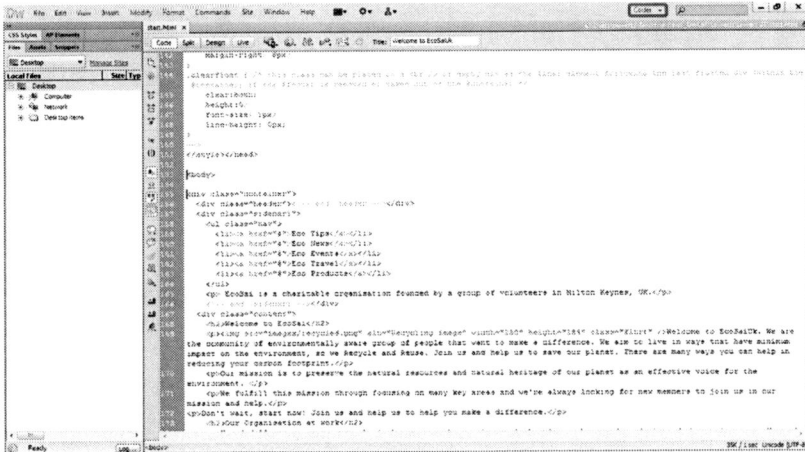

One more, as an example: the new **Mobile Applications Workspace**:

These are just a few examples of workspaces in Dreamweaver. Take a few moments and explore the other workspaces.

When working in Dreamweaver, you have a choice of four **View Modes** that suit your needs:

- **Code View,**

- **Split View,**

- **Design View,** and

- **Live View.**

3 Switch back to **Designer** workspace. The View Modes appear at the top of the document window as shown here:

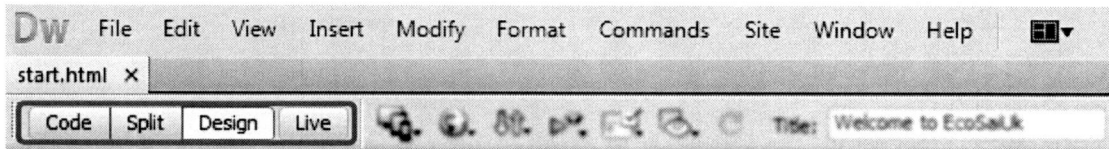

4 Click on the Code View button to switch to the Code View:

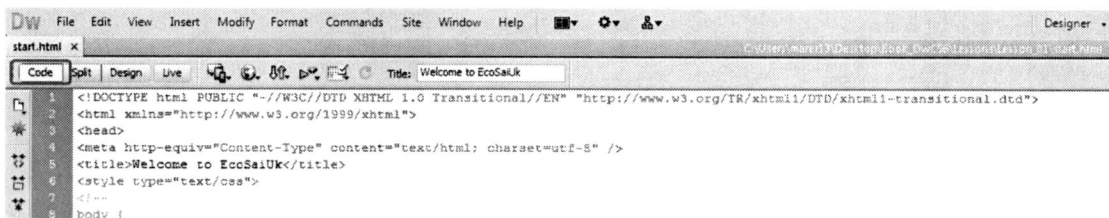

Code View focuses on the code. What you see is the HTML code of the page, the structure of the page. If you like coding, you will be spending a lot of time in this View Mode. When working in Code View, you also get access to a variety of coding tools – situated on the left hand side by the edge of the screen.

5 Click on the Design View button to switch to the Design View:

Design View focuses on working visually in Dreamweaver. When you switch to the Design View, Dreamweaver turns into a WYSIWYG editor (What You See Is What You Get), so what you see is a close preview of what you're going to see in the web browser.

6 Click on the Split View button to switch to the Split View:

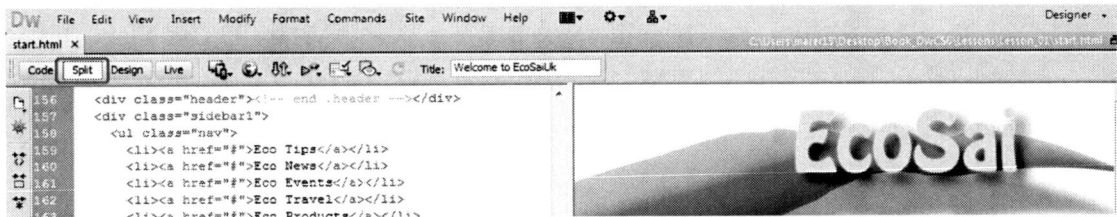

Split View gives you a mix of both: Code and Design at the same time. You can change the arrangement of the Code and Design windows by choosing **View > Split Vertically** (this option will split the windows either vertically or horizontally. You can also change which window appears on what side by choosing **View > Design View on Left** or **Design View on Top**.

7 And finally the Live View. Click on the Design View and then the Live View button:

Live View allows you to preview the page using a web browser engine (WebKit), so what you see in Live View is what you should see in the WebKit web browser (i.e. Chrome, Safari). Notice that when you launch Live View, any visual aids in Dreamweaver (i.e. dotted lines, etc.) disappear. That's because you won't see these things in the web browser. Live View is a great feature that allows you to quickly preview the page you're working on without going into a web browser. And Live View is interactive as you're going to find out in the future chapters.

NOTE: You should notice one more big difference between Design View and Live View. Did you notice the shadow behind a page? Not? Pretty impressive, isn't it? You're going to learn how to create it later on.

Welcome screen

Welcome screen appears when you start Dreamweaver and every time you have no documents open. You can choose to hide the Welcome screen, and later on display it if you change your mind. If you hide the Welcome screen, the document window will be blank.

8 Close the page and the Welcome Screen will appear:

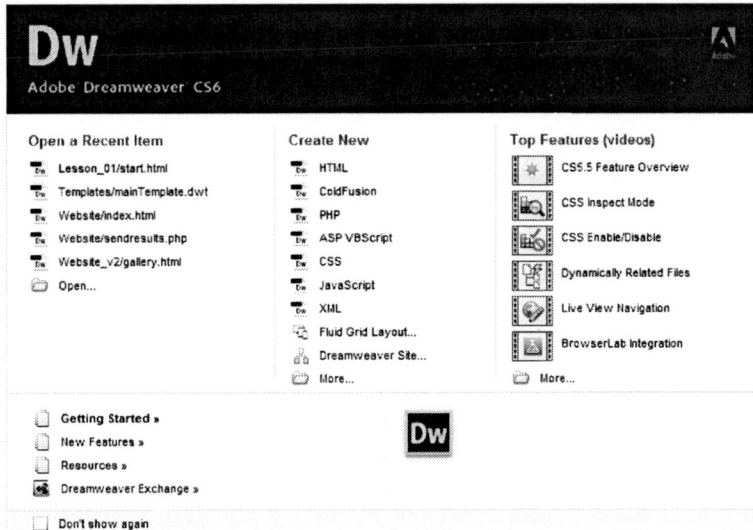

If you want to hide the Welcome screen, select **Don't show again** option on the Welcome screen (bottom left corner). I personally would encourage to leave it on as it gives you access to loads of very useful options.

If you have hidden the Welcome screen and want to bring it back, select **Edit > Preferences** on Windows (**Dreamweaver > Preferences** on a Mac) and select the Show Welcome screen option.

If you are new to Dreamweaver, you will find the Welcome screen very useful. Let's have a look on what options the Welcome screen provides and how to use them effectively.

Starting from left:

Open a Recent Item - a list of the recent files you worked on appears here, you can also browse to open a document by clicking on Open button at the bottom.

Create New - you can create a variety of different documents such as HTML pages, CSS, JavaScript, and many more. This is your starting point if you want to create a blank HTML page or a new CSS stylesheet. You can also define a new Dreamweaver Site by clicking on Dreamweaver Site button at the bottom.

Top Features (videos) - these are links and by clicking one of these links you can watch videos hosted on Adobe website about some of the new features in Dreamweaver CS6.

Working with Documents

In the next lesson you're going to learn the basics of creating, opening, and saving the documents in Dreamweaver.

Dreamweaver's Welcome screen allows you to create new HTML pages. However, you can also use CSS Starter pages to quickly create HTML pages with pre-designed layouts (Create New > HTML on the Welcome screen creates just a blank document) and start adding content in a matter of minutes. To access CSS Starter pages, you're going to use the menu File > New. More about it a bit later on.

How websites work

Let's start with some basics before we jump into building web pages.

When you type in a web address in the address bar, i.e. *http://bbc.co.uk*, you connect to the web server (a remote computer) and the web browser downloads all the required files into the memory and renders (displays) a web page. Web browser is rendering the page based on the HTML code that was created either by a user or by Dreamweaver.

There are many web browsers to choose from and all of them are free. Some web browsers come pre-installed with your operating system, i.e.:

*   if you run Mac OS, you have Safari,

*   if you run Windows, you have Internet Explorer

*   if you run Linux, you have Firefox or Konqueror

The most popular web browsers are (with their worldwide market share as of end of 2011):

*   **Mozilla Firefox – 38.7%**

*   **Google Chrome – 32.3%**

*   **Internet Explorer – 21.7%**

*   **Apple Safari – 4.2%**

*   **Opera – 2.4%**

Most browsers are also cross-platform (Windows, Mac, and Linux) – two most popular browsers in the World today, **Firefox** and **Chrome**, are examples of these browsers.

When building web pages using Dreamweaver, Dreamweaver is going to create all HTML code for you, so you don't have to worry about the knowledge of HTML, even though it helps to know a bit of HTML.

Domain Names and Servers

When you type in a website address (such as *www.adobe.com*), you enter the website's domain name that was purchased by the website owner. The website is located on a web server.

A web server is just a machine like a computer with constant access to internet and with the ability to handle massive traffic from thousands of users. It needs constant access to internet so that your website is available 24 hours a day. Websites are usually hosted on web servers maintained by web hosting companies. These companies charge a fee to host your website, some big companies have their own servers.

There are many hosting companies to choose from and if you do a bit of research, you'll find one that suits you. I'm going to refrain from recommending any hosting company, I'll just say that I had some bad experience with one of the big hosting providers in the UK so I would highly recommend a small hosting company focused on delivering great customer service. The prices for web hosting usually start from about £3 a month ($5 a month).

You will need to purchase your own domain name as well as web hosting. Your domain name will be the address of your website, i.e. one of my domain names is marekmularczyk.com. You can buy your domain name from your hosting provider and you pay either yearly or 2-yearly fee. Here are some examples of fees for domain names:

Per year pricing	1 year	2 years
.COM New	$11.99*	$11.99*
.CO New	$29.99 $11.99	$29.99 $20.99
.INFO New	$10.69* $1.99*	$10.69* $6.34*
.NET New	$14.99* $9.99*	$14.99* $12.49*
.ORG New	$14.99* $9.99*	$14.99* $12.49*
.ME New	$19.99 $8.99	$19.99 $14.49
.MOBI New	$17.99* $6.99*	$17.99* $12.49*
.US New	$19.99 $6.99	$19.99 $13.49
.BIZ New	$14.99* $5.99*	$14.99* $10.49*
.CA New	$12.99	$12.99
.CC New	$19.99	$19.99
.WS New	$14.99	$14.99
.ASIA New	$19.99* $8.99*	$19.99* $14.49*
.TV New	$39.99	$39.99

	TLDs	1 year	2 years
?	.com	FREE	$9.95
?	.net	FREE	$9.95
?	.org	FREE	$9.95
?	.we.bs	FREE	$4.50
?	.info	FREE	$9.95
?	.biz	FREE	$9.95
?	.us	FREE	$9.95

This brings you to the end of the first lesson and it is time to move on to the next lesson.

In the next Lesson you're going to learn a bit about HTML and CSS.

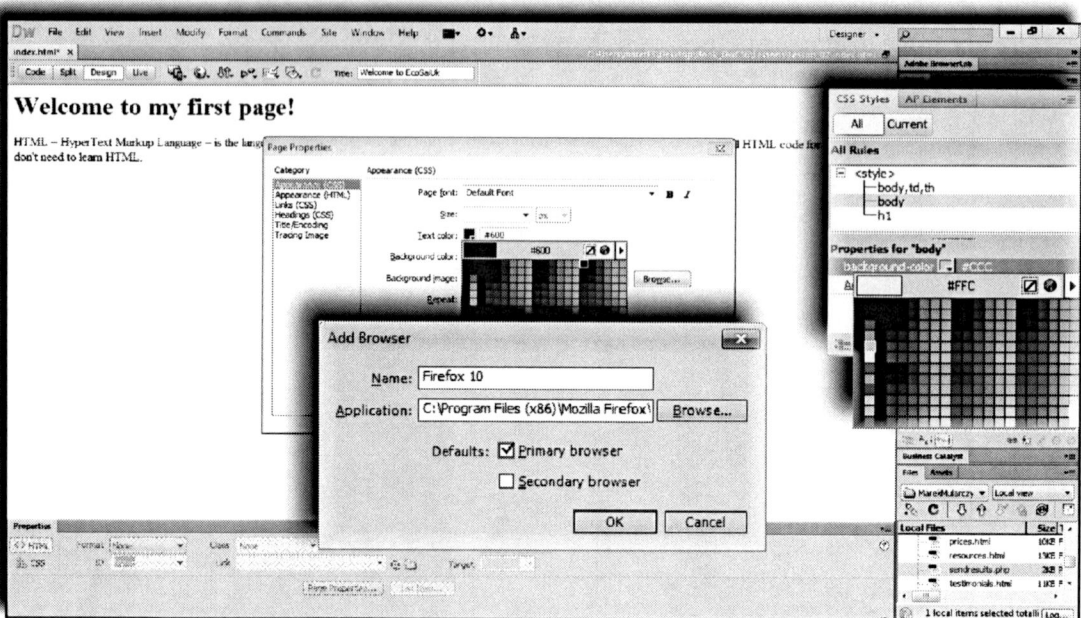

Lesson 2

HTML and CSS Basics

In this lesson you're going to familiarize yourself with HTML and CSS and learn how to:

- create HTML code using a Text editor

- understand how HTML syntax works

- create HTML with Dreamweaver

- differentiate HTML and CSS

- apply CSS formatting to the pages

This lesson will take about 1 hour 15 minutes to complete.

What is HTML?

HTML – HyperText Markup Language – is the language used for creating web pages. As you create pages in Dreamweaver, Dreamweaver will create all HTML code for you, so you don't need to learn HTML. Because of the nature of HTML web pages (it's just a text), you can easily edit your web pages with any text editor while away from your computer/Dreamweaver. Using Dreamweaver to create HTML code makes your life so much easier as Dreamweaver will take care of everything for you.

Even though you don't need to know HTML, it's good to know some basics of HTML as sometimes it is just easier to make amendments using the HTML code (Code or Split View).

HTML standard we're using is XHTML 1.0 Transitional, that's the standard approved by World Wide Web Consortium or W3C – the governing body behind the web standards. We will touch on HTML 5 later on as well, but because it is not a standard yet, we'll still be using XHTML 1.0 Transitional. When using Dreamweaver you don't need to worry about that as Dreamweaver will insert all necessary code for you.

Basic HTML Structure

```
<html>
    <head>
    <title> My first web page. </title>
    </head>
    <body>
    <h1> Welcome to my first web page! </h1>
    </body>
</html>
```

Let me explain the code above. The properly structured HTML page contains HTML tags, most of which consist of opening and closing tags (there are some exceptions as usual but don't worry about that now). The opening tag consists of lesser than and greater than symbols with a tag inside, i.e.. <html>. The closing tag uses the same symbols and it also includes the backslash, i.e.. </html>.

Now, you're going to do some coding using a text editor and then you'll jump into Dreamweaver. This will give you an idea of what to expect.

1 Start by opening a text editor, the simpler the better, i.e. you can use TextEdit on Mac or Notepad on Windows. (NOTE: If you're using TextEdit on a Mac, use **Plain Text** instead of Rich Text).

2 In the empty window type the basic HTML code:

```
<!DOCTYPE html PUBLIC "-//W3C//DTD XHTML 1.0 Transitional//EN"
"http://www.w3.org/TR/xhtml1/DTD/xhtml1-transitional.dtd">

<html xmlns="http://www.w3.org/1999/xhtml">

    <head>

    </head>

    <body>

    </body>

</html>
```

This is the basic code for every web page. Are you scared a bit? I guess so.

The first line of code is the Doctype declaration. In simple terms, it tells the web browser what document type are you using so that it can properly render the page (Dreamweaver will add all this content).

NOTE: If you were to create an HTML 5 document, the first line would read:

```
<!doctype html>
```

Shocked? Well, you should be! That's it! No URLs, that even the web designers that have been designing websites for many years would need to copy and paste. Nothing about the HTML version either.

What you've got so far are the HTML tag as well as:

<head> - head section would normally contain content for web browsers and search engines like page title, description and keywords;

<body> - content on the page that will display in the browser window. All the content goes within <body> tags.

3 Now you'll add a heading on a page. Before closing body tag add:

```
<h1> Welcome to my first page! </h1>
```

4 Save the file as **mypage.html** using Save As command. In the dialogue box that opens choose **All Files** from the Save As type drop-down menu. Save the page in Lesson_2 folder.

5 Open a web browser (Firefox, Safari or Explorer).

6 Choose **File > Open**. Navigate to the location where you saved the file and select **mypage.html**. Click **Open/OK**.

Congratulations! You have just created your first web page and it didn't even require a lot of coding.

7 Back in the text editor, below the line enclosed within h1 tag, add another line:

```
<p>This is the first paragraph below the main heading.</p>
```

so now your code should read:

```
<!DOCTYPE html PUBLIC "-//W3C//DTD XHTML 1.0 Transitional//EN"
"http://www.w3.org/TR/xhtml1/DTD/xhtml1-transitional.dtd">
<html xmlns="http://www.w3.org/1999/xhtml">
    <head>
    </head>
    <body>
        <h1>Welcome to my first page!</h1>
        <p>This is the first paragraph below the main heading.</p>
    </body>
</html>
```

8 Save the page.

9 Navigate to your web browser and load the updated page.

Congratulations! You have done very well.

Now, without wasting much time you're going to move on to Dreamweaver and start creating a simple web page using Dreamweaver instead of a text editor. You'll find out how much easier and faster it is.

Creating HTML pages in Dreamweaver

Let's start with a very frequently asked question:

"If I can create my pages with any text editor, why would I use Dreamweaver and spend all these money buying it, when I get a free text editor with my operating system?".

You will see in the coming lessons, why Dreamweaver is so much better than text editors and there are many reasons for that. But, you'll find out one reason right now. I don't want to keep you impatiently waiting.

You're going to recreate the same page this time in Dreamweaver.

10 Open Dreamweaver if it's not already open and on the Welcome Screen click on **HTML** in the **Create New** column:

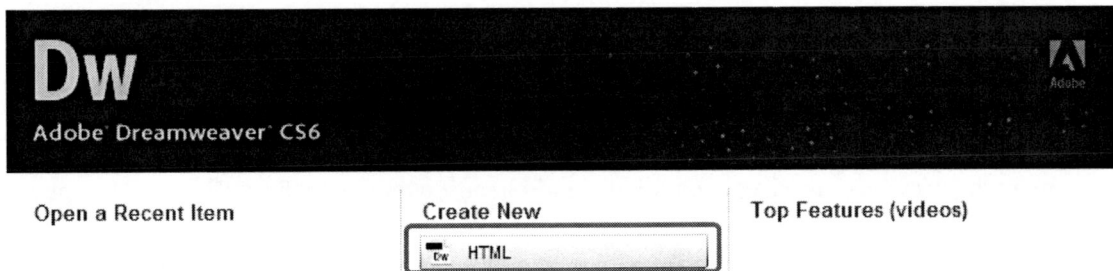

11 When a new document opens, if you don't see the Design View click on **Design View** button in the top left corner of the document window.

You should now see just a blank document with no content, yet. However, behind the scenes, Dreamweaver added some content for you already, even though you haven't done much!

12 Click on Split View button to see the code and the design as on the screenshot below:

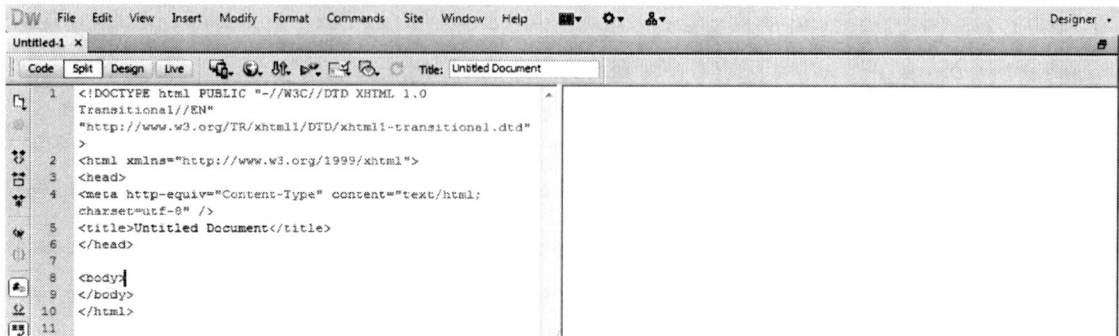

Even though you don't have any content on the page yet, Dreamweaver has already added all necessary content to the HTML code. Wow! Let's add some content.

13 Return to Design View, it will be easier to work in Design View most of the time.

14 As in the previous exercise, you added a main heading on a page first. Click on the page and type **Welcome to my first page!**

15 Leave the cursor blinking in the first line and in the Properties panel at the bottom of the screen change the **Format** drop-down menu to **Heading 1**.

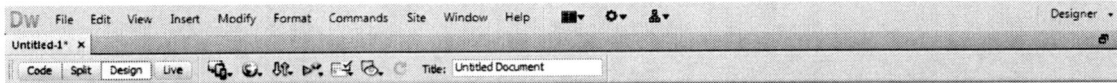

Welcome to my first page!

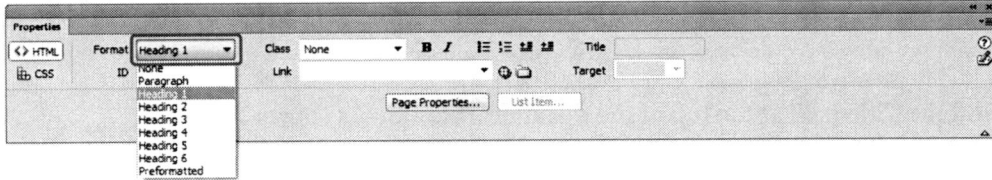

As simple as that! The text has changed to a heading. Isn't it much easier and faster then doing it in a text editor? Of course it is. Next step will be to add a paragraph of text below.

16 Place the cursor at the end of the heading and press Enter/Return to move the cursor to the next line.

17 Start typing text. Here's an example of a text I've added:

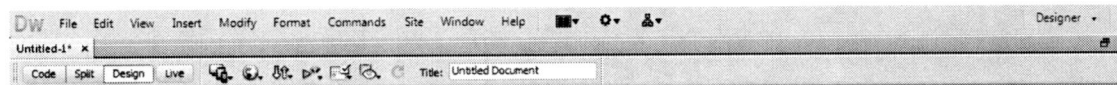

Welcome to my first page!

HTML – HyperText Markup Language – is the language used for creating web pages. As you create pages in Dreamweaver, Dreamweaver will create all HTML code for you, so you don't need to learn HTML.

Have you noticed that the text changed to a Paragraph automatically? You didn't do anything, you didn't have to. When you pressed Enter/Return to move cursor to a new line, Dreamweaver changed formatting to Paragraph. How great is that?! The Properties panel should say Paragraph.

You're not going to leave the page like that, you're going to add some more content and then you're going to customise it with some CSS. Now, you're going to add the page title and then you'll save the page and preview it in the web browser.

18   Find the Title field at the top of the document window as shown here:

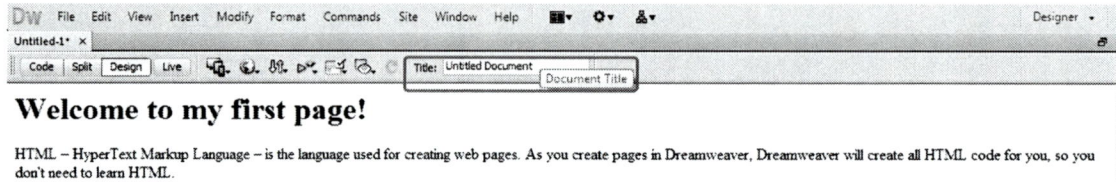

19   In the Title field type **Welcome to EcoSaiUk** and press Enter/Return.

20   Save the page by choosing **File > Save As...** and save it as **index**. Save the page in the Lesson_02 folder as shown below:

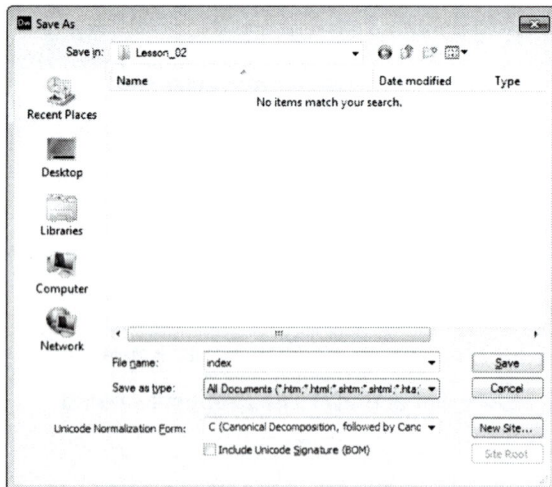

NOTE: The reason why you saved the page as **index.html** is because index is the name of the home page on every website. Also, notice that when using Dreamweaver you don't need to add .html, Dreamweaver does it for you.

It's time to preview the page in the web browser.

21 With the page still open choose **File > Preview in Browser** and choose the browser that appears there (it may be Internet Explorer or Safari, it depends on your operating system).

The page opens in a web browser.

Now you can see, that you managed to create a page in Dreamweaver in a fraction of the time it took you to do it in a text editor. And you didn't do much coding, you spent most time in the Design View.

What if you want to use a different web browser? Let's deal with that now. You can use any web browser that is installed on your computer to preview the pages you are about to create. I personally use Mozilla Firefox, as an example.

Before you decide which web browser you want to use, make sure it's installed on your computer first. Here are a few links where you can download the most popular web browsers:

- *Mozilla Firefox – Windows, Mac, Linux -* http://goo.gl/7ICv2

- *Google Chrome – Windows, Mac, Linux -* http://goo.gl/KIwr

- *Apple Safari – Windows, Mac -* http://goo.gl/cNp2

22 Choose **File > Preview in Browser > Edit Browser List...** This opens

Dreamweaver Preferences dialogue box where you're going to add a new browser.

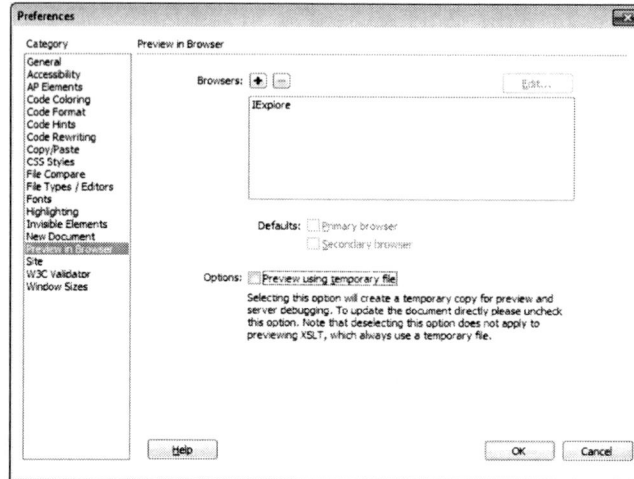

23 In the dialogue box click on the plus sign (+) to add a new browser.

24 In the dialogue box that appears (shown on the next page) type the name (I use name

and version of the browser) and click **Browse** button next to Application.

This will take you straight to Program Files folder on Windows or Applications on Mac.

Find the location of the browser and accept it. You can also check **Primary browser** or

Secondary browser if you want to use keyboard shortcuts.

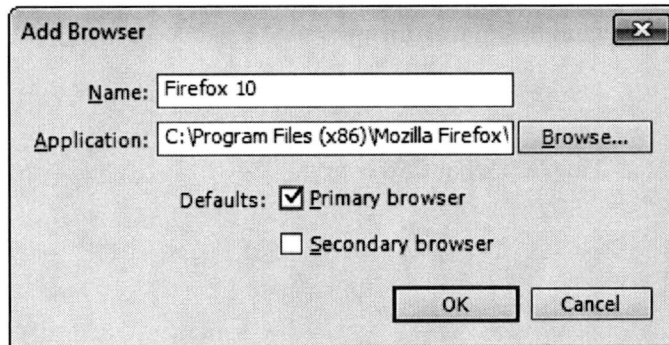

25 When done, click **OK** to accept.

If you defined a web browser as your primary or secondary web browser, you will now see a keyboard shortcut next to the name of the browser, so from now on you can use a keyboard shortcut to preview web pages in this web browser. What if you don't use keyboard shortcuts? Here's what you can use:

26 With the page open, click on the Globe icon on the top of the document window and choose the name of the web browser you want to use:

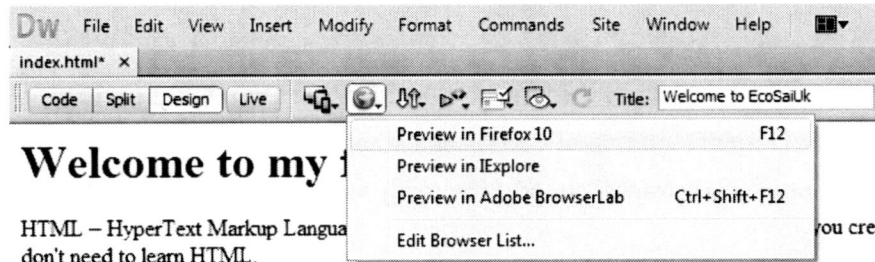

27 The page opens in your chosen web browser.

It's time for some CSS. I'll explain what CSS is first.

What is CSS?

Do you know how the web pages were created in the past? Have you created one? In the past, to simulate a multicolumn layout web designers were using tables. However, HTML-based formatting using tables was quickly deprecated from the language, and the cascading style sheets (CSS) were introduced. CSS avoids all the problems we had designing HTML layouts. And it is much faster to change layout with CSS.

Here's how we differentiate HTML from CSS. HTML is used to add content to your pages, while CSS is used to present the content, style it. So basically:

• *HTML > Content,*

• *CSS > Presentation.*

CSS (Cascading Style Sheets) was developed by the **World Wide Web Consortium** (W3C), and the latest official implementation of CSS specification is CSS2 (CSS3 is still work in progress, even though some web browsers support it already and we will start using it later).

Formatting pages with CSS

You're going to start by customising the text on the page you have created earlier.

28 Open **index.html** if you closed it.

29 In the Properties panel click on **Page Properties** button.

30 When **Page Properties** panel opens, click on **Appearance (CSS)** category on the left side so that you will customise the page using CSS and not HTML.

31 Click on the colour swatch next to **Text color** and choose the colour for the text from the colour picker that opens:

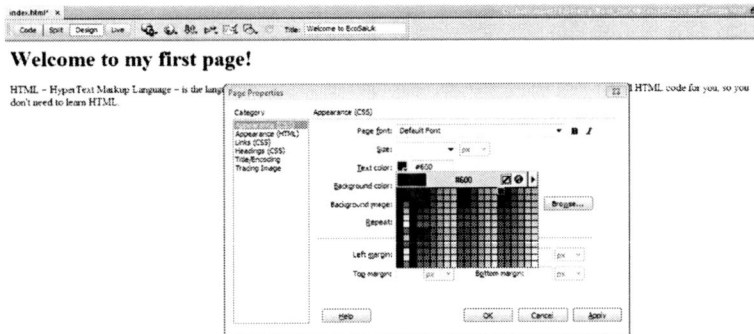

32 Click Apply and the text on the page will change colour like on the screenshot above.

33 Click on the colour swatch next to **Background color** and choose the colour for the text from the colour picker that opens. Click Apply.

Can you see how easy it is to customise the page with CSS? Next, you're going to change how the heading looks with some more CSS.

34 Reopen the **Page Properties** dialogue box if you closed it.

35 Click on **Headings (CSS)** category on the left. The heading you used for the main heading was Heading 1, so that's what you're going to customise now.

36 Click on the colour swatch next to **Heading 1** and apply a colour. Click **Apply** to see how the colour of the heading changes.

37 Now make the heading smaller. Click on the drop-down menu next to Heading 1 and choose **24** for size. Click **Apply**. The heading gets smaller.

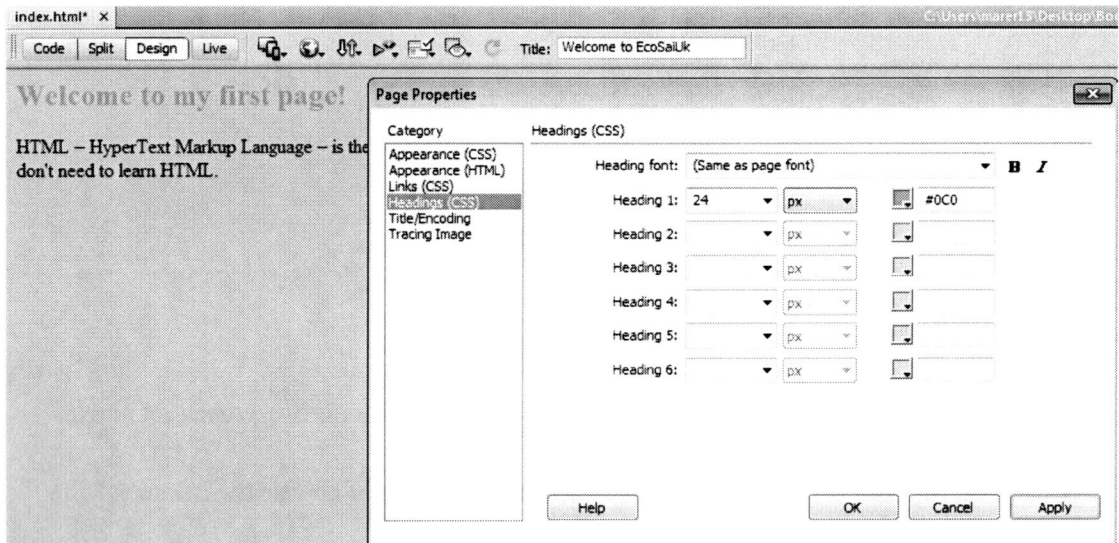

38 Click OK to accept the changes and close the dialogue box to return to the page.

You're going to make one more change here. You're going to change the default font family for the web page.

39 Click on **Page Properties** button in the Properties panel (if you don't see it, choose **Modify > Page Properties** from the menu).

40 Choose the **Appearance (CSS)** category and click on the drop-down menu next to **Page font**.

41 Choose one of the fonts listed here, I chose Tahoma. We will talk more about fonts in the future lesson, for now just choose one of the fonts from the list.

42 Click Apply to see how the font family for the entire web page changes. If you like it, click OK.

43 Preview the page in a web browser.

Look into the **CSS Styles** panel. CSS Syles panel has two buttons on the top. For now, just make sure that All is selected. CSS Styles panel is divided into two sections. When you highlight the rule in the top section called All Rules, the bottom section called Properties will display all the properties associated with this property.

NOTE: If you don't see the rules in the top section, and you see the plus sign (+) next to the word <style>, then click on it to expand it.

Here's what the CSS Styles panel looks like:

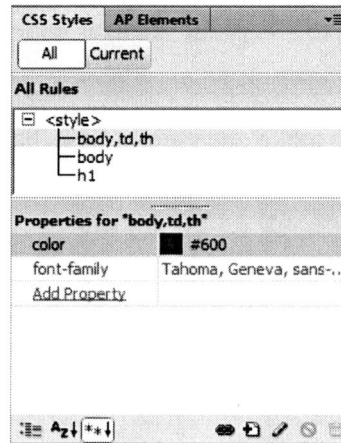

From now on, you'll be using the CSS Styles panel for changing rules. It displays all rules applying to the page elements. Give it a go.

44 In the CSS Styles panel highlight the **body** rule. In the bottom part of the CSS Styles panel, Properties for Body, you should see a property called **background-color**.

45 Next to **background-color** property click on the colour swatch and change the colour:

That's how you can make changes to CSS rules. In the future lessons you'll be creating new CSS Rules using the CSS Styles panel as well.

Now you see how easy it is to format your page with CSS in Dreamweaver. CSS Styles panel is very easy to use and at the same time it is a powerful feature offering you the full control of your page formatting.

Congratulations! You have successfully finished another lesson.

Just before you finish with this chapter, I want to share a few more words about HTML and CSS with you. HTML was never intended to do all the customization/presentation of the web pages you were to create. HTML lacked a standard way to format the text and load the fonts (when we talk more about the fonts, you'll find out more on how to load the fonts dynamically from the internet to expand number of fonts you can use in your web pages).

Creating page layouts, as an example, was a very difficult task with HTML and required using the tables. Nowadays, we just use CSS for that and it is so much easier and more future proof than using HTML table-based layouts. HTML-based formatting was actually deprecated from the HTML language and CSS-based formatting was widely accepted as a proper way to design layouts. CSS allows you to limit your HTML code to just the content, and do all the styling within CSS. And you are going to learn some tips and tricks using CSS3, the latest "incarnation" of CSS that is becoming more and more popular and most web browsers support it already (not Internet Explorer in most cases, which doesn't come as surprise).

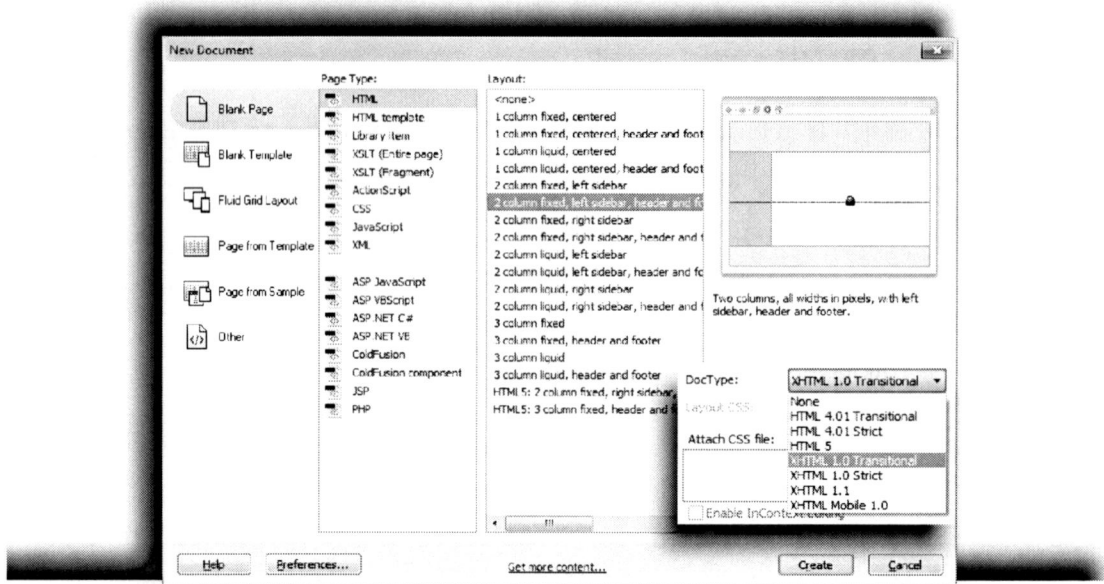

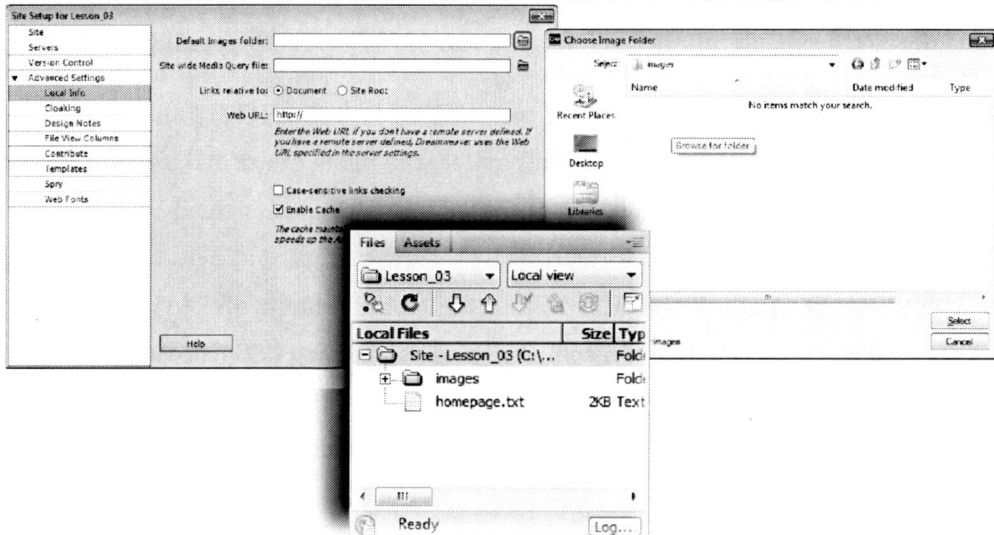

Lesson 3

Quick Start - Set Up a Website

In this lesson you're going to familiarize with Dreamweaver's web building features and learn how to:

- Define a New Dreamweaver Site

- Establish local root folder

- Create a new page using CSS Starter pages

- Modify the page title and add Metadata

- Insert Text from an external file

- Customise your page with CSS

This lesson will take about 1 hour 15 minutes to complete.

Set Up a new Dreamweaver Site

The power of Dreamweaver lies in its ability to quickly and easily create websites as well as in its web management tools. Dreamweaver is used for creating the complete website. The web pages created inside Dreamweaver will share the same layout and common elements (when using Templates, more on that later). Once you've finished building your website, you can quickly upload it to the web server using Dreamweaver's fantastic upload features within Files panel (one of my favourites).

A Site, in Dreamweaver, refers to the local location (on your computer) where all the files that are used on a website are stored. Before you start creating web pages, you should define your site first. The Dreamweaver Site is the local version of your website.

You're going to start by setting up a new Dreamweaver site. Prepare for a ride of your life, fasten your seat belts (just kidding).

1 Copy Lesson_03 to your computer if you haven't done so yet.

2 Open Dreamweaver if it's not already open.

3 Open New Dreamweaver Site dialogue box by clicking on **Dreamweaver Site** button on the Welcome Screen, or by choosing **Site > New Site**.

4 **Site Setup** dialogue box opens. In the **Site Name** field, type **Lesson_03**.

Next, you need to set up a Local Site Folder. This is a folder, where you store the files you are working with (every page you create in Dreamweaver will be automatically saved within your Local Site Folder).

NOTE: Keep all the files you use on your website in the same main folder within your Local Site Folder to make sure, that when you upload the site to the web server the links will work properly.

5 In the **Local Site Folder** field, click on the folder icon to the right and navigate to the Lesson_03 folder containing the files for this lesson. Double-click on the Lesson_03 folder and then click **Select** (Windows) or **Choose** (Mac) to choose this folder as your local root folder. Don't click Save yet.

Even though this is not required, it is a good practise to keep separate content in separate folders. It is very common to keep images, PDFs, videos, and sounds in separate folders. If you look at the structure of the Lesson_03 folder, you're going to notice images folder inside the main folder, that's the folder containing images. That's why Dreamweaver helps you here by giving you option to define the images folder. If you define the images folder for your site, and later try to insert images from other locations, Dreamweaver will copy the images to your defined images folder within the site.

6 To define images folder (to point Dreamweaver to the images folder), click on the arrow next to the **Advanced Settings** category on the left to reveal a list of tabs. Select **Local Info** category.

7 Next to **Default Images** folder field, click the folder icon. When the dialogue box opens, navigate to the images folder located inside Lesson_03 folder and click **Select** (Windows) or **Choose** (Mac).

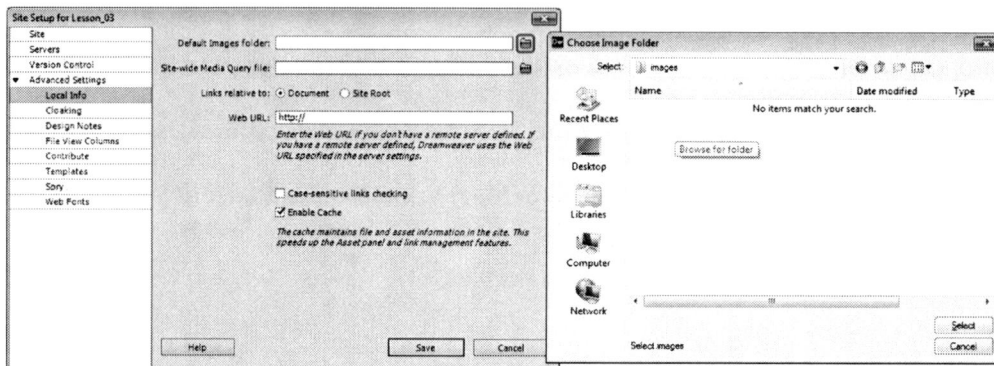

8 Click Save in the Site Setup dialogue box to save and close.

Your Files panel should display the images folder and a text file called homepage.txt. The site name should also appear as shown on the screenshot on the next page. There are no pages here, yet.

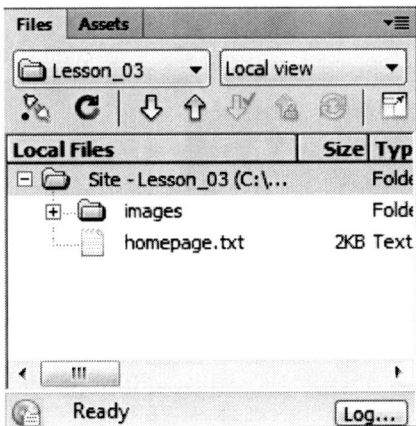

Congratulations! You have successfully defined your first site in Dreamweaver. Now, you're ready to create your first web page.

Create your first Web Page

Dreamweaver's Welcome screen gives you a quick access to a number of pages you can create, i.e. HTML pages, PHP pages, etc. However, when you use Welcome screen to create a new HTML page, Dreamweaver creates a blank page. There are some limitations to using this options, but more on that in just a moment. You're going to create a new page using Welcome Screen first.

9 Click on **HTML** in the Create New column on the Welcome Screen.

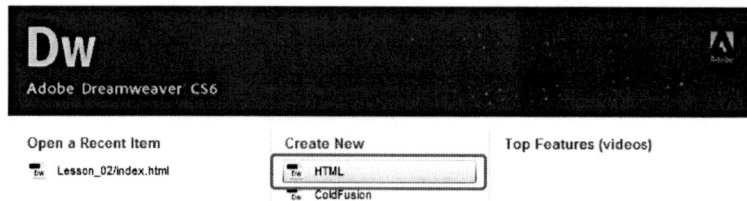

This opens a blank new document. You don't even get to choose whether you want it to be an HTML4, XHTML, or HTML5 document. And there is no content here, no columns or header or footer. Just a blank document. Not that useful for a new user.

10 Close the document – **File > Close**.

Here's what you're going to do now. You're going to create a new HTML document using one of the presets, called CSS Starter Pages, one with 2 columns, header and footer. This will be an XHTML 1.0 document (more on that in just a moment), and in the future you're going to be creating HTML5 documents! How great is that?!

Dreamweaver's CSS Starter pages

Dreamweaver CS6 comes with 16 layouts (starter pages) that use pure CSS/HTML - the best practise in web design. These starter pages were created by experts and were tested to make sure they work cross-platform in all major web browsers.

All these starter pages are web standards compliant. Adobe included popular one, two, and three - column layouts in either fixed or liquid set ups. I hear you asking: "What's the difference between fixed and liquid layouts?" Here you go:

Fixed layouts are specified in fixed dimensions in pixels,

 i.e. 950px wide;

Liquid layouts are specified in relative measurements in percentage,

 i.e. 90% wide

Fixed layouts used to be more common (and they still are quite common) as you can decide how wide your page is going to be and keep it that size all the time, i.e. 950px all the time. If you go for a liquid layout, your web page is going to change its width based on the viewer's browser window, i.e. when they resize their browser window or use a small screen, your page will resize (to keep it 90% width all the time).

Responsive web design

Liquid layouts are becoming more and more popular with the wide spread of "responsive web design". Responsive web design appeared because users use so many different devices to access websites. It used to be easier with computer screens as you could predict the screen resolution. It gets more complicated when the screen resolution (or web browser window) changes. We can use responsive web design to embrace flexibility of the web devices.

There are three main elements in responsive web design:

- flexible, grid-based layout

- flexible images

- CSS media queries

For now, we'll focus on fixed layouts.

11 Choose **File > New** to create a new document.

12 In the **New Document** dialogue box choose **Blank Page** in the first column, **HTML** in the second, and you're going to see the CSS Starter Pages presets in the third column:

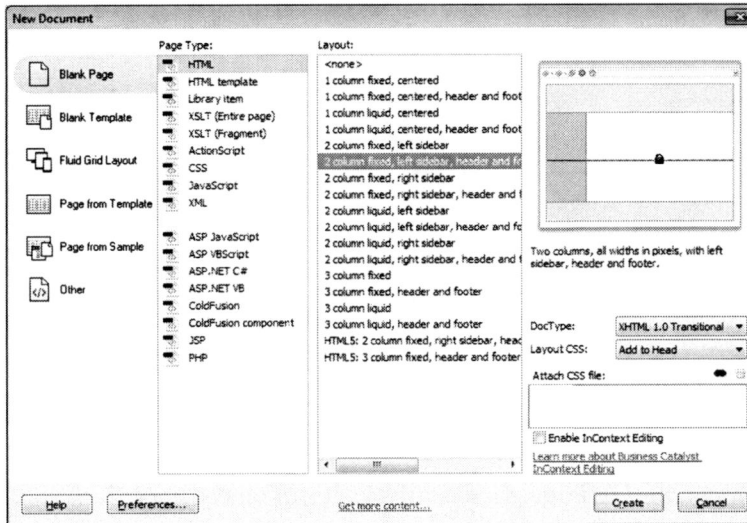

13 In the last column choose the preset **2 column fixed, left sidebar, header and footer** as on the screenshot above.

On the right hand side you'll see a preview of the page with a padlock icon on it. The padlock means that the size of the page is set in pixels and it's locked to this size. That will be fine for now. In the bottom right corner you'll find the DocType drop-down menu. More on DocType on the next page:

DocType (Document Type declaration)

DocType: XHTML 1.0 Transitional ▼

Layout CSS: None
                 HTML 4.01 Transitional
                 HTML 4.01 Strict
Attach CSS file: HTML 5
                 XHTML 1.0 Transitional
                 XHTML 1.0 Strict
                 XHTML 1.1
                 XHTML Mobile 1.0

☐ Enable InContext Editing

Selecting one of the document type definitions from the DocType drop-down menu makes your page compliant with one of the standards, i.e in this case XHTML 1.0 Transitional. In the future lessons you will be using HTML 5, but for now we'll stick to XHTML 1.0 Transitional as this is a standard DocType.

DocType declaration is supported in all major web browsers (Firefox, Opera, Chrome, Safari, Iexplorer). DocType specifies the rules for the markup language (HTML), so that the web browsers render the content correctly.

14 From the DocType drop-down menu choose **XHTML 1.0 Transitional** and click Create.

Dreamweaver creates a new document with some content, your task will be to fill the page with content and then customise it with some CSS.

15 Highlight the main heading that reads **Instructions** and change it to **Welcome to EcoSai UK**.

This is the main heading on a page and it is formatted as Heading 1 – you can see it in the Properties panel, just place your cursor in the heading:

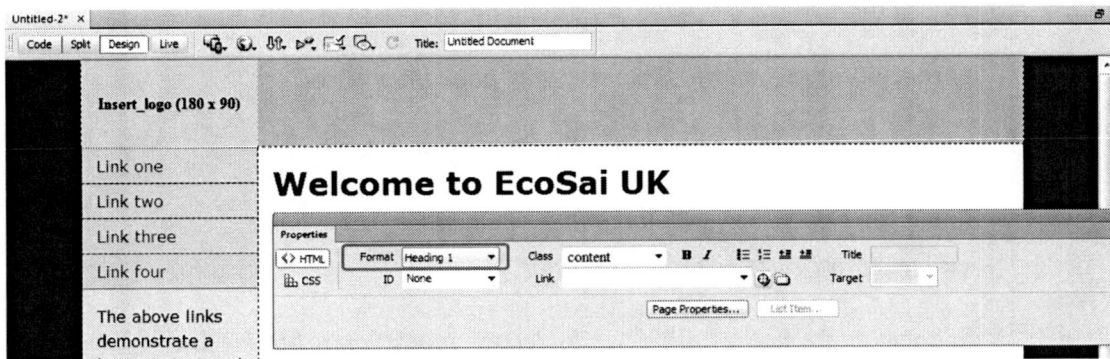

It's time to save the page.

16 Choose **File > Save As...** and save it as **index**. Click **Save**.

Naming conventions for pages

There are some naming conventions when creating HTML documents that you need to follow. These naming conventions are common in web design, whether you use Dreamweaver or a text editor to create pages. To make sure you achieve consistency between different web browser and that your pages render correctly in all the web browsers, you need to follow these four rules when naming your HTML documents:

- no spaces - mypage.html is correct, my page.html is not,

- no special characters - no characters like: &, %, ?, !,

- do not start the name with a number - you can create a page products2.html, but not 2products.html,

- do not start the name with a capital letter - myCSSpage.html is fine, MyCSSpage.html is not.

17 Preview the page in the web browser.

18 Back in Dreamweaver, highlight all the text on the page that appears below the main heading and delete it by pressing Delete key.

19 Navigate to the Files panel and double-click on **homepage.txt** file to open it. The file opens in Dreamweaver!

20 Highlight all the text except the main heading on the top and copy it to the clipboard (you can use **Edit > Copy**).

21 Once the text has been copied to the clipboard you can close the text file (**File > Close**).

22 Place the cursor below the main heading and choose **Edit > Paste Special**. Paste Special dialogue box opens.

23 In the Paste Special dialogue box click **Paste Preferences**.

24 Dreamweaver Preferences dialogue box opens in the **Copy/Paste** category:

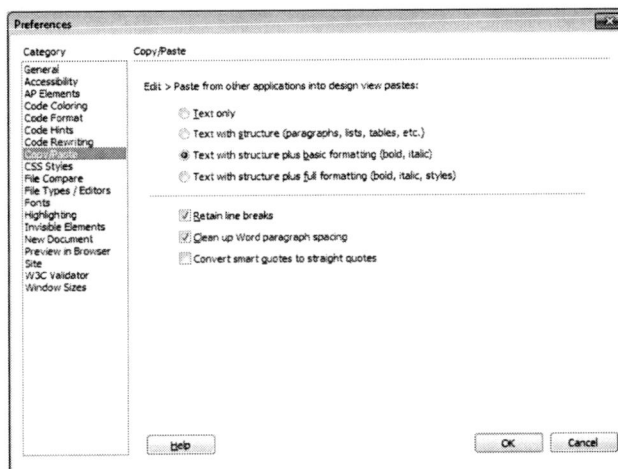

25 On the right-hand side set the **Edit > Paste** option to **Text with structure plus Basic formatting.** Click OK.

From now on, Dreamweaver will use the document structure from the text file that you copy to the clipboard and paste into Dreamweaver.

26 When the dialogue box closes and **Paste Special** dialogue box appears again, click OK.

27 Place the cursor after the sentence **Welcome to EcoSaiUK** (this will become a subheading) and press Enter.

28 Place the cursor inside the subheading **Welcome to EcoSaiUK** and format it as **Heading 2** using the Format drop-down menu in the Properties panel.

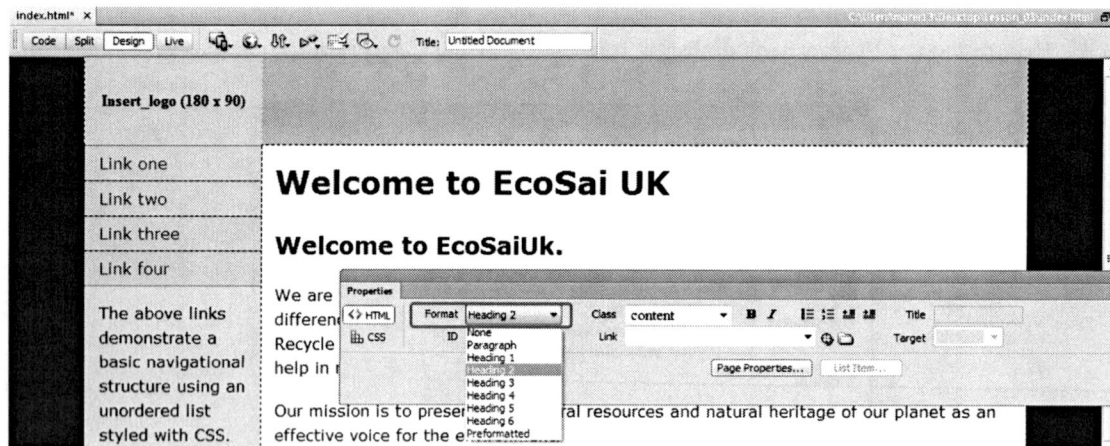

Leave the subheading formatted as Heading 2, we'll talk more about headings in the next lesson.

Now, you're going to add the header image, you're going to replace the image placeholder in the header (Insert_logo) with a proper header image.

29 Select the **Insert_logo** image placeholder in the header and press Delete key on your keyboard to delete it.

30 Navigate to the **Insert panel > Common** category, and choose **Images > Image**:

31 Navigate to the images folder and choose **header.jpg**. Click OK.

32 Now, you'll get prompted for Accessibility Attributes. Type **EcoSaiUK header image**, and press OK.

The header image appears on the page. Congratulations! You have successfully inserted text and image on the page. Your page starts looking better. There is only one challenge here. The image is a bit narrower than the page itself. You're going to fix it with a bit of CSS. For now, you'll preview the page.

33 Preview the page in the web browser.

Just before adjusting the image and customising the page even more, we'll talk about metadata.

Add Metadata

Let's start with some explanation of what the Metadata are. Metadata, or meta elements, are usually used to specify things like page description, keywords or page title. Metadata can be used by search engines as well as by web browsers, and they always go inside the <head> element.

There are three most common types of meta tags:

- title

- description

- keywords

The **Title** tag appears in the web browser, depending on the web browser it may appear on the tab like in Firefox or on the top of the application frame like in Explorer – both browsers side by side here:

Some web browsers will add their own name after the title of your website, as Internet Explorer is doing here.

The **Description** tag gives you a chance to decide what is going to appear directly below the title of your website in the search performed using a search engine. Here's an example of a description as it appears in the Google search:

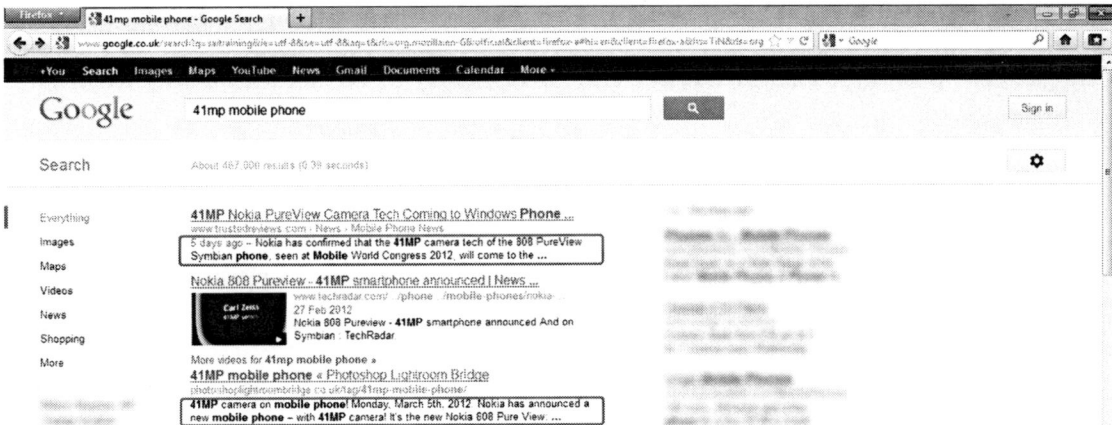

The **Keywords** tag allows you to add extra text for crawler-based search engines to index them with your website. These would typically be keywords that users may type when searching for your website.

You're going to start with a page title.

34 Place your cursor in the **Title** field at the top of the document window and type **Welcome to EcoSaiUK**. Press Enter on your keyboard.

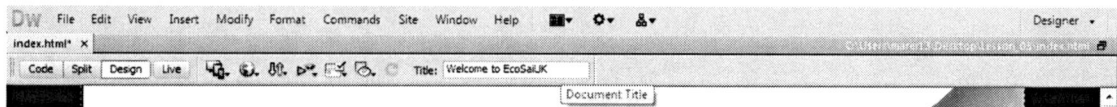

It's time for a description of the web page.

35 Choose **Insert > HTML > Head Tags > Description** and when the Description dialogue box opens, type **EcoSaiUK are the community of environmentally aware group of people that want to make a difference** and click OK.

You won't see any change on the page because the Description doesn't appear on the page. Here's how you find it:

36 Switch to Split View and notice the Description appear in the top part of the code, within the <head> tag.

37 If you want to alter the Description then place the cursor in the code in the line for description and the Description will appear in the Properties panel:

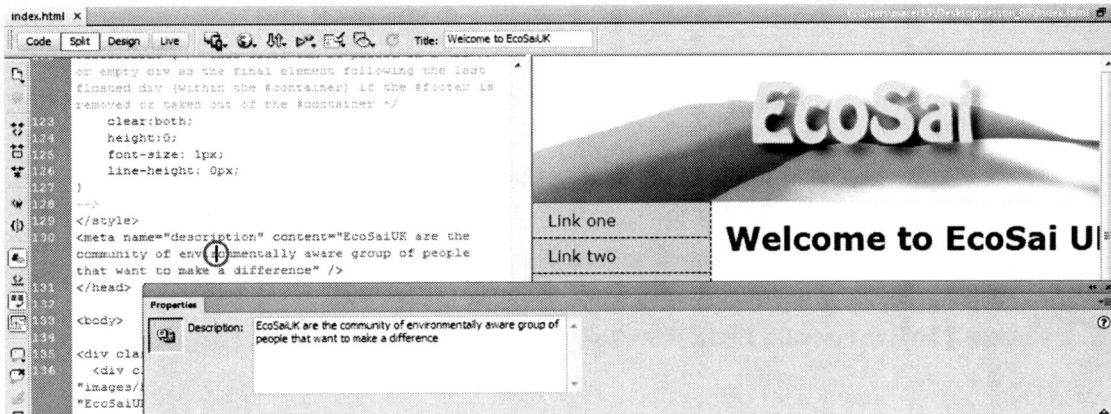

Now, you're going to add keywords to finish adding metadata.

38 Switch back to Design View and choose **Insert > HTML > Head Tags > Keywords**. When the Keywords dialogue box opens, type **eco sai uk, organic, eco, environmentally-friendly, eco products, organic products, eco organisation, based in the UK, volunteers, recycle, reuse, save the planet, eco forums, eco tips** and press OK.

39 Save and preview the page in the web browser of your choice. Notice the page title in the web browser.

Congratulations! You have successfully added metadata to the web page. Now that you've added metadata to the page, you're going to customise the menu in the sidebar and then the footer.

40 Highlight the text that reads **Link one** in the sidebar and change it to **Eco Tips**.

41 Highlight **Link two** and change it to **Eco News**.

42 Change **Link three** and **Link four** to **Eco Events** and **Eco Travel** respectively:

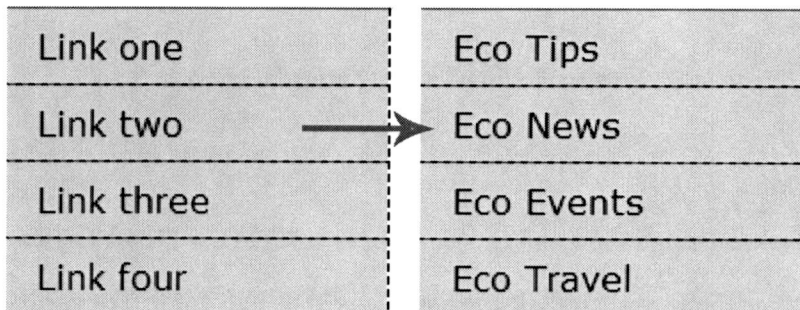

Link one	Eco Tips
Link two	→ Eco News
Link three	Eco Events
Link four	Eco Travel

In the original menu, as you may have noticed in the Lesson 1, there were five menu elements, so you need to add one more. You would have thought that placing the cursor in the last line and pressing Enter key would help, but not. It's not how it works here. You'll fix it quickly using the code.

43 Highlight one of the menu elements (it doesn't matter which one) and click on **Split View** button. The line you selected is highlighted in the code.

44 Notice that the menu is built using a list, an unordered list to be precise. Select the entire line including opening and closing **li** tag.

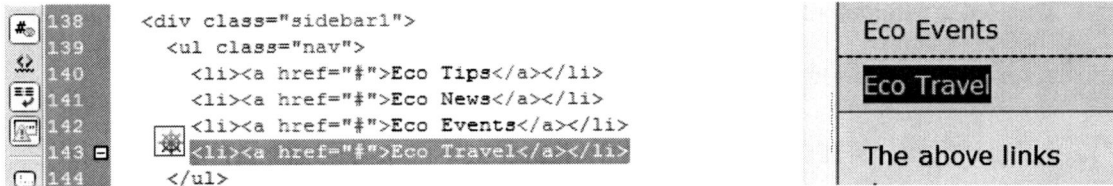

```
138    <div class="sidebar1">
139       <ul class="nav">
140          <li><a href="#">Eco Tips</a></li>
141          <li><a href="#">Eco News</a></li>
142          <li><a href="#">Eco Events</a></li>
143          <li><a href="#">Eco Travel</a></li>
144       </ul>
```

Eco Events
Eco Travel
The above links

45 Copy the line to the clipboard **Edit > Copy**, place the cursor in the line that starts with **</ul>** and press Enter to create an empty line.

46 Move the cursor to the empty line and paste the code **Edit > Paste**.

47 Click on the Design View button and change the last menu item to **Eco Products**.

48 Save and preview the page.

Your menu is ready for now. You're going to customise the menu in the sidebar with some CSS in the next lesson. Now, you're going to customise the footer.

49 Scroll to the bottom of the page, so that you can see the footer. Remove all the content from the footer.

50 In the empty area in the footer type **2012 Copyrighted. EcoSaiUK. All rights reserved.**

51 The footer will look nicer and more professional when you add a copyright symbol. Place the cursor at the beginning of the line.

52 Choose **Insert > HTML > Special Characters > Copyright.** You will now see a nice copyright symbol in the footer, and without using any graphics that would slow the page down!

That's it for this lesson. You have done an amazing job so far, congratulations!

In the next lesson, you're going to make more changes to the page, customise it more, and use text more.

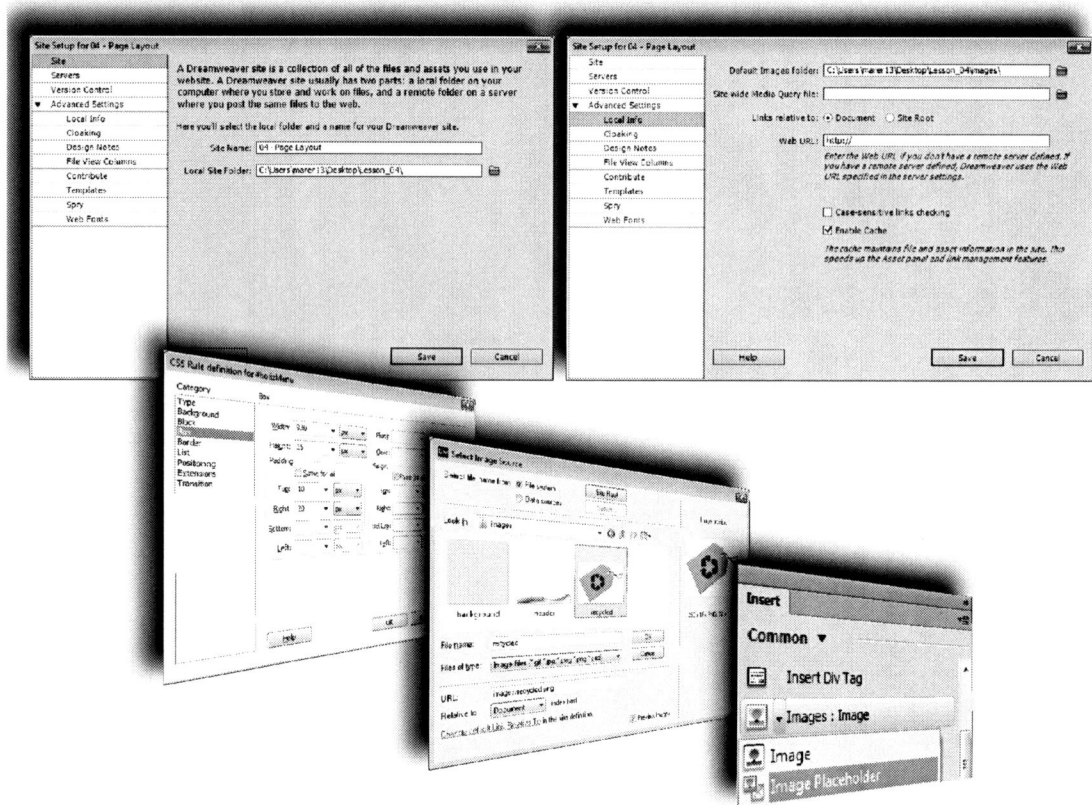

Lesson 4

Create a Page Layout

In this lesson you're going to familiarize with Dreamweaver's page layout techniques and learn how to:

- Plan your page layout

- Customise a pre-defined CSS layout

- Add text based menu

- Modify the footer with CSS

- Wrap text around an image

This lesson will take about 1 hour 15 minutes to complete.

Your audience

Before you start designing your website in Dreamweaver, you need to decide on the purpose of your website. This one question will define how the pages are going to be layed out. And the second most important question you need to ask yourself is the audience of your website. Your layout will depend on these two things. The amount of content will also define the layout of the pages. Is your website going to display information for your visitors or maybe it is going to sell some products? What age are your primary visitors? Are they adults, teenagers, children?

It's usually a good idea to start by doing some research. In our case, we're designing a website for a fictitious eco/organic charity organisation that wants to increase audience's awareness on the topic of ecology, recycling, and green lifestyle.

One of the important factors to consider when building a website is the internet connection your visitors are going to use? High-speed broadband connection? 56Kb dial-up? If someone is using a slow internet connection, they don't want to wait for ages for the graphics to load. That's why we'll be using graphics in smaller amounts here.

What if someone is using a mobile phone to access your website? Things to consider are things like the technology you are going to use. As an example, if they use iPhone or iPad, they won't have Flash Player (iPhone and iPad are the only modern mobile devices that don't run Flash Player). So you may want to use graphics or JavaScript/JQuery for some animations instead of using Flash animations. We will talk about these technologies in detail in later lessons.

What is the screen resolution of the display of your audience? This will determine how big you make your website (how wide).

What operating system/web browser are they using?

Here are some statistics from W3C (World Wide Web Consortium) and Gartner (end of 2011):

Operating systems' market share - Desktops:

> Windows - ca.80%

> Mac OS - ca.10%

> Linux – ca.10%

Operating systems' market share – Mobile Devices (acc. to data from Gartner):

> Android (Linux) – 52.5%

> Symbian – 16.9%

> iOS (Apple) – 15%

> Blackberry – 11%

> Windows – 1.5%

Web browsers market share (Febr 2012):

> Mozilla Firefox – 36.6% (down from 44% last year)

> Google Chrome – 36.3% (up from 20% last year)

> Internet Explorer – 19.5% (down from 28% last year)

> Apple Safari – 4.5% (up from 4% last year)

Current average screen resolution is higher than 1024 x 768 px (computers). 1024x768 and below resolution only accounts for 14% of displays.

The website we're working on here, is a website for a fictitious charity dedicated to sharing their knowledge of eco living with their visitors. This means, that the visitors will come from different backgrounds and different age groups.

Wireframing

Once you've decided on your audience, you need to decide on the number of pages within your website. Also, you need to draw/sketch what the page layout will look like - this is a wireframe.

Start by creating thumbnails (you can do it on a piece of paper) for the pages. Thumbnails should include the connections between the pages as shown below:

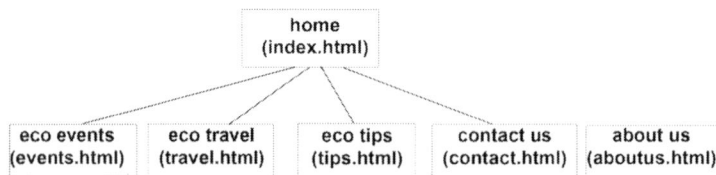

All the pages link to the home page, so that the visitor could navigate back to the home page from any page.

Once you've got number of pages worked out, the next step is to create a visual representation of the website's layout. That's where the Wireframe comes in. Ask yourself these questions:

- *how many columns do I need?*

- *do I want a sidebar on left or right?*

- *what goes into sidebar?*

- *where do I position all the objects on a page?*

etc.

Because in the western culture people read from left to right, and from top to bottom, EcoSaiUK website will have two-column layout with a sidebar on the left. The sidebar will hold the menu, and the right column will be the main content area on the page. The website will also be centre-aligned within a web browser window.

Some companies like their websites to be left-aligned to the edge of the browser window, however, if someone uses a high-resolution screen (1900px wide or more), they will see a lot of empty space on the right. If you centre your website (EcoSaiUK website is going to be 950px wide), a person using 1900px wide screen will see 500px space on the left and 500px space on the right.

Here's an example of a wireframe for a website:

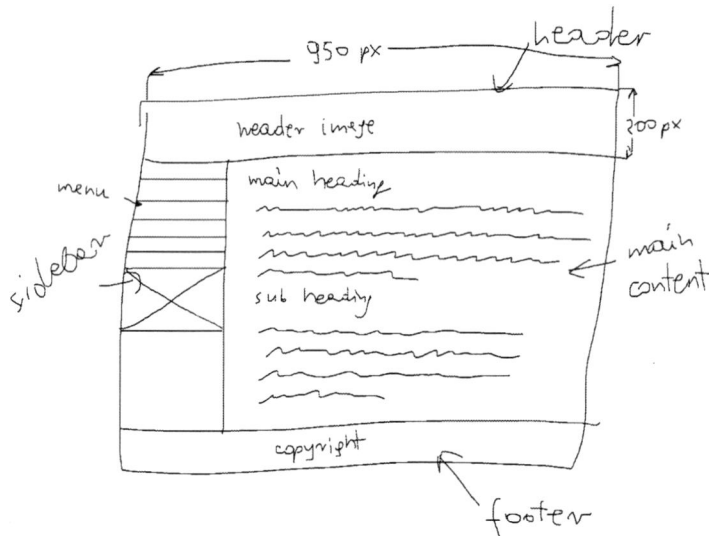

NOTE: Sometimes designers create full-colour mockups of the web page using graphics editors like Adobe Photoshop or Fireworks.

Enough of theory. Now it's time to start customising the web page you were working on in the previous lesson.

Customise a pre-defined CSS layout

The predefined CSS Starter pages are a good point to start in the process of creating pages. They're fantastic at this stage of your learning process as you don't know how to create page layout from scratch yet. Don't worry, you will learn how to do it in the future lesson. For now, CSS Starter pages are quick to create and easy to customise.

In the previous lesson, you have created a new page from one of the CSS Starter pages. In this lesson, you are going to build on that by customising the page as we left it at the end of the previous lesson.

Let's get to work then.

1 Launch Adobe Dreamweaver CS6, if it is not already open.

2 If you see the Welcome Screen, click on **Dreamweaver Site** button to define a new Site.

NOTE: If you don't see the Welcome Screen (you may have disabled it through the Dreamweaver Properties), choose **Site > New Site** from the menu. The Site Setup dialogue box appears.

3 In the **Site Name** field, type **04 – Page Layout**.

4 In the **Local Site Folder** field, click on the folder icon to the right and navigate to the Lesson_04 folder containing the files for this lesson. Select it.

5 Click the arrow next to the **Advanced Settings** category on the left to reveal a list of tabs.

Select **Local Info** category and next to **Default Images folder** field, click the folder icon.

When the dialogue box opens, navigate to the images folder located inside Lesson_04 folder

and click Select (Windows) or Choose (Mac).

Your Site Setup dialogue box should look like this:

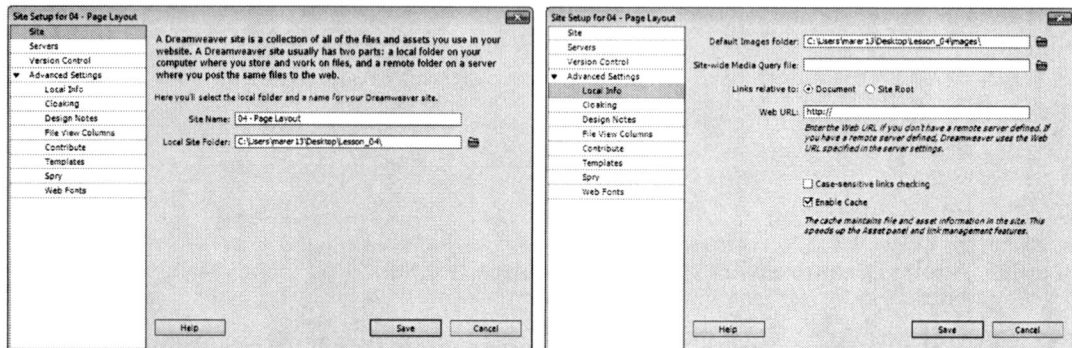

6 In the Site Setup dialogue box click **Save**.

Your Files panel should display the images folder and site name. You will also notice the page

you have created in the previous lesson. This is the page you are going to work on in this

lesson, so that in the future lesson you could convert it into a Template.

7 Open **index.html** from the Files panel (double-click on it). You're going to customise the sidebar first.

8 Highlight all the text below the menu in the sidebar and delete it.

9 With the cursor still blinking in the sidebar, insert an image placeholder by going to the Insert panel and selecting **Images > Image Placeholder**:

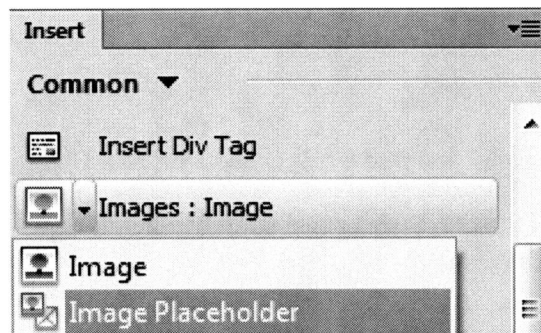

10 When the **Image Placeholder** dialogue box opens, type **sidebar_image** in the Name field, set Width to **150px** and Height to **180px**, give it a grey colour and set Alternative text to **Sidebar image**. Click OK.

Now, you're going to add a temporary caption to the sidebar image.

11   Click directly after the image placeholder and press Enter to move the cursor to the new

line.

12   Type **Add caption here**.

If you remember from the first lesson, the original home page didn't have any background in

the sidebar. It was white from the content behind it. Let's remove the background colour from

the sidebar.

13   Go to the CSS Styles panel and find a rule called sidebar1. Highlight it and click on Edit

Rule icon at the bottom of the CSS Styles panel as shown here below:

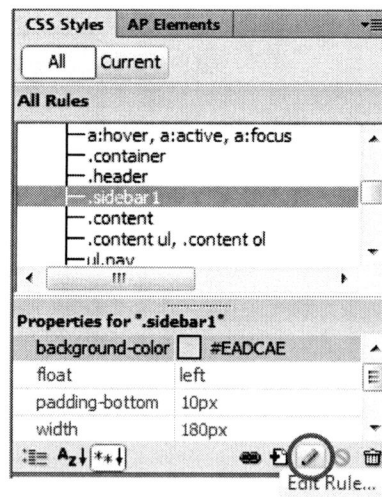

14 This opens CSS Rule Definition dialogue box. Select **Background** category and delete the value for **Background-color**. Simply leave the field empty.

15 Click **Apply** and the background colour will disappear. Well done. Click **OK**.

Now, you're going to remove the background behind the text in the sidebar (menu). Just a bit more CSS...

16 Place your cursor in the sidebar and in just a few seconds you will see this icon:

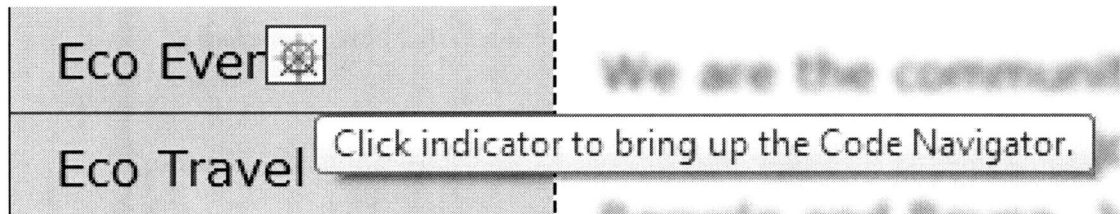

This is your good friend, Code Navigator, a very useful feature in Dreamweaver.

Let me explain on the next page.

Code Navigator

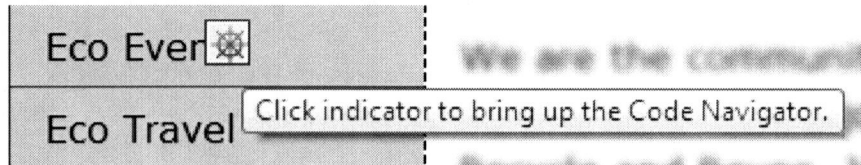

Eco Ever ⚙

We are the comm...

Eco Travel

Click indicator to bring up the Code Navigator.

Code Navigator displays a list of code related to particular location on a page. You can use it to navigate to related code sources. When you click on a link in Code Navigator, it opens the file containing the relevant code. Dreamweaver will basically take you to that particular piece of code, to that particular rule.

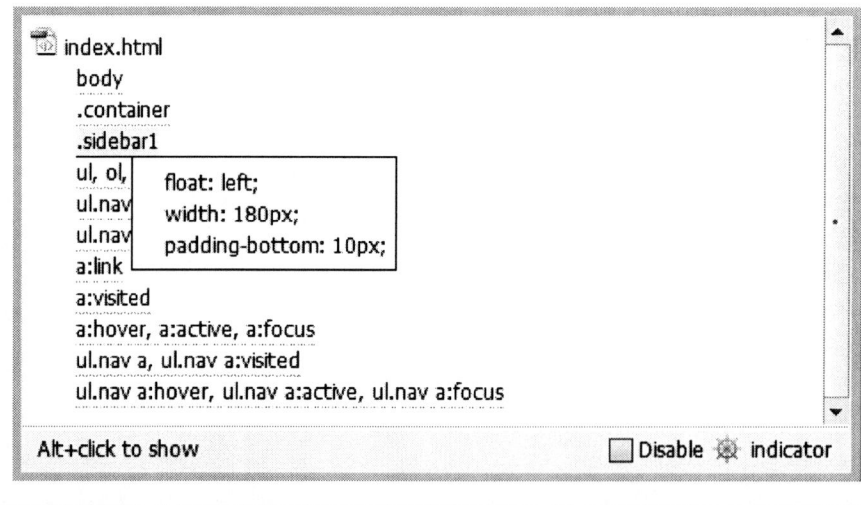

---

index.html
  body
  .container
  .sidebar1
  ul, ol,   float: left;
  ul.nav   width: 180px;
  ul.nav   padding-bottom: 10px;
  a:link
  a:visited
  a:hover, a:active, a:focus
  ul.nav a, ul.nav a:visited
  ul.nav a:hover, ul.nav a:active, ul.nav a:focus

Alt+click to show   ☐ Disable ⚙ indicator

17 Back in Dreamweaver, click anywhere inside the menu in the sidebar, and when the Code Navigator icon appears, click on it to reveal the relevant code.

You're going to use it to find the rule that will change the background colour of the sidebar.

18 When the relevant code drop-down menu appears, start moving the cursor over the rules and notice how the properties appear! How great is that?!

19 For starters, if you don't know much about CSS, start looking for a property called **background** or **background-color**. The rule we're looking for here is the one before the last: **ul.nav a, ul.nav a:visited**.

20 Click on the **ul.nav a, ul.nav a:visited** rule. This will change the view of the document to the Split View and the cursor will be blinking inside the rule you selected! How clever!

But notice another very interesting thing that has just happened. In the CSS Styles panel, the same rule is now selected! And if you look carefully into the Properties section, you will notice the light green background colour!

21 Navigate to the CSS Styles panel and highlight the background-color property. Click on the trash icon to delete it.

22 Preview the page in the web browser and save all the changes when prompted.

Add text based menu

In this part of the lesson, you're going to add a text based menu directly below the header. You'll do a bit of coding and use a bit of CSS.

23 Switch to Split View so that you can see the Design and the Code View at the same time.

24 Find the ending code for the header (you can start by clicking on the header image, this will highlight the code for you). It should look like this:

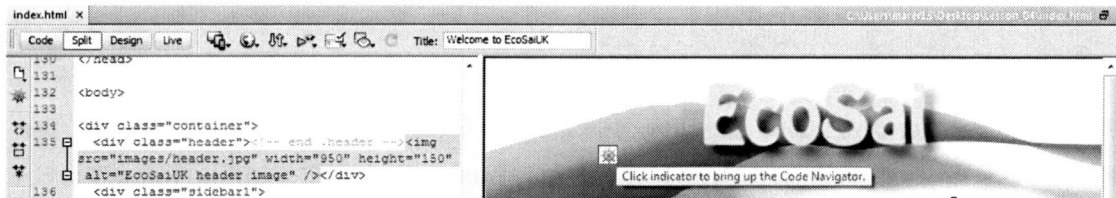

25 Place the cursor after the closing div tag and just before the opening div tag for the sidebar, and press Enter to move the cursor to the new line:

The first step will be to create a new div tag for the horizontal menu you're about to create. Next, you'll add text for the menu and add some CSS to customise it.

26 On a new line in the code type the following code (notice how Dreamweaver gives you drop-down menus as you keep typing, I love that feature in Dreamweaver):

```
<div id="horizMenu"> </div>
```

27 Between opening and closing div tags add the following text for the menu:

```
Home | About Us | Contact Us
```

so that the code looks like this:

```
<div id="horizMenu"> Home | About Us | Contact Us </div>
```

That's the menu. Press F5 on the keyboard to update changes and you will see the menu appear on the page.

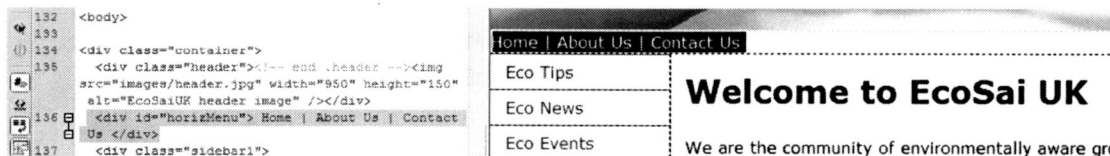

Now it's time to customise the menu. You're going to move the menu to the right, adds some space above and below the menu and change the text properties.

First thing you'll need to do is to create a new CSS rule for the horizontal menu you have just created.

28 Navigate to the CSS Styles panel, highlight the rule **.header**, and click on **New CSS Rule** icon at the bottom of the CSS Styles panel:

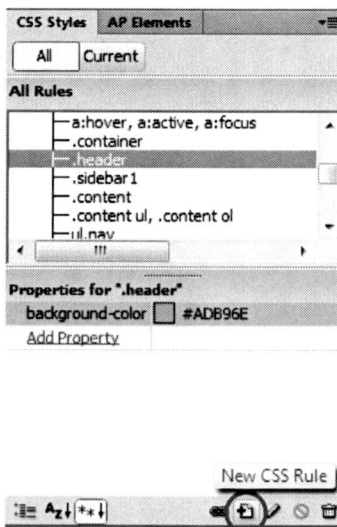

29 When the New CSS Rule dialogue box opens, set the options as on the screenshot below and press OK:

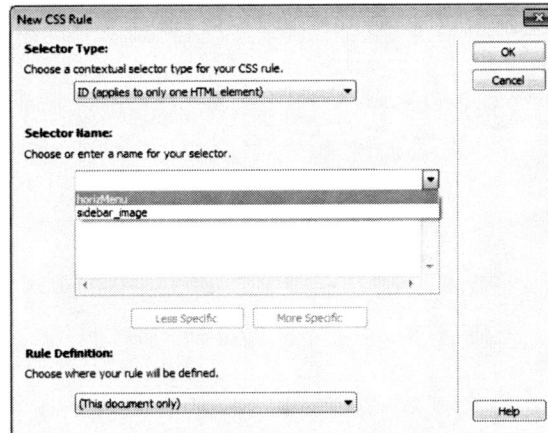

30 In the CSS Rule definition dialogue box, go to **Block** category and set Text-align to **right**. This will move the text to the right.

31 Go to the **Type** category and set Font-size to **90%**.

This will set the size of the text to 90% of the default size on a device that's being used to access the web page. We're using percentage units to accommodate different devices (computers, mobile phones, and tablets).

32 You can click **Apply** to see how the text changes. It moves to the right and gets a bit smaller. Perfect.

33 If you still have CSS Rule Definition dialogue box open, go to **Box** category and set the options as shown here:

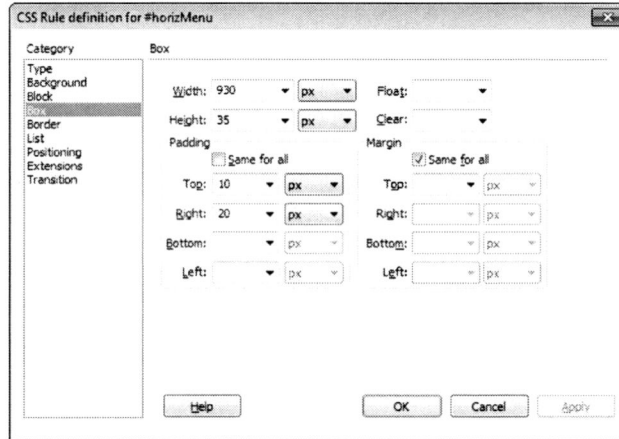

Everything in this category of the CSS Rule Definition dialogue box will be explained to you in the next lesson as we'll talk more about CSS and we'll talk about CSS Box Model.

34 For now, make changes and click OK.

Modify the footer with CSS

It's time to modify the footer with some CSS.

35 Switch back to Design View and scroll the page so that you can see the footer.

Here's what you're going to do here:

- centre the text,

- reduce the size of the text,

- change the background,

- add a text menu.

Let's get to work!

36 In the CSS Styles panel search for the footer rule. Once found, highlight it and click on the Edit icon as shown on the next page:

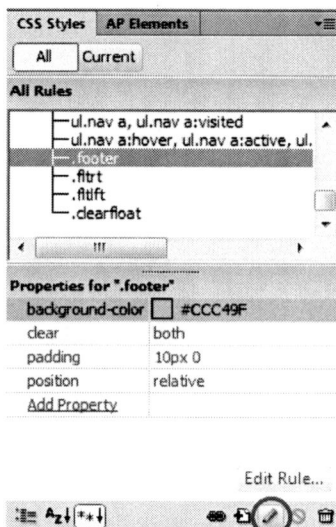

37 In the CSS Rule Definition dialogue box go to **Block** category and set Text-align to

center. This will move the text to the centre.

38 Go to the **Type** category and set Font-size to **90%**.

39 Now change the background colour to a shade of grey by going to **Background**

category and clicking on the colour swatch next to **Background-color**. Set the colour and

click OK to apply the effect.

NOTE: If you want to make the background very light grey (like the footer in the first lesson),
instead of using a colour swatch, type the value next to **Background-color** like the one
shown on the next page:

CSS Rule definition for .footer   ▣

Category   Background
Type
Background
Block   Background-color: [ ] #DDDDDD
Box
Border   Background-image: [_____] ▼ [Browse...]

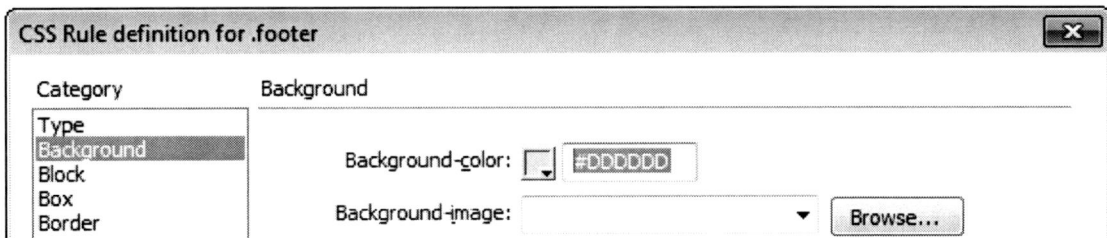

40 Finally, add the text menu below the copyright. Place the cursor at the end of the line and press Enter to move the cursor to a new line. On a new line type the text menu like this:

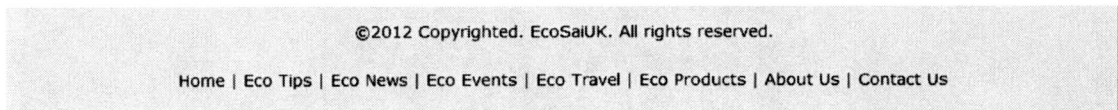

©2012 Copyrighted. EcoSaiUK. All rights reserved.

Home | Eco Tips | Eco News | Eco Events | Eco Travel | Eco Products | About Us | Contact Us

One more final step. The content in the footer now seems to be a bit too big.

41 Edit the footer rule once again and in the **Type** category and set Font-size to **80%**. Press OK.

In the next lesson as you'll go deeper into CSS you are going to make some more changes to the footer to customise it.

Now the last part of this lesson – adding an image and setting the text to float around it – a very popular effect in desktop publishing.

Wrap text around an image

42 Scroll page to the top and place your cursor at the beginning of the first paragraph that starts with **We are the community**. You're going to insert an image here.

43 Go to the Insert panel and choose **Images > Image** as shown here:

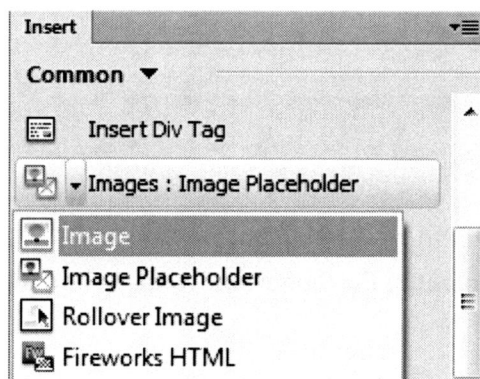

44 In the **Select Image Source** dialogue box navigate to the images folder and choose **recycled.png**.

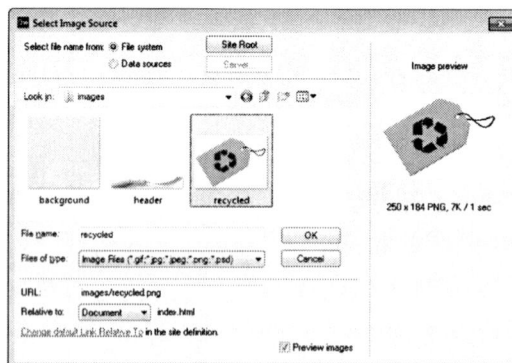

45 In the **Image Tag Accessibility Attributes** dialogue box, in the **Alternate text** field type **Recycled logo** and press OK.

46 The image will by default appear on the left, so you're going to move it to the right and float the text around it now. Select the image on the page if it's not already selected.

47 Go to the Properties panel and from the **Class** drop-down menu choose **fltrt**:

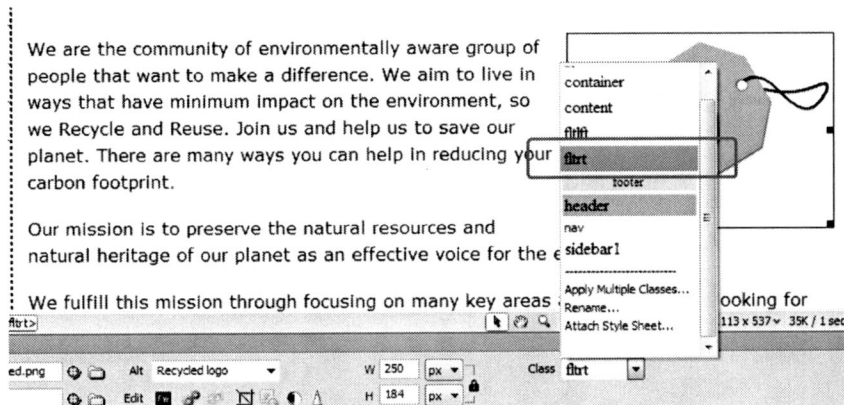

Congratulations! You have successfully finished the lesson! Well done.

Lesson 5

Working with Text, Tables and CSS

In this lesson you're going to start working with text and learn how to:

- Insert and customise Headings and Paragraphs

- Use Web Fonts

- Add text from other sources

- Create Ordered/Unordered Lists

- Format text with CSS

- Add Tables

This lesson will take about 1 hour 30 minutes to complete.

Headings and Paragraphs

In HTML, there are six headings' tags - **\<h1\>, \<h2\>, \<h3\>, \<h4\>, \<h5\>**, and **\<h6\>**. Every web browser will format the content between one of these tags as a heading. Headings are used to organise the page into meaningful sections. If you look through any book, you'll notice that every chapter has a title or the chapter number as a heading. The same with web pages.

\<h1\> heading in HTML has the most semantic meaning and it is also the biggest on the page. All other headings are descending in order with \<h6\> being the less important among headings and being the smallest as well.

On your web page, the name of the page will appear as the main heading \<h1\>, and the subheadings will appear as \<h2\> elements.

1 Launch Adobe Dreamweaver CS6, if it is not already open.

2 Define a new Dreamweaver Site using either Welcome Screen or **Site > New Site** menu.

3 In the Site Name field, type **05 – Text**.

4 In the Local Site Folder field, click on the folder icon to the right and navigate to the Lesson_05 folder containing the files for this lesson.

5 Select Lesson_05 folder, and click Open (Windows) or Choose (Mac). Then, click Select (Windows) or Choose (Mac) to choose this folder as your local root folder.

6 Click the arrow next to the **Advanced Settings** category on the left to reveal a list of tabs. Select **Local Info** category and next to **Default Images folder** field, click the folder icon. When the dialogue box opens, navigate to the images folder located inside Lesson_05 folder and click Select (Windows) or Choose (Mac).

7 In the Site Setup dialogue box click **Save**.

8 Choose **File > Open**, and select **index.html**.

Now you're going to define headings on the page.

9 Place the cursor inside the main heading that reads **Welcome to EcoSai UK** and check the Properties panel, it should be a Heading 1. If it's not then change the formatting to **Heading 1**.

This will be the main heading for each page. All subsequent headings will become sub-headings and you're going to format them as Headings 2.

10   Place your cursor at the beginning of the line that reads **Our Organisation at work**,

press Enter to move the text to the new line and format it as **Heading 2** (Properties panel):

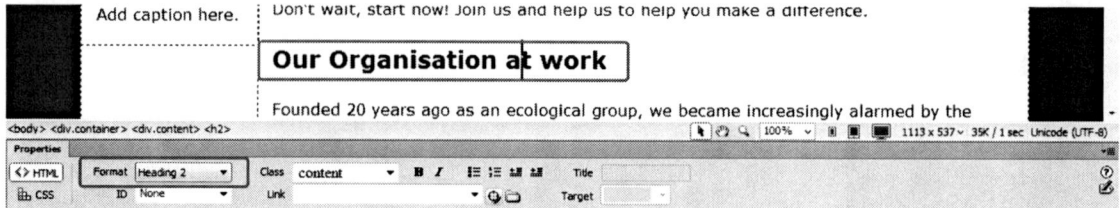

It's time change the appearance of the headings.

11 Go to the CSS Styles panel and check if there are rules for Heading 1 and Heading 2, i.e.

rules **h1** and **h2**.

There should be none except for one rule for all headings **h1, h2, h3, h4, h5, h6, p**, but this
rule only defines margin and padding, so you're going to create new CSS rules for headings on
the page.

12 In the CSS Styles panel, highlight the rule **.content** (that's the right column), place the

cursor inside Heading 1 on the page (this will help a lot) and click on **New CSS Rule** icon at

the bottom of the CSS Styles panel as shown on the next page:

Because you placed the cursor inside the heading, Dreamweaver will try to help you and will suggest creating a Compound rule for Heading 1 inside Content area. This is great, you're just going to change it slightly. You're going to leave the rule as Compound, but you will make it slightly less specific.

13 Leave the Selector Type as **Compound**, in the Selector Name area click **Less Specific** button once so that it reads **.content h1**. Leave Rule Definition as **This document only** and click OK.

NOTE: Whether you leave the Selector Name as .container .content h1 or .content h1, doesn't make any difference because the content area is contained within a container area anyway. You used less specific rule to make it easier to read in the CSS Styles panel and in the code.

14 In the **CSS Rule Definition** dialogue box, in the **Type** category, set the Font-size to something smaller like 140% and change the colour to a shade of green. When done, click OK.

Welcome to EcoSai UK

We are the community of environmentally aware group of

15 Scroll the page down to find the subheading – Heading 2 and repeat Steps 12, 13 to create a new CSS Rule **.content h2**.

16 Make the heading smaller than the main heading, set it to **120%** and change its colour to the same shade of green as previously.

Our Organisation at work

Founded 20 years ago as an ecological group, we became increasingly

It's time to set some defaults for the entire web page. Let's do some CSS. To set the defaults for the entire web page (or entire website), you need to edit body rule. In this case, you're going to set the default font-family, font-size and font colour for the entire web page.

17 Find the body rule in the CSS Styles panel, highlight it and click on the Edit button at the bottom of the panel.

18 In the Type category you will find some settings here already. Let's change the Font-family. Click on the drop-down menu next to it. This reveals the list of fonts.

FONTS ON WEB PAGES

There are two ways of including fonts on a web page. The first one, the traditional one, is to use fonts installed on user's computer. The second one is Web Fonts. We'll talk about Web Fonts in just a moment. Let's talk about the traditional approach of using fonts on a web page.

When using a traditional method of using fonts on web pages, method supported by Dreamweaver for a very long time, and the only way we used to use fonts on web pages until quite recently, you rely on fonts that are installed on your visitor's computer (or mobile device). Because of that, the list you just saw in the CSS Rule Definition dialogue box, is a limited list. That's because there are only a limited number of fonts that all users have. It's a bit like using a text editor, like LibreOffice Writer, where you can choose any font installed on your computer, but only the fonts installed on your computer. If you then email the document you created to a friend of yours, he or she may not have the same font on their computer. They will see a default font on their system.

The same with web pages. You are free to use any font you want on a web page you're creating, but if someone doesn't have the same font on their device, the default font will be used. That's why you get a drop-down menu when choosing the font, to give users a choice:

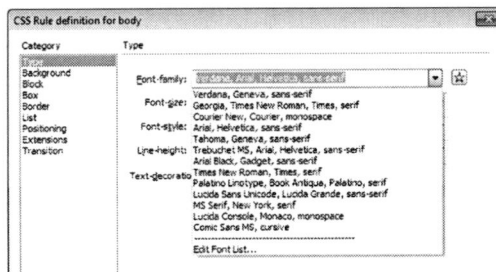

19 From the drop-down menu choose **Verdana, Geneva, sans-serif**.

Verdana will be your default font, but if someone doesn't have Verdana, then Geneva or any other sans-serif font will be used instead.

20 Leave the rest as it is and click OK.

Now, you're going to use Web Fonts for the headings.

WEB FONTS

Web Fonts started becoming popular quite recently and many web designers started using them in their web design workflow. Web Fonts are "downloadable" fonts that can be used on web pages with CSS. You can add Web Font to your website by "pointing" to it so that it loads into the web browser when a visitor comes to your website. This means that when a visitor comes to your website, the web browser downloads all HTML, CSS and the Web Fonts as well.

Interesting enough, Web Fonts work in all major web browsers. The example we're going to use here are Google Web Fonts. They're quite easy to add to your pages with just a few steps.

Use Web Fonts

21 Let's add a Web Font to the main heading on a page. Open your web browser and go to Web Fonts website:

> *http://www.google.com/webfonts*

22 When the page opens, click **Start choosing fonts**. You'll see a list of fonts available (at the moment of writing 489).

Woow! That is a lot of fonts you can use! Isn't it incredible? You don't have to rely on these 8 or 9 standard fonts, now you can use hundreds! And here's another amazing thing: Near the top of the page there is a field where you can type in (or paste) the text you use on the page. Let's do that!

23 Navigate back to Dreamweaver (keep Web Fonts page open) and open the page we were working on if you closed it.

24 Highlight the main heading – Heading 1 – and copy it to the clipboard.

25 Back in the web browser, paste the text from the clipboard in the **Preview Text** field as shown on the next page:

Google web fonts

	Word	Sentence	Paragraph
Showing			
489	Preview Text:	Welcome to EcoSai UK ▾	Size: 28 ▾ px Sorting: Trending ▾

26 Now that you see what the fonts look like, find the font you like (I chose **Kaushan Script** here):

Normal 400

Welcome to EcoSai UK

Kaushan Script, 1 Style by Pablo Impallari

27 Once you've found the font you like, click **Quick-use** on the right to open the page with steps to use the font.

28 Step 1 will be to choose the style you want

NOTE: Only choose the style you're going to use on a web page to avoid loading too many fonts/styles. Also, check the Page Load on the right, ideally it should be on the green, so the font will load quickly without slowing down the web page:

1. Choose the styles you want:

☐ *Kaushan Script*
  ☑ *Normal 400*

Grumpy wizards make toxic brew for the evil Queen and Jack

Page Load
39

29 Step 2 is to choose the character set you're about to use. In most cases, the default Latin will be fine.

30 Step 3 is to add the code to the page that will load the font from the server. Copy the code that appears here:

3. Add this code to your website:

```
<link href='http://fonts.googleapis.com/css?family=Kaushan+Script' rel='stylesheet' type='text/css'>
```

31 Navigate back to Dreamweaver, go to Code View and paste the code in the <head> section as shown here:

```
146  -->
147  </style>
148  <link href='http://fonts.googleapis.com/css?family=Kaushan+Script' rel='stylesheet' type='text/css'>
149  <meta name="description" content="EcoSaiUK are the community of environmentally aware group of people that want
     difference" />
150  <meta name="keywords" content="eco sai uk, organic, eco, environmentally-friendly, eco products, organic product
     organisation, based in the UK, volunteers, recycle, reuse, save the planet, eco forums, eco tips" />
151  </head>
```

32 The final step, Step 4, is to integrate the font into CSS. Copy the code from Step 4.

33 Back in Dreamweaver, find the rule for the main heading **.content h1** and paste the code within the curly braces, so the rule now looks like this:

```
.content h1 {
    font-family: 'Kaushan Script', cursive;
    font-size: 140%;
    color: #005A00;
}
```

34 Save the page and preview it in a web browser. Enjoy your new Web Font on a web page!

35 Add the same font to the subheading **h2**. Repeat Step 33 for **.content h2** rule.

36 Save all the changes and preview a page in a web browser.

And that's how you use Web Fonts with just a few steps.

Add text from other sources

Often you may be working on a website and you will be provided with text that goes on web pages. You may be given text documents in different file formats. One of the most popular file formats for text is RTF – Rich Text Format supported by many text editors. You may also use TXT files for some simple text without extra formatting. If you use a .txt file, you can open it within Dreamweaver without using any external editor.

In this exercise you're going to replace the page you were working on with an Eco Tips page.

37 Open **index.html** if it's not already opened and replace the main heading that reads **Welcome to EcoSai UK** with **Eco Tips**.

38 Save the page as **tips.html** using **File > Save As...**

39 Once you've saved the page, close **index.html**.

40 Highlight all the text below the main heading and delete it.

41 Navigate to the Files panel and double-click on **ecoTips.txt**. It opens here in Dreamweaver.

42 Highlight all the text and copy it to the clipboard using **Edit > Copy**.

43 Close ecoTips.txt and back to tips.html choose **Edit > Paste** to paste the text.

The first line of the text displays the same text as in the heading, so you'll need to remove it.

44 Highlight the line that reads **Eco Tips** below the main heading and press Delete key on your keyboard ot delete it. Leave the space between the main heading and the rest of the text.

The text you have just pasted on this page contains two subheadings, two sections within the text. They will need to be formatted as Headings 2.

45 Highlight the line that reads **EcoLiving at home** and format it as **Heading 2**:

Eco Tips

EcoLiving at home

Buy rechargeable batteries

46 Repeat the process for the second subheading that reads EcoLiving at work.

47 Save and preview the page in a web browser.

Create Ordered/Unordered Lists

Text should be formatted to give it some meaning, and that's the reason behind using text formatting like lists. Lists are easier to read than blocks of text. In this exercise, you will use lists to display a number of ideas on saving the planet and living a more ecological life at home and at work.

48 Highlight all the text between the first and second subheading:

EcoLiving at home

Buy rechargeable batteries
Buy local fruits and vegetables
Use reusable containers
Install energy efficient light bulbs
Turn the thermostat down
Turn off the lights in the rooms you are not in
Buy recycled paper

EcoLiving at work

49 Change the text into an unordered list by clicking on this icon in the Properties panel:

EcoLiving at home

- Buy rechargeable batteries
- Buy local fruits and vegetables
- Use reusable containers
- Inst
- Turr
- Turr
- Buy

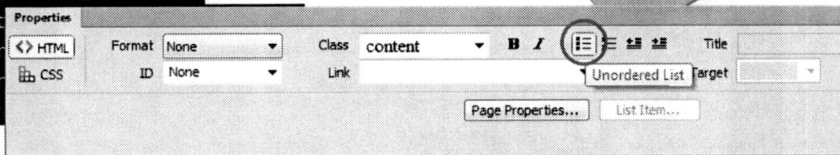

50 If you prefer to use an ordered list, click on the icon next to unordered list icon in the Properties panel.

51 If you want to customise the list (you may want to use squares instead of bullets), choose **Format > List > Properties...** from the menu with the cursor inside the list.

52 **List Properties** dialogue box opens, where you can choose either squares or bullets from **Style** drop-down menu:

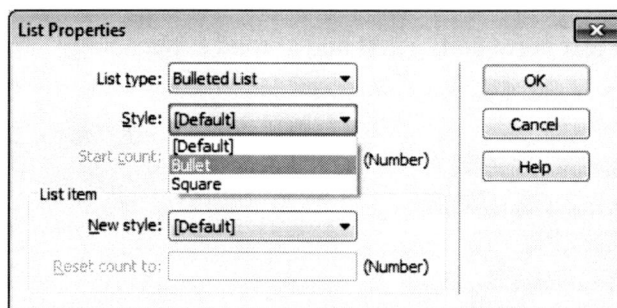

53 Repeat Steps 48 – 52 for the sections of text below the second subheading, so that the page looks like this:

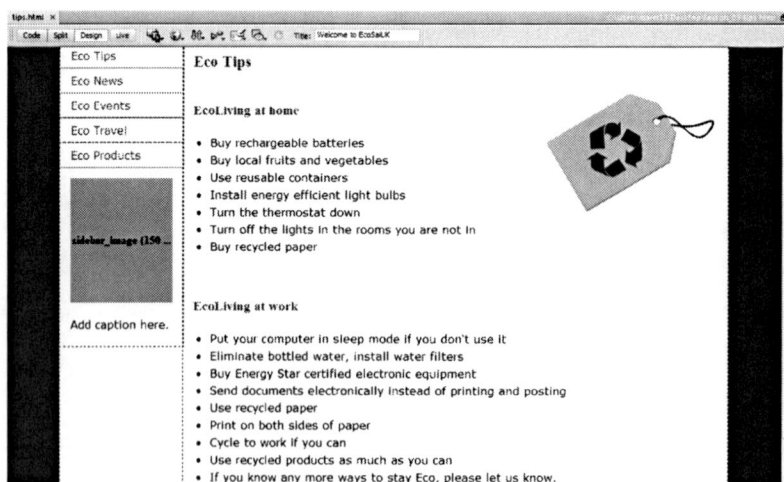

Add Tables

In the past tables were widely used for page layout, but now it is a thing of the past. We don't use the tables for layout purposes any more (even though you can see many websites built this way on the internet). Nowadays, and we have been doing it for over 10 years now, we use CSS for creating layouts. Don't get me wrong, we do still use tables, but not for layout purposes. We do use tables for presenting information, i.e. price lists, products list, or events lists as in this lesson.

One of the reasons why we don't use tables for layout any more is because they're harder to customise, format than using CSS.

54 Start by opening a page **events.html**.

55 Place the cursor below the main heading and type **Eco Events 2012**.

56 Format it as **Heading 2** and press Enter to move the cursor to a new line.

57 Insert a table by choosing **Insert > Table** or if you use the Insert panel click on **Table** in the Common category.

58 Set the following options for the table: **3** for Rows, **4** for Columns, **90%** for Table width, **1** for Border thickness, and set the Header to **Top** by clicking on Top. Press OK.

Just before you start adding content, you're going to customise the table. First, you're going to centre the table on the page using CSS. In the past, you would highlight the table on the page and aligned it to the centre using Properties panel (HTML), but as you already know, nowadays we're using CSS instead. To keep all the CSS rules in order, you will create a new CSS rule for a table under the .content rule. That's because the table is placed inside the div tag called content.

59 In the CSS Styles panel select the **.content h2** rule.

60 On the page, place the cursor anywhere inside the table and using the Tag Inspector at the bottom of the document window, click on **<table>** tag to select the entire table:

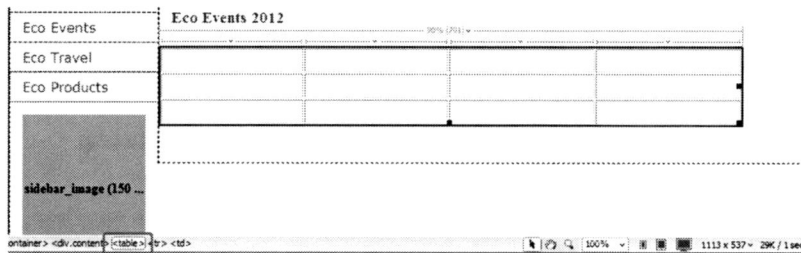

61 Click on **New CSS Rule** icon in the CSS Styles panel. Set Selector Type to **Compound**, Selector Name to **.content table** (just click once on Less Specific), Rule Definition to **(This document only)** and click OK.

62 In the CSS Rule dialogue box select **Box** category, deselect Same for all for Margin, and choose **auto** for Right and Left. Click OK.

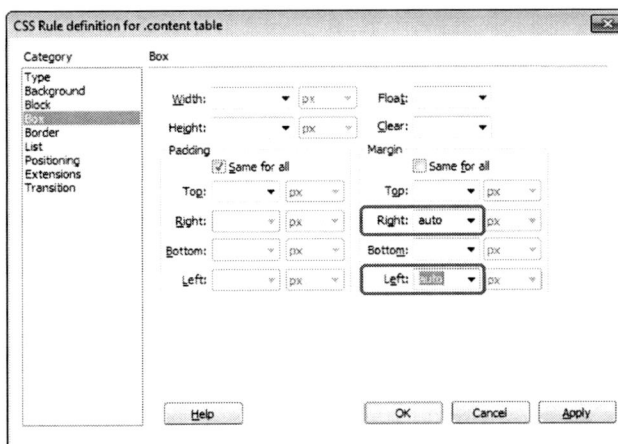

63 Add some data to the table. Add content as shown on the screenshot here:

Eco Events 2012

Date	Event	Location	Price
January 5th	Eco Living seminar	London	£20
January 23rd	Healthy Living workshop	Winchester	£25
February 5th	Organic Food in your kitchen	Milton Keynes	Free

NOTE: To add a new row in a table, place the cursor in the last cell and press Tab key on your keyboard. Alternatively, right-click in the last row and choose Table > Insert Row as shown here:

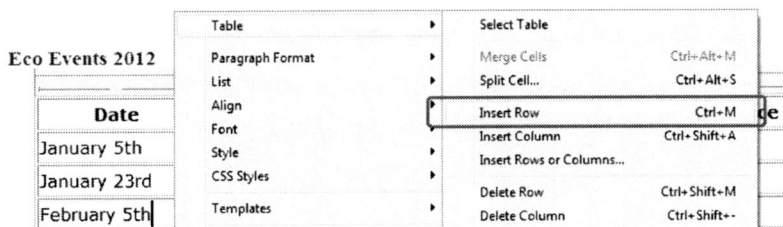

This is great, but if you have a table already created somewhere and if it is an .html file, you could easily copy and paste it here. Let's give it a go.

64 In the Files panel there is a file called **eventsTable.html**. It's a page with just a table. Open the file.

65 Highlight the entire table (you can use the Tag Inspector as in the Step 60) and copy the table to the clipboard: **Ctrl+C/Cmd+C** or **Edit > Copy**.

66 Back to events.html highlight the entire table and paste the table using either **Ctrl+V/ Cmd+V** or **Edit > Paste**.

How great is that! The entire table was replace with a new table! Very impressive in my opinion.

67 Save and preview the page in a web browser.

Your page should look like on the screenshot here:

Home | About Us | Contact Us

Eco Tips

Eco News

Eco Events

Eco Travel

Eco Products

Sidebar image

Add caption here.

Eco Events

Eco Events 2012

Date	Event	Location	Cost
Mar 10th	Nature Preserve Hike	Peak District National Park	Free
May 1st	May Day Parade	London	Free
June 12th	Mountain hike	Snowdonia National Park	Free
June 30th	Glaciel Park Tour	Iceland	£99
July 15th	Beginners Backpacking	Lake District National Park	£45
August 13th	East Trail Hike	Snowdon	£70
September 1st	3-Day Backpack	Black Mountains, Peak District	£199
October 10th	Book Club	Milton Keynes	Free
November 3rd	Day hike in Cotswolds	Cotswolds	£25
December 7th	Nature Photography hike	Devon	£99

Congratulations! You have successfully finished Lesson 5! Well done.

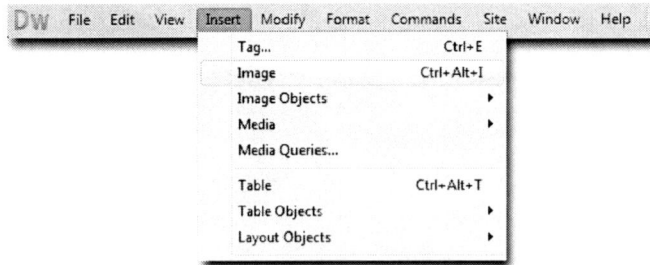

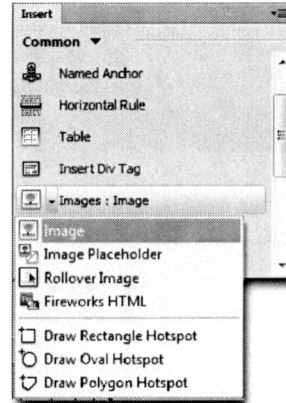

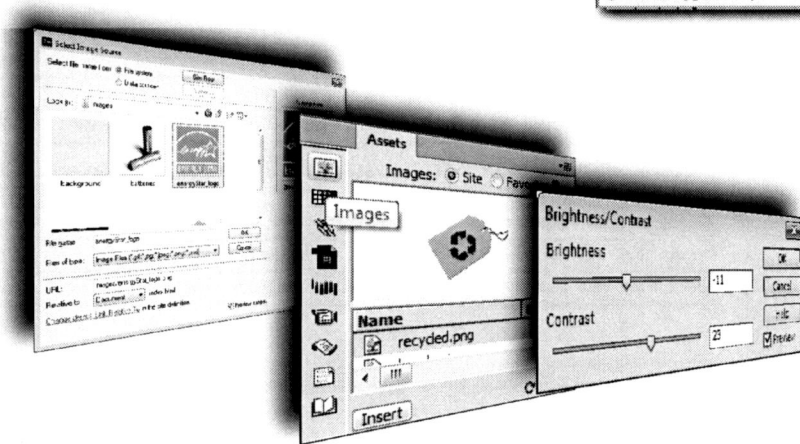

Lesson 6

Images

In this lesson you're going to start working with images and learn how to:

- Differentiate File Formats

- Add Images to the web pages

- Use Assets panel

- Import images using Adobe Bridge

- Import images from Photoshop or Fireworks

- Use Photoshop Smart Objects

- Edit images with Dreamweaver

This lesson will take about 1 hour 30 minutes to complete.

Basics of Images on the web

Images are a big part of web design process. All web pages use images as they bring life to them. And, inserting images in Dreamweaver is very easy as you're going to learn in this lesson.

In design world, there are two kinds of graphic/images:

- **vector graphics,**

- **raster graphics**

Vector graphics are created with mathematical calculations. This allows vector images to be resized without losing quality. Vector graphics are basically a number of lines, shapes and curves described with maths.

However, because vector graphics are created with maths, they're mainly used for logos, line art and drawings. Most logos are built with vector graphics. When creating a vector image, the mathematical formulas determine where to put the dots that create the image to get the best results when displaying the image. These formulas can produce an image that's scalable to any size with great quality.

Vector images are usually saved in these file formats:

- **AI**

- **EPS**

- **PICT**

However, the above three file formats are not supported by the web browsers, hence they're mostly used in vector applications like Adobe Illustrator, and then exported to SVG (Scalable Vector Graphic).

Raster graphics, or bitmap images as we call them, are composed from pixels - little, perfectly square dots of colour.

Raster images are much more popular on the web than vector graphics. Raster images are built from thousands and even millions of pixels that produce the final image. Each pixel within image has certain colour.

What mostly affects the quality of raster images, is the resolution. Resolution is a number of pixels within one inch. The more pixels per inch, the higher resolution of the image and the better the quality. Unfortunately, the higher the resolution the bigger the file size. Luckily, when you're building the websites, the images are only going to be displayed on screen and they don't need a higher resolution. The images on the screen are using a resolution of 72 dpi, so the file size will be much smaller if you compare it with an image that is going to be printed and uses a resolution of 300.

The screenshot on the next page illustrates the quality of the image at the resolution of 300dpi (on the left) and 72dpi (on the right) zoomed in to show you the difference it makes.

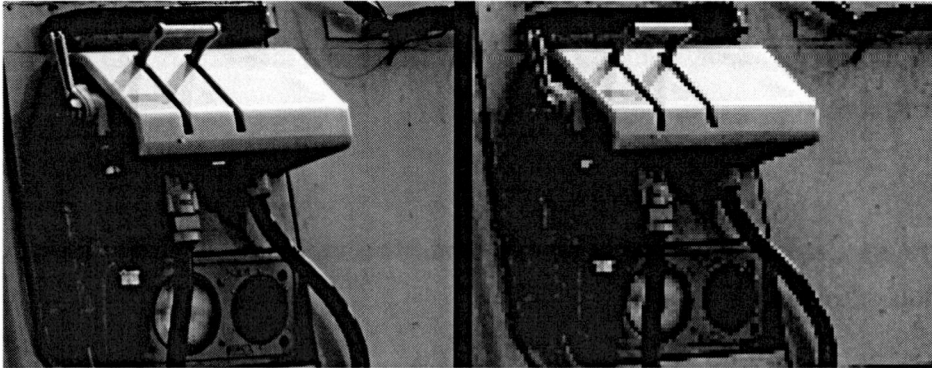

You can clearly see how pixelated is the image at 72dpi.

Because one of the most important factors when building websites is the speed at which the page loads into a web browser, you'll be optimizing the images and the images will be much smaller than the entire web page.

Colour is another important factor when preparing images for the web. Screens (nowadays you need to bear in mind portable devices like mobile phones and tablets as well) display only a fraction of the colours that human eye can see. And they display different levels of colour:

- mobile phones usually support up to 65,000 colours (with more and more mobile phones displaying even more)

- computer screens support up to 16.7 millions of colours.

The more colours image contains, the bigger the file size. That's why you'll look for compromise between resolution, file size and colour to get optimal quality with small file size so images load quickly on a web page.

Differentiate File Formats

The most popular file formats on the web are: **JPEG, PNG**, and **GIF**. All of these file formats are compatible with all the web browsers.

GIF

GIF stands for Graphics Interchange Format and it was one of the first file formats created. GIF doesn't use lossy compression (as JPEG does), but instead it limits the file size by limiting number of colours in the image. GIF is limited to only 256 colours, so it's not well suited for photographs, as they contain gradients and soft edges and millions of colours. It is very popular for elements like:

- logos, illustrations, buttons, and web interfaces.

JPEG

JPEG stands for Joint Photographic Experts Group and it is a file format that was created in 1992 to deal with the limitations of GIF file format. It reduces the file size by using the lossy compression. When you save a JPEG, you decide how much information you want to retain in the image and the more information you retain (the higher the quality setting) the bigger the file size. Your aim would be to reduce the file size as much as possible while retaining good quality of the image without creating distortions.

JPEG is the most popular file format and one of its powerful features is support for unlimited resolution. That's why it is a default choice for images on the web and a default file format on most digital cameras as a way of storing images on a memory card.

One big disadvantage of JPEG file format is lack of support for transparency.

PNG

PNG stands for Portable Network Graphic and it was created in 1995. PNG incorporates some of the best features of both GIF and JPEG:

- it supports transparency, unlimited resolution, and lossless compression.

Even though PNG has been around for a long time, its adoption wasn't fully implemented until recently as Internet Explorer 6 and earlier didn't support transparency in PNG files. PNG is also a great file format for saving screenshots and many scanners use PNG as their default fie format for saving scans.

Add Images to the web pages

1 Launch Adobe Dreamweaver CS6, if it is not already open.

2 Define a new Site. If you don't see the Welcome Screen (you may have disabled it through the Dreamweaver Properties), choose **Site > New Site** from the menu. The Site Setup dialogue box appears.

3 In the Site Name field, type **06 - Images**.

4 In the Local Site Folder field, click on the folder icon to the right and navigate to the **Lesson_06** folder containing the files for this lesson.

5 Select Lesson_06 folder, and click Open (Windows) or Choose (Mac). Then, click Select (Windows) or Choose (Mac) to choose this folder as your local root folder.

6 Click the arrow next to the **Advanced Settings** category on the left to reveal a list of tabs. Select **Local Info** category and next to **Default Images** folder field, click the folder icon. When the dialogue box opens, navigate to the images folder located inside Lesson_06 folder and click Select (Windows) or Choose (Mac).

7 In the Site Setup dialogue box click Save.

8 Choose **File > Open**, and select **index.html**. You're going to start by replacing the recycled logo on the homepage.

9 Select the recycled logo on the page and press Delete key on your keyboard to remove it.

There are many ways of inserting images onto your web pages. Here are a few examples:

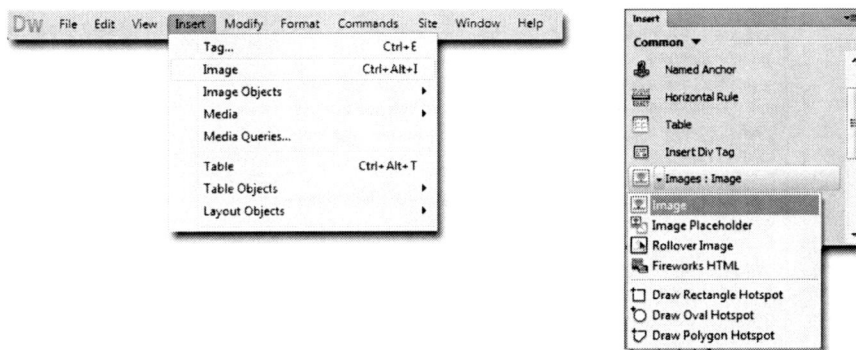

As you can see from the screenshot, you can insert images using Insert panel or Insert menu.

10 With your cursor still blinking where the image was, insert a new image using one of the methods and select **grass.jpg**. For alternate text type **Grass image** and press OK.

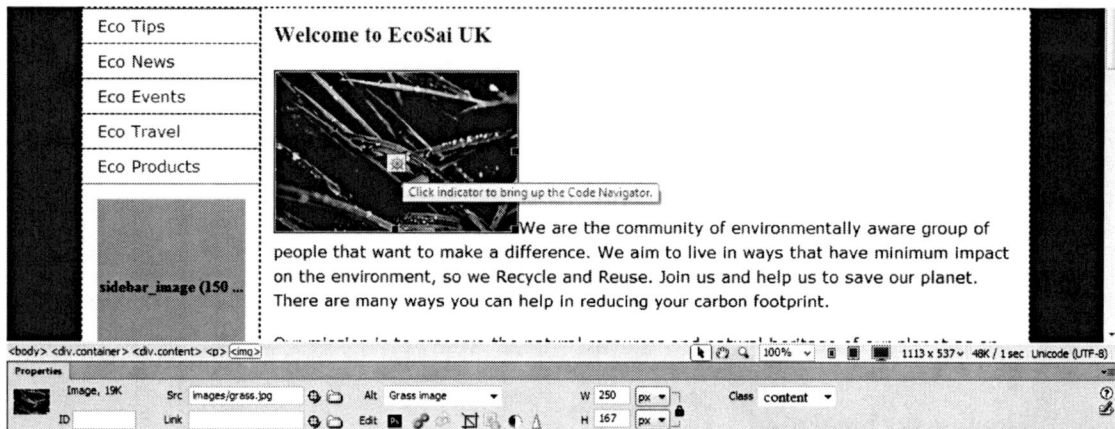

11 If the image doesn't appear in the same place, but it appears on the left, move it to the right by setting its class to **fltrt** as shown here:

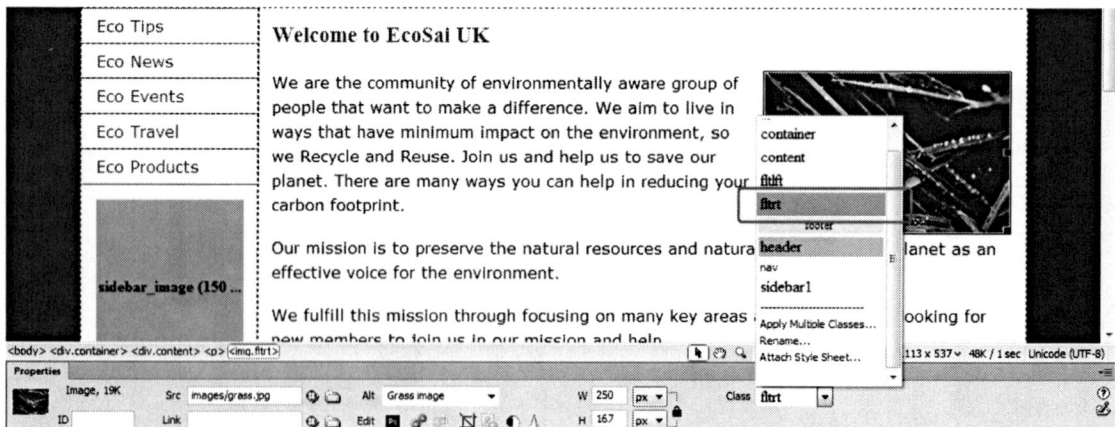

Now the image should appear on the right. Now, you're going to deal with this header image that appears to be not wide enough. You have two options:

- • - you could resize the image (make it wider), or

- • - you could resize the container (make it narrower)

You should avoid resizing graphics in Dreamweaver, so you're going to make the header a bit narrower and you're also going to insert this image once again, but this time as a background image, so it won't be that easy to be downloaded from the website.

12 Select the header image and check its dimensions using the Properties panel:

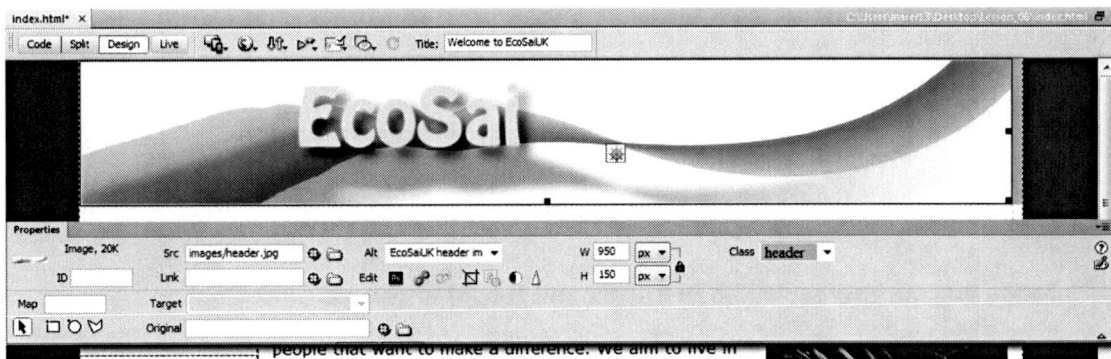

As you can see from the screenshot, the image is 950px x 150px.

13 Remove the image by pressing Delete key on your keyboard (with the image selected).

14 The header collapses, that's normal. That's because there is no content in the header. Find **.header** rule in the CSS Styles panel and edit it to bring up the CSS Rule Definition dialogue box like the one shown here:

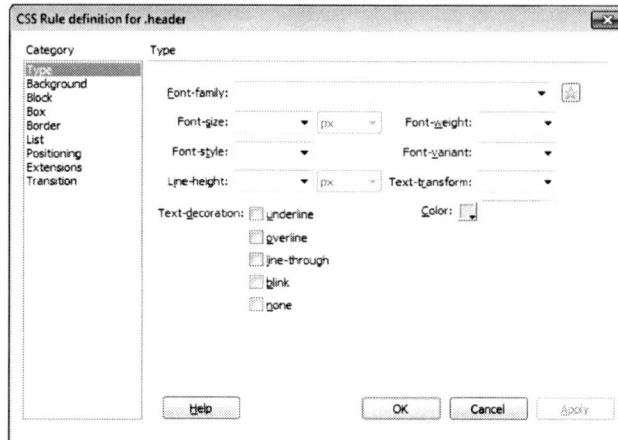

15 In the Background category set background-image to header.jpg.

16 In the Box category set Width to **950px** and Height to **150px**. Click OK.

The image appears in the header section once again, but this time it's a background image.

17 Save and preview in the page in a web browser.

Next step will be to resize the page so it's a bit narrower, the size of the header image (950px).

18 Back in Dreamweaver, in the CSS Styles panel find a rule **.container** and edit it.

19 In the **Box** category, change the Width to **950px** and click OK.

Don't worry if it looks like something went wrong. It didn't. The page is now 950px wide, the same width as the header graphic. The right column, .content, moved below the sidebar. Before you do anything, I would suggest to preview the page in a web browser first.

20 Preview the page in a web browser once again.

If the page still looks the same (it should), now you'll start looking for reason why this happened. I'll give you a minute. I'll wait...

Ok. That's enough time... Here's what happened if you haven't worked it out:

The .content column moved down because it doesn't fit here any more. Each column has its own width defined in pixels. Because you've reduced the width of the web page, you'll need to resize one of the columns as well.

Let me show you what I mean (you can check the CSS):

- The page is now 950px wide;

- The .sidebar is 180px wide;

- The .content is 780px wide.

- 180px + 780px = 960px.

Because the sidebar is narrow anyway, let's make the right column a bit narrower (10px).

21 Change the width of the right column, **.content**, to **770px** using the CSS Styles panel.

The page is "back to normal". Well done.

22 Save and preview the page in a web browser.

In the next step, you're going to add an image in the sidebar.

So far, you have an image placeholder in the sidebar. Now it will be replaced by an image.

23 Select the image placeholder in the sidebar and notice the properties of it – **150px x 180px**.

24 Double-click on the image placeholder. This opens **Select Image Source** dialogue box like this one:

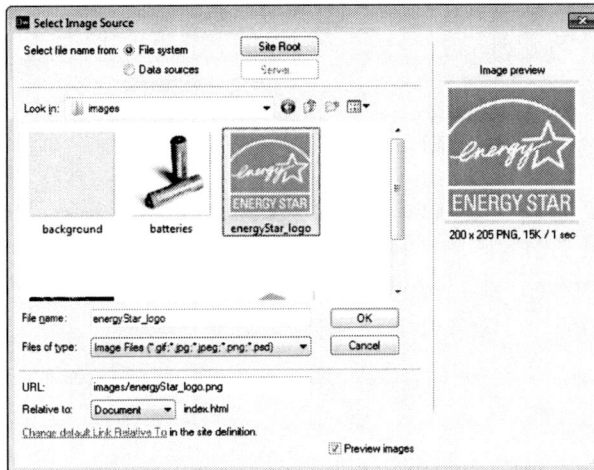

25 In the dialogue box select **energyStar_logo.png** and click OK (You can also double-click on the image).

Notice two things. First, the image is a bit bigger than the sidebar, that's ok for now, you're going to fix it later in this lesson. Second, you weren't prompted for an Alternative text, were you? No, because you replace an existing image or image placeholder. So, in this case you'll need to add an Alternative text using the Properties panel.

26 With the image still selected, type **Energy Star logo** in the Alt section in the Properties panel as shown on the screenshot here:

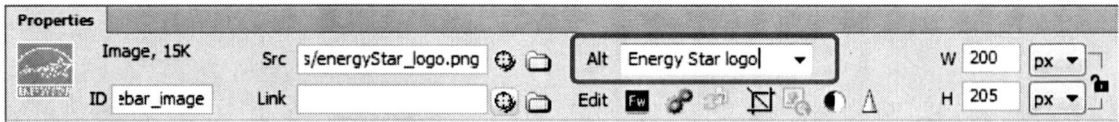

Before you start editing images, let's talk about the Assets panel first.

Use Assets panel

Assets panel displays assets for the site associated with the document that is active in the Document window. That's why you will need to define a Dreamweaver site before using the Assets panel.

Assets panel provides two ways of displaying assets as shown below:

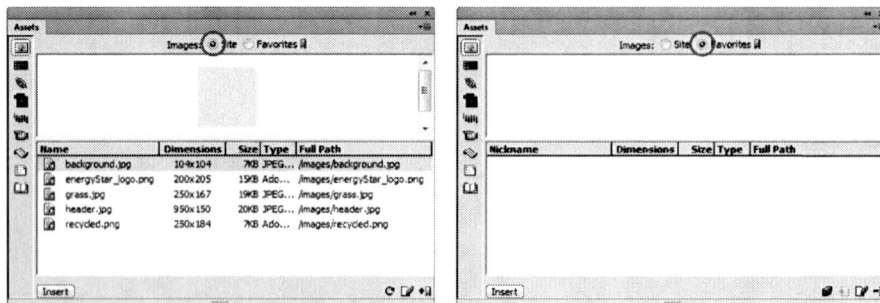

Site List   Favorites List

NOTE: If you don't see the Assets panel, choose **Window > Assets**.

Site list shows all of the assets in your site (to access images, click on the first icon in the top left corner - icon that looks like a tree).

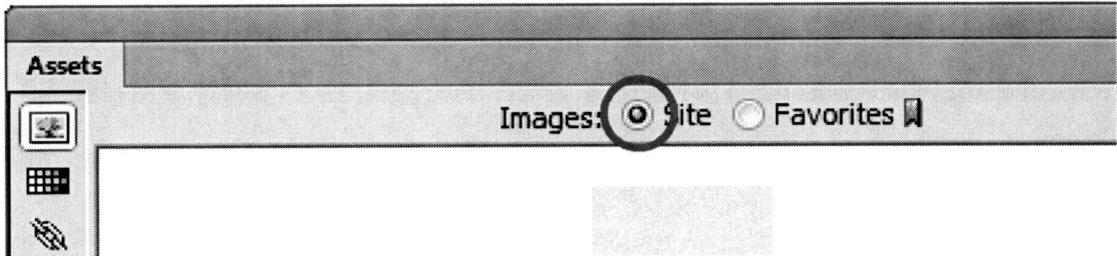

Favorites list only shows assets that you have chosen, so it should be empty.

To access the Site list or the Favorites list, click on one of the buttons on the top of the Assets panel. By default, assets are listed alphabetically so it's easier to find them. If you prefer, you can change the sorting of images by clicking on one of the columns: Name, Dimensions, Size or Type.

There are a number of different categories in the Assets panel and as you move your cursor over the icons on the left side, the descriptions appear as shown on the screenshot:

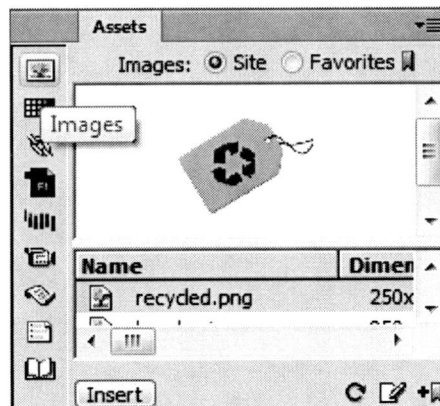

NOTE: Did you notice something interesting about the Assets panel? Did you notice that the Assets panel doesn't display all the images? Did you notice that there are more images in the images folder than in the Assets panel? If this happened, click on Refresh icon at the bottom of the Assets panel and the batteries image should appear as well.

You can also use the Assets panel to insert images on web pages. That's what you're going to do now.

27 Open **tips.html**.

You're going to move the recycling logo to the second section of the page – EcoLiving at work - and then you're going to insert another image in the first section – the image of the rechargeable batteries.

28 Click on the recycling logo, hold the mouse button down and drag it to the beginning of the second section.

When you release the mouse button, the image will automatically appear on the right side in the second section as shown on the screenshot on the next page (before and after):

Eco Tips

EcoLiving at home

- Buy rechargeable batteries
- Buy local fruits and vegetables
- Use reusable containers
- Install energy efficient light bulbs
- Turn the thermostat down
- Turn off the lights in the rooms you are not in
- Buy recycled paper

EcoLiving at work

- Put your computer in sleep mode if you don't use it
- Eliminate bottled water, install water filters
- Buy Energy Star certified electronic equipment
- Send documents electronically instead of printing and posting

Eco Tips

EcoLiving at home

- Buy rechargeable batteries
- Buy local fruits and vegetables
- Use reusable containers
- Install energy efficient light bulbs
- Turn the thermostat down
- Turn off the lights in the rooms you are not in
- Buy recycled paper

EcoLiving at work

- Put your computer in sleep mode if you don't use it
- Eliminate bottled water, install water filters
- Buy Energy Star certified electronic equipment
- Send documents electronically instead of printing and

Well done! You have dragged and dropped an image into another location on a page! And if you look at the properties for the image, it kept its properties like class and Alternative text! Very impressive.

29 Now with the Assets panel open, click on **batteries.jpg** and drag the image onto the page. When your cursor appears at the beginning of the first section of the page, release the mouse button.

30 When the Image Tag Accessibility Attributes dialogue box opens, type **Rechargeable batteries image** and press OK.

31 The image will appear on the left side of the page, so set the Class drop-down menu in the Properties panel to **fltrt** so that the image moves to the right side of the page.

Congratulations! Well done! It's time to move on to the next section. We'll talk about adding images using Adobe Bridge and Photoshop and Fireworks and you are going to resize the image in the sidebar you inserted earlier in this lesson.

Import images using Adobe Bridge

Adobe Bridge is an essential application for web designers. It is a cross-platform file browser and you can use Adobe Bridge to quickly browse directories of images. It is fully integrated with Dreamweaver. You can launch Bridge straight from Dreamweaver to browse through the images before you drag them into your page.

32 Open **tips.html** if you closed it. Remove the image placeholder in the sidebar.

Now, you will use Bridge to drag and drop an image onto your web page.

33 Launch Adobe Bridge by choosing **File > Browse in Bridge...**

NOTE: You could just launch Bridge on its own from the list of applications (Applications on Mac and Program Files on Windows), but there is a reason why you are launching Bridge from Dreamweaver. Here's why:

If you launch Bridge from Dreamweaver, Bridge will automatically open and navigate into your site folder! How great is that? So now, you should have Bridge opened pointing to Lesson_06 folder.

34 Double click images folder to open it. If the images thumbnails are small, resize them using slider in the bottom right corner of Bridge:

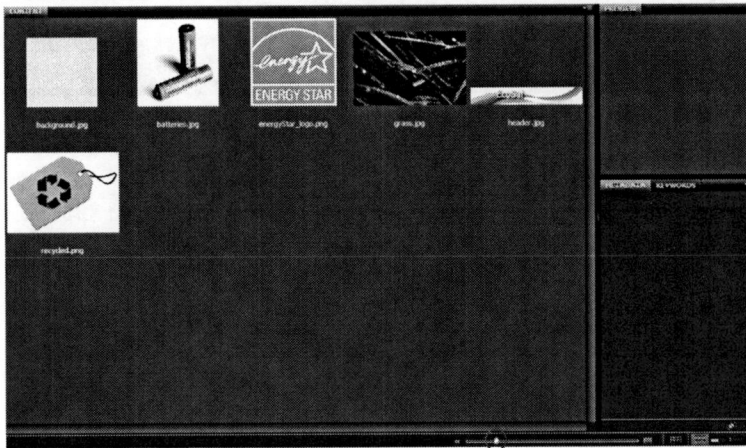

NOTE: To make sure you work with the same workspace and the arrangement of the panels is the same, make sure you are working in the Essentials workspace. You'll find the name of the workspace in the top right corner of the Bridge interface as shown on the screenshot on the next page:

ESSENTIALS   FILMSTRIP   METADATA   OUTPUT ▼

Bridge has a fantastic feature called Compact Mode. You're going to use it to insert an image on a page in Dreamweaver. What is exciting about the Compact Mode is that when you activate it Bridge interface gets smaller so you can see the other applications (and that's great because you want to see Dreamweaver), but it also stays on top of other applications! All the time! Very exciting feature in Dreamweaver. I love using it.

35 To activate Compact Mode in Bridge click on the **Compact Mode** icon in the top right corner of the application window as shown here:

ESSENTIALS   FILMSTRIP   METADATA   OUTPUT ▼   🔎▾

> 📁 images   ▨ ▭ ▾ | ★ ▾   Sort by Filena Switch to Compact Mode

36 With Bridge and Dreamweaver visible (you can move Bridge to a side so you can see the Dreamweaver page clearly) find the image **energyStar_logo.png**, then click and drag it onto the page.

37 When the cursor appears in the sidebar, below the menu, release the mouse button to drop the image.

38 Type **Energy Star logo** in the Alternate text field in the Image Tag Accessibility Attributes dialogue box and press OK.

Congratulations! You have successfully inserted an image on the page using Adobe Bridge and its Compact Mode. Well done! You can close Bridge now.

Import images from Photoshop or Fireworks

Adobe Photoshop and **Adobe Fireworks** are both excellent applications used for editing and optimising graphics for the web. Normally you would prepare your graphics in Photoshop or Fireworks and save them as GIF, PNG or JPG. However, you can also copy and paste images between Photoshop / Fireworks and Dreamweaver. In this exercise, you're going to use Adobe Photoshop.

NOTE: if you don't have Photoshop or Fireworks, you can download free trial versions of these applications from Adobe website at www.adobe.com.

39 Open Photoshop and choose **File > Open**. In the Open dialogue box navigate to the PSD folder within your site and choose **header.psd**.

40 When the image opens, choose **Select > All** and **Edit > Copy**. This selects and copies the image to the clipboard.

41 Back in Dreamweaver, open **index.html**, place your cursor in the bottom section of the page before **Founded 20 years ago....** and choose **Edit > Paste**.

42 Now, you're going to see something new in Dreamweaver CS6 – **Image Optimization** dialogue box:

Our Organisation at work

Founded became increasingly alarmed by the degradatio zens, business leaders, like-minded environn o create a balance between growth and environm

We organise energy expos, workshops dship of our environment and recycling programs and activities that encourage sustainable practices.

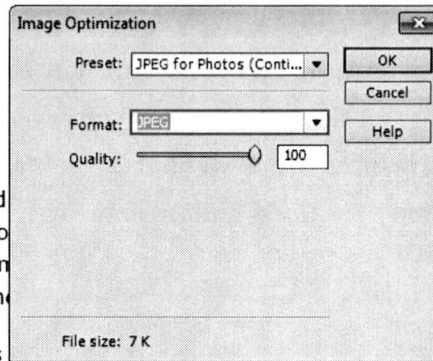

43 Set the Preset and Format to **JPEG** and set the Quality to **100**. Press OK.

44 In the Save Web Image dialogue box that appears save the image as **header_cropped**.

45 In the Image Description dialogue box type **EcoSaiUK logo**.

46 Align the image to the left by setting the Class to **fltlft**. Done.

NOTE: I used Photoshop as an example here but Fireworks could be used in the same way.

Use Photoshop Smart Objects

This is one of my favourite features in Dreamweaver (one of many as you may know so far). Dreamweaver supports use of Photoshop's Smart Objects – native Photoshop PSD files that can be used in Dreamweaver and optimised for use on the Web.

PSD is a native Photoshop format that supports everything you do in Photoshop, whether it's creating layers, using layer styles/effects, anything you can think of. Because PSD supports layers, PSD files are very big, much bigger than JPG, PNG, or GIF files. PSD files are also not supported by the web browsers, what makes sense if you think about their file size. You don't want to place a 2 or 3MB file on your web page, do you?

When you try to place a PSD file on a web page in Dreamweaver, Dreamweaver is going to save it to one of the supported file formats (GIF, PNG or JPG). However, when you save a Smart Object to one of these file formats Dreamweaver will keep a live connection to the original PSD file. This is the workflow for PSD files that Adobe recommends. If you make any changes to the PSD file, a red arrow will appear on the image on your web page in Dreamweaver to let you know that the original file has changed.

Have a look at the screenshot to see what I mean:

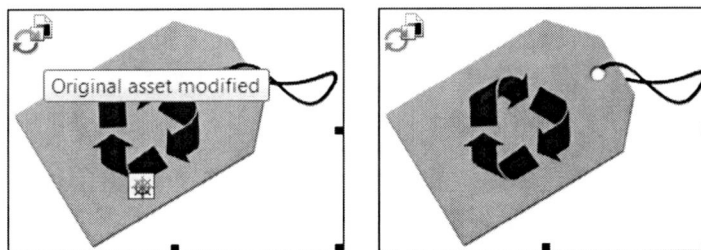

The image with two green arrows is the image that is up to date with the original PSD file, the image with one red arrow is the image that is "out of sync" - PSD file has changed, but the image on the page hasn't updated yet.

In this part of the lesson you're going to replace the image header_cropped in the second section of the page with the PSD version of it and you will import it as a Smart Object.

47 Open **index.html** if you closed it.

48 Remove the **header_cropped.jpg** image from the page.

There are many ways of inserting PSD files (the same ones as when inserting JPEGs or PNGs). You can use one of the methods you prefer:

- **Insert panel**

- **Insert menu**

- **Assets panel**

49 Using one of you preferred methods for inserting images insert an image **header.psd** from the PSD folder.

50 In the Image Optimization dialogue box accept the defaults and press OK.

51 In the **Save Web Image** dialogue box save the image as **header.jpg** in the images folder.

52 When the **Image Tag Accessibility Attributes** dialogue box opens, type **Header image small** and press OK.

NOTE: In previous versions of Dreamweaver (before CS6), Image Preview dialogue box used to open, now you just get the Image Optimization dialogue box instead.

53 Now align the image to the left. In the Properties panel choose **fltlft** from the Class drop-down menu.

54 Preview the page in a web browser and save it when prompted.

55 Back to Dreamweaver notice the icon that appears in the top left corner of the image. This icon identifies that this image is a Smart Object.

Add caption here.   **Our Organisation at work**

Founded 20 years ago as an ecological group, we became increasingly alarmed by the degradation of the environment. We work with citizens, business leaders, like-minded environmental groups and government officials to create a balance between growth and environmental preservation.

The green circular arrows indicate that the original image is the same as the image placed on the page. If you change the original image, the arrows will change and you'll see it in just a moment. You'll change the original file outside Dreamweaver.

56 Launch Adobe Photoshop and open **header.psd** using **File > Open**.

57 When image opens, choose **Image > Adjustments > Hue/Saturation**. You're going to colorise the image a bit.

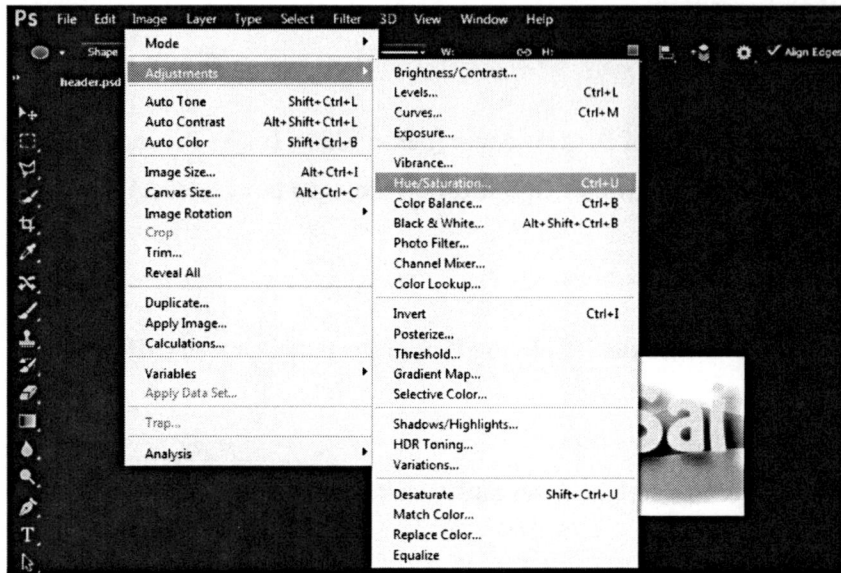

58 Move the **Hue** slider to change the colours within the image:

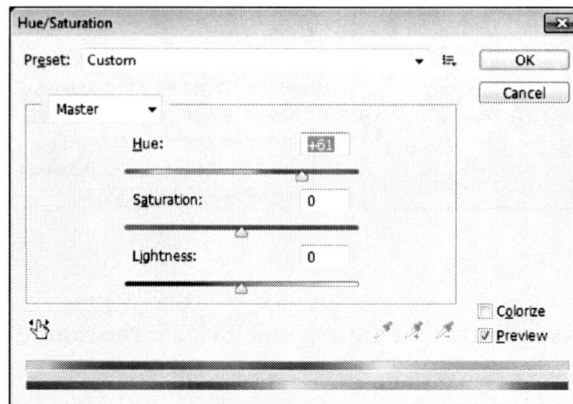

59 Save the file by choosing **File > Save** or pressing **Ctrl+S** on Windows or **Cmd+S** on Mac and close Photoshop.

60 Back to Dreamweaver, notice how the icon on the image changed.

Dreamweaver indicates that the original file has changed. You don't have to update the file now. You can do it later on. So how do you update the image? It's really simple.

61 Right-click image and choose **Update from Original** in menu.

The image has updated. As you can see, Photoshop Smart Objects are great in designing process. They're perfect for images that are often updated.

Congratulations! Well done. Now you can move on to the last section of this lesson. We'll talk about editing images.

Edit images with Dreamweaver

One of the most important factors when preparing images for the web is to optimise them, in other words, to balance the quality of the image with pixel dimensions and file size. When preparing images that go on the web page, you would use a graphics editor i.e. Adobe Photoshop or Adobe Fireworks. But what if you want to edit an image that's already been placed on the page? Dreamweaver offers some features that you can use to modify an existing image without having to use an external graphics editor. Obviously, ideally you would use an editor like Photoshop or Fireworks, but if you just want to make some simple edits, you can use Dreamweaver for that. You will start by resizing the image in the sidebar.

62 Back to **index.html**, select **energyStar_logo.png** in the sidebar.

If there is a gap between the image and the sidebar edge on the left, you'll fix that first. The gap appears when the image ends up being inside a paragraph.

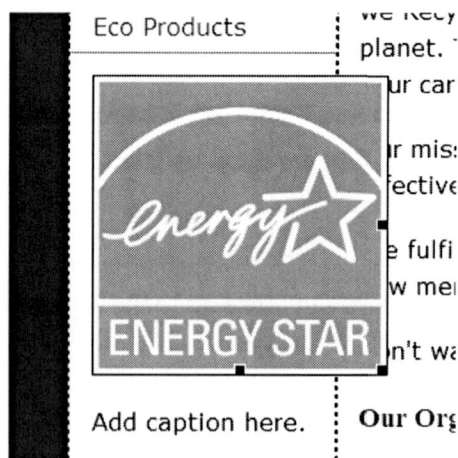

63 Click on the Split View button to see the code as well as the design. Keep image selected.

64 The code for the image will be highlighted and around it you will see the opening and closing <p>tag. Delete it.

65 Go back to Design View and the image will now be nicely aligned to the left:

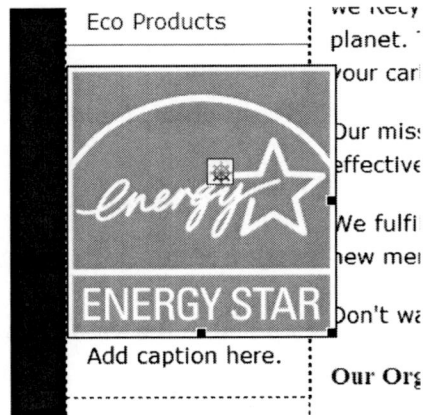

66 Now hold down the Shift key on your keyboard and start resizing the image using its bottom right corner handle until it fits into the sidebar.

NOTE: You can keep looking at the Properties panel as you are resizing the image and when the width (W) reaches 180px release the mouse button and then Shift key (sidebar is 180px wide).

Here's the information about the images you can find in the Properties panel:

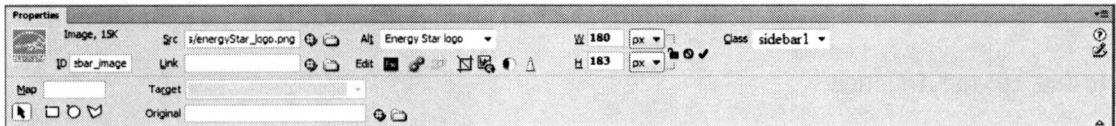

Starting from the left, you'll find:

- the file size in the top left corner (**Image, 15K**),

- below the file size a field called ID (**sidebar_image**),

- the dimensions of the image (**W** and **H**),

- moving to the right Src field - location of the file (**images/energyStar_logo.png**),

- directly below - link field (more on that in the lesson on navigation),

- Alt field for Alternative Text for Accessibility,

- Edit section (more on that in just a moment),

- and finally Width and Height (W and H).

Look at the image in the sidebar. Does it look nice and crispy? Is it sharp? I bet it isn't. Here's what to do to make it look better:

67 Select the image and in the Properties panel click on **Resample** icon as shown here:

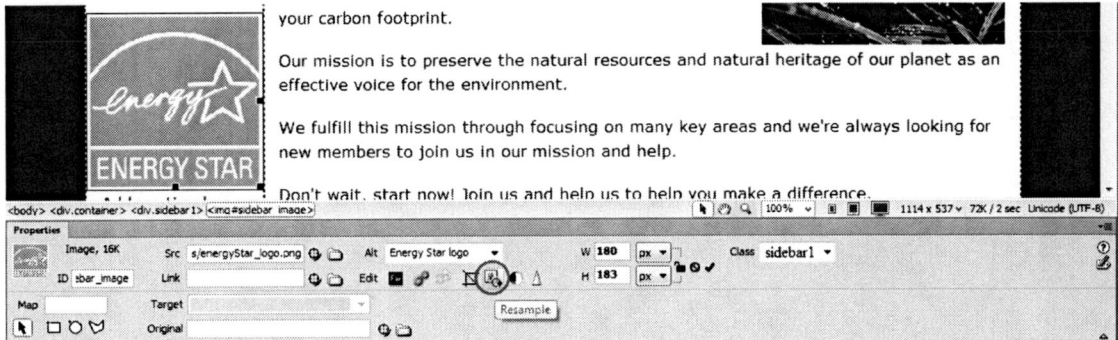

68 A dialogue box will appear warning you that you are about to change the image permanently. That's fine. Click OK.

69 Check the image. It now looks much better than before.

This is one of the options for simple edits of images in Dreamweaver. Next to Resample icon (to the left) you can see the Crop icon that can be used for cropping images (not resizing, cropping). The icon on the right, on the other hand, can be used to improve the brightness and contrast of the image. That's what you're going to do now.

70 With the image still selected, click on **Brightness and Contrast** icon:

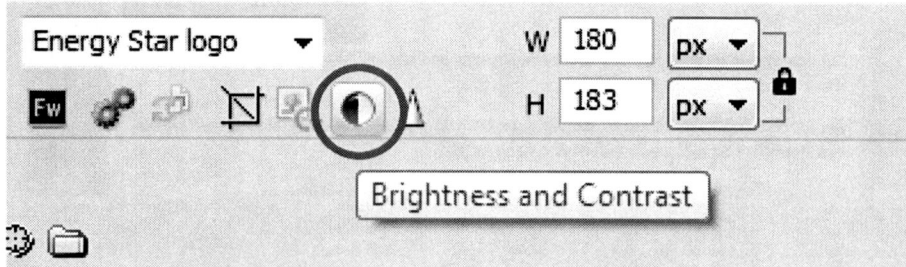

71 A dialogue box will appear warning you that you are about to change the image permanently. That's fine. Click OK

72 In the **Brightness/Contrast** dialogue box adjust the sliders to your liking and press OK.

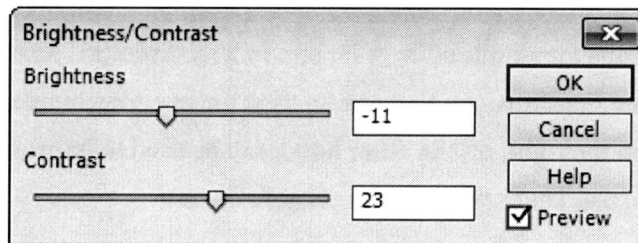

Very well done. These are a few examples on how you can edit images on web pages in Dreamweaver.

Congratulations! You have successfully completed the lesson.

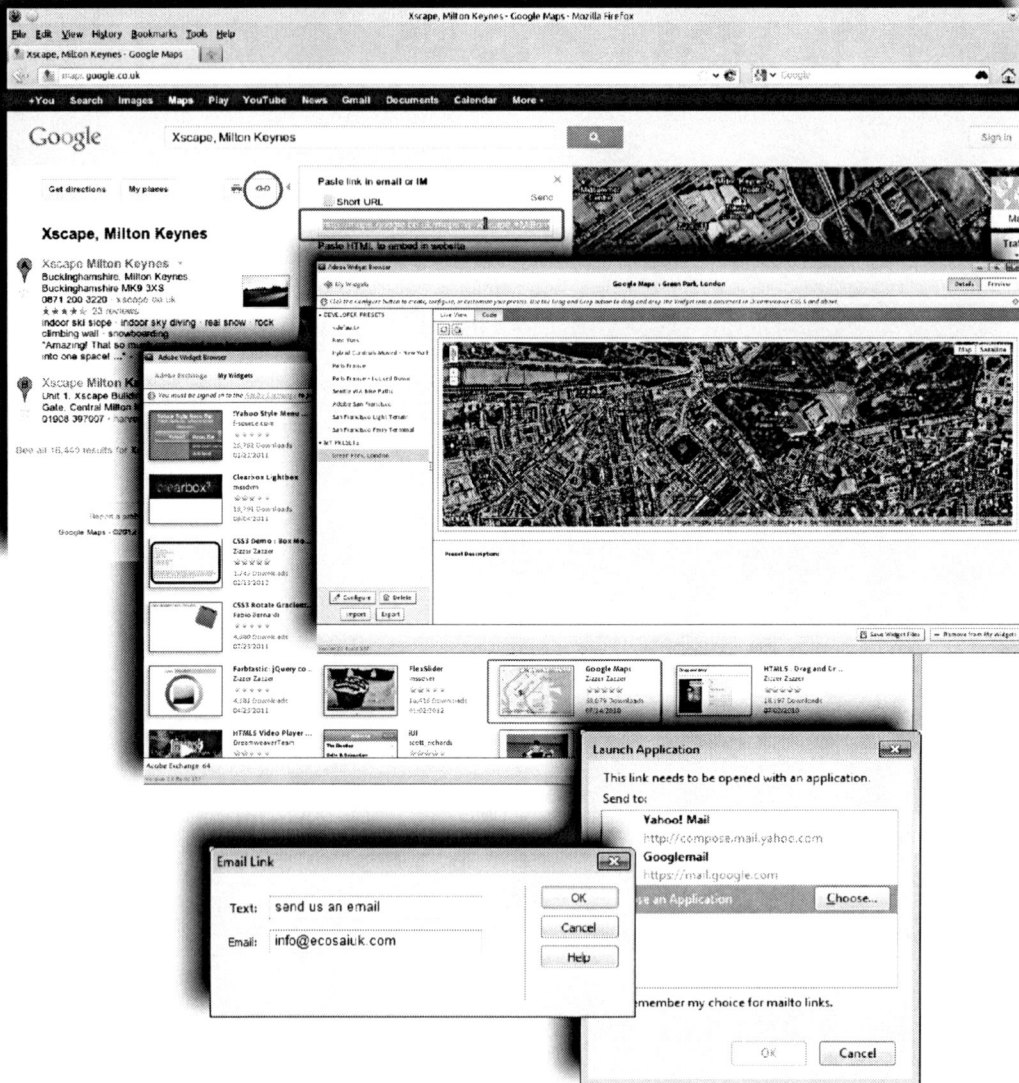

Lesson 7

CSS and Navigation

In this lesson you're going to start working with navigation and learn how to:

- Create internal links

- Create links to external websites

- Create Live Google Map with Widget Browser

- Set up e-mail links

- Insert drop-down menu using Spry

- Customise drop-down menu with CSS

This lesson will take about 1 hour 30 minutes to complete.

Hyperlinks

The Web would be a boring place without hyperlinks (or just links as they're often called). Can you imagine browsing through internet without ability to click on a link to open another page? If we didn't have links, every time you wanted to see something new, you would need to open a new tab in your web browser manually and type in the web address. Can you imagine typing in an address like this:

https://www.adobe.com/cfusion/mmform/index.cfm?name=notify-me-ccm

I don't think so, I wouldn't want to type that in... I think you get the idea.

What are Hyperlinks you may be asking? Hyperlink, or link as we usually call it as it's shorter, is an element on a page that has a connection with another element on the same computer or on the Internet.

Here's how the World Wide Web Consortium define a link:

> *" A hyperlink (or link) is a word, group of words, or image that you can click on to jump to a new document or a new section within the current document. "*

When you move the cursor over a link in a Web page, the arrow will turn into a little hand.

Links are specified in HTML using the <a> tag. The behaviour of the hyperlink is specified by HTML, as in the example below:

<a href="http://www.adobe.com/products/dreamweaver.html" target="_blank"> Adobe Dreamweaver CS6 </a>

Here's a quick overview of the code:

- **a** is an HTML element that defines a link

- **href** is an attribute that points to page or file (in this case a web page)

- the address of a web page or a file that is going to load upon click follows the href attribute and appears in quotes

- **target** attribute defines whether the link is going to open in a new tab/window or is going to reload the content within the same window, we'll talk about it later in this lesson

- after the > symbol comes a text that is going to be visible to the visitor

- finally, the closing tag **</a>** defines the end of the link

How do you recognise a link, you may ask? If you have a link on a page, when you move your cursor over it it changes into a hand icon like this:

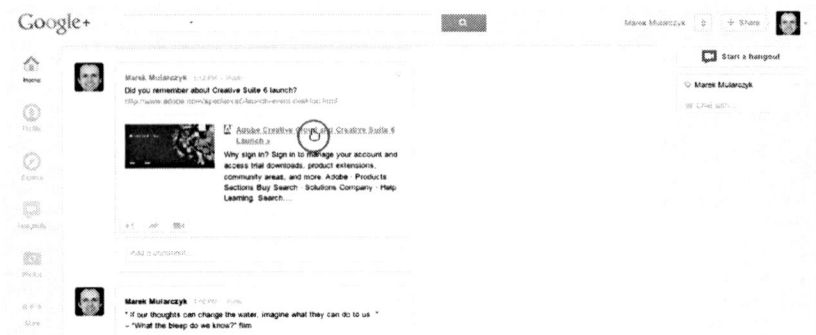

Links – Internal vs External

There are two main kinds of hyperlinks (links):

- internal

- external

Internal links navigate to another page or file that could be downloaded within the same website, i.e. About Us page or Contact page etc.

External links navigate to an external website or a file somewhere else on the Internet, not on the same website. An example could be a link on my blog pointing to a Download page on Adobe website.

Create Internal links

Now you're going to learn how easy it is to create links in Dreamweaver.

1 Launch Adobe Dreamweaver CS6, if it is not already open.

2 Define a new Site.

3 In the Site Name field, type **Lesson_07**.

4 In the Local Site Folder field, click on the folder icon to the right and navigate to the Lesson_07 folder containing the files for this lesson.

5 Select Lesson_07 folder, and click Open (Windows) or Choose (Mac). Then, click Select (Windows) or Choose (Mac) to choose this folder as your local root folder.

6 Click arrow next to the Advanced Settings category, select Local Info category and next to Default Images folder field, click the folder icon. When dialogue box opens, go to images folder inside Lesson_07 and click Select(Windows) or Choose(Mac).

7 In the Site Setup dialogue box click Save.

8 Choose **File > Open** and select **index.html**.

9 When the page opens, place your cursor in the horizontal section directly below the header. That's where you're going to create a text based menu.

You're going to add links to the pages: Home, About Us, and Contact Us as well as to the menu in the sidebar on the left.

10 Highlight the word **Home** in the horizontal menu section and choose **Insert >**

Hyperlink. In the dialogue box that appears leave the Text as Home and in the Link section

below click on the folder icon.

11 In the Select File dialogue box choose **index.html** and accept it.

12 For Target click on the drop-down menu next to it and choose **_self**. Click OK.

13 Save the page and preview it in a web browser. Inspect the link by positioning your

cursor over it. Your cursor should change to a hand icon which indicates a link on a page.

14 Back in Dreamweaver highlight the word **About Us**.

15 This time use the Insert panel, and in the Common category click on **Hyperlink**.

16 As there is no About Us page yet, in the dialogue box that appears leave the Text as

About Us and in the Link section below type **#**.

NOTE: Hash (#) symbol creates a so-called "dummy link" - a link that doesn't link to anywhere but allows you to check the link interaction, so you can see your cursor changing to a hand icon when you're over the About Us link, but when you click on it, nothing happens.

17 For Target click on the drop-down menu next to it and choose **_self**. Click OK.

18 Save the page and preview it in a web browser. Inspect the link by positioning your cursor over it.

19 Let's do one more. Highlight the word **Contact Us**, and this time using the Properties panel add following information as on the screenshot here:

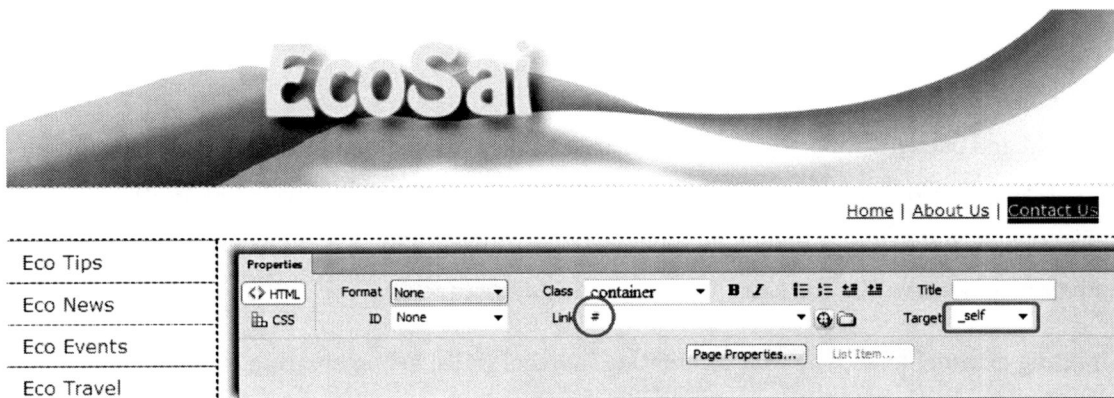

If you look in the Files panel, you will notice that we actually have Contact Us page.

20 Relink the last link, so it's pointing to **contactus.html**.

As you may have noticed, the links on the page appear with the text being underlined. That's the normal behaviour with links. You're going to customise the links with CSS a bit later.

21 Save the page and preview it in a web browser.

Congratulations! You have successfully added links to the horizontal menu.

Create links to external websites

Internal and external links work very similar, and they are defined in HTML code in a similar way. However, external links when clicked take visitor to an external website. Another difference is that external links open in a new web browser tab or window unlike internal links which open within the same browser window/tab.

Creating external links is as easy as creating internal links. When creating external links you can use the same method you used earlier.

22 Start by opening a web browser of your choice and navigate to Google Maps.

You're going to create a link to a map with your chosen location, we'll use it as the location of the office of our fictitious company.

23 When the page opens, find the map of the location of your choice (in my case I'm using *http://maps.google.co.uk* for the address but feel free to use the address that works best for your country.

24 When the map with your chosen address loads, zoom in or out as needed to customise the map.

25 Once you're happy with the way the map looks, click on the chain icon at the top of the page as shown here and copy the link:

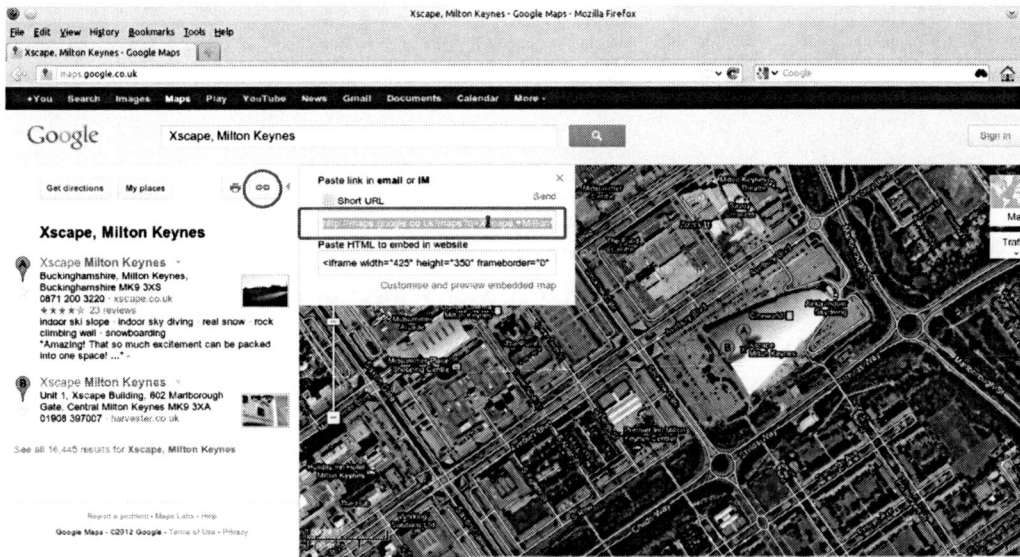

26 Back in Dreamweaver open **contactus.html**.

27 Highlight the text that reads **Map of our location**.

28 In the Properties panel paste the code you copied in Step 25 in the Link section (you can use Ctrl+V / Cmd+V).

29 For Target click on the drop-down menu next to it and choose **_blank** . This will open the link in a new browser tab or a new browser window.

30 Save the page and preview it in a web browser. Inspect the link by positioning your cursor over it. Your cursor should change to a hand icon which indicates a link on a page.

31 Click on the link and your web browser should open a new page in a new tab (or window) with a map. Close the web browser and navigate back to Dreamweaver.

Congratulations! You have successfully added an external link that opens a map with your location. Well done. Now let me show you how to insert a live map on a web page using Widget Browser. You will need a free Adobe account to use the Widget Browser so if you don't have one, you can create it at www.adobe.com or just sit and read.

Live Google Map with Widget Browser

Adobe Dreamweaver Widget Browser is an application built into Dreamweaver, built on Adobe AIR, that one can use to add widgets to web pages. Widget Browser can be used to browse and configure widgets before inserting them on web pages. As the widget is being configured by the user, the user can save the configuration for later use.

In this exercise, you are going to create your own Google Map and then you are going to insert it on a web page.

Here's what the Widget Browser looks like with Google Maps widget highlighted:

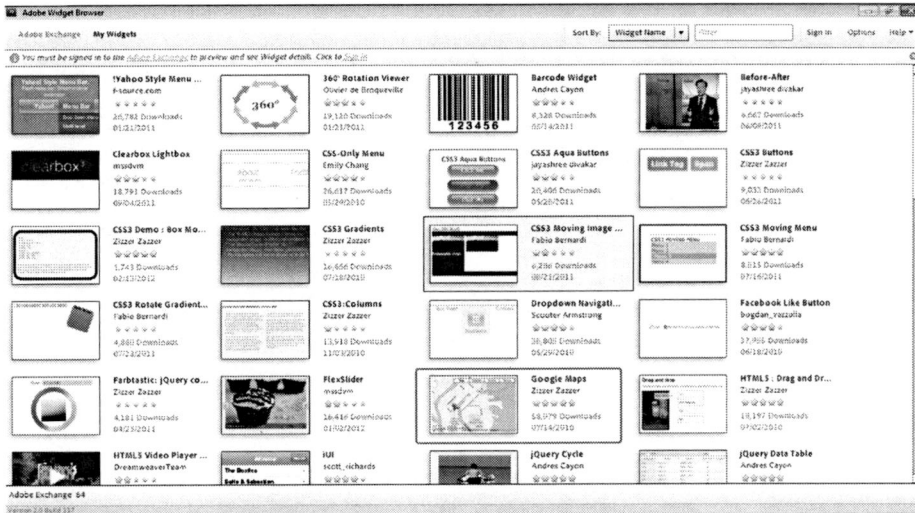

32   Open the Widget Browser by clicking on this icon:

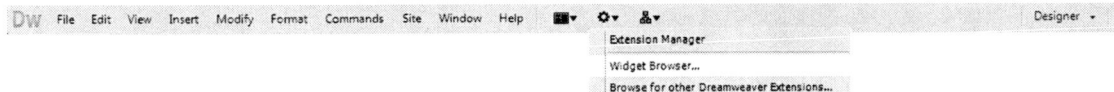

33   This opens Widget Browser as on the screenshot above.

34 Click on the Google Maps widget and a dialogue box will open for you to log in with your adobe account as shown here:

35 Once you're logged in, you are going to see the Google Maps widget. Click **Add to my widgets** in the bottom right corner of the screen as shown here:

36 Once you're on the screen with your widgets, click on Google Map widget to start customising it.

37 When the Google Maps widget opens, you will see the preview of the widget on the right and any existing presets on the left:

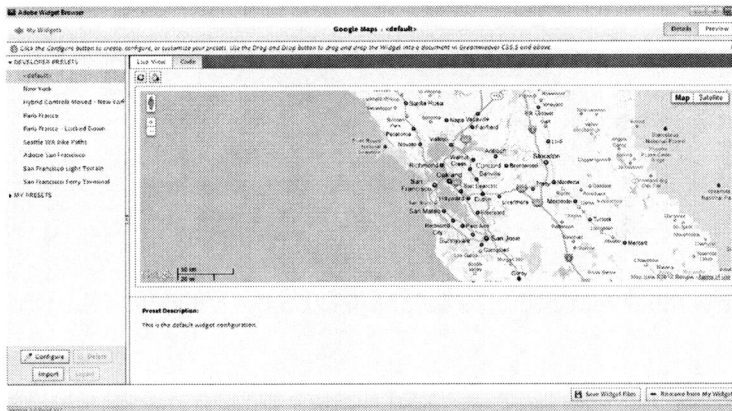

38 Start customising the widget by clicking **Configure** in the bottom left corner.

39 Now start adjusting Latitude, Longitude, and Zoom to create your own custom map. You can also set the Map Type, I used Hybrid.

Here's the map of Central London I created, you can see the settings I used:

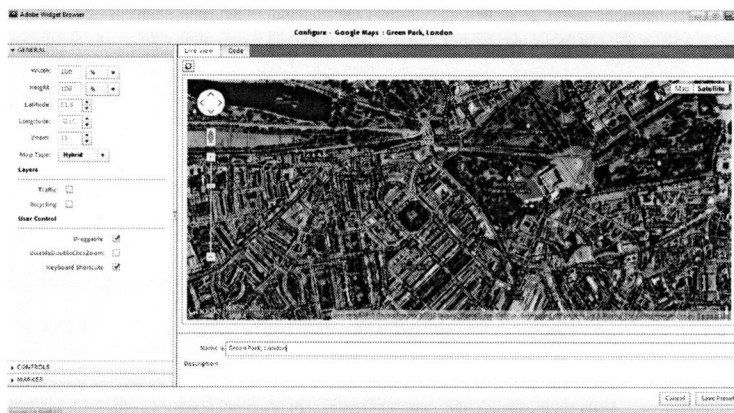

40 Once you've created your preset, it will appear on the left side of the window:

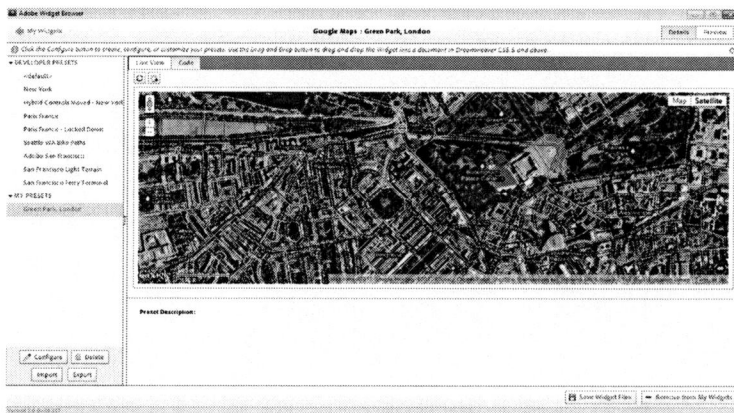

41 Close the Widget Browser and return to Dreamweaver.

42 Back in Dreamweaver, still on contactus.html, scroll down the page and find the line that reads **Map of our location (opens in new window).**

43 Delete **(opens in new window).**

44 Place the cursor on the line below and insert the widget by going to Insert panel and choosing **Widget:**

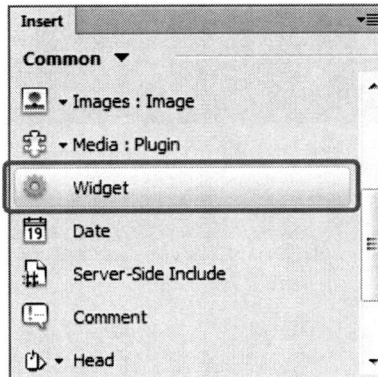

45 In the Widget dialogue box that appears choose your preset and press OK:

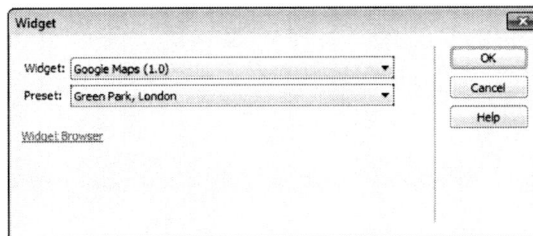

46 Save and preview the page in the Live View or in the web browser if you prefer.

Congratulations! You have successfully created your own map and inserted it onto a web page! Well done.

Set up E-mail links

Adding Email links to your website allows your visitors to communicate with you in an easy way. Modern web browsers will even give the users a choice on how they want the email to be sent - either using their email client or using one of the web based email services. And, adding email links in Dreamweaver is very simple.

As usual, there are a number of ways to create Email links, it's very similar to creating hyperlinks. So, let's get started.

47 Open **index.html** and navigate to the bottom of the page.

48 Highlight **send us an email**.

49 In the Insert panel click on **Email Link**:

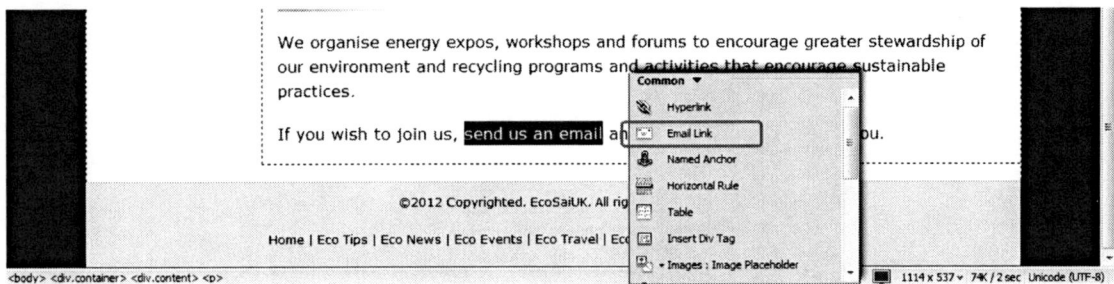

50 In the Email Link dialogue box type in an email address and press OK:

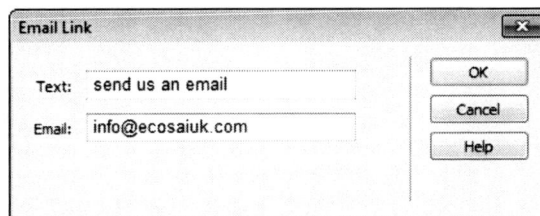

51 Preview the page in the web browser and test the link.

Depending in the web browser you're using, you're going to have different effect from clicking the email link. In the past, web browser would look for an Email client on your computer and would open it (Internet Explorer still does it).

Nowadays, modern web browsers like Firefox, give you an option to choose what you want to do. You can use one of the web mail services like Googlemail or Yahoo Mail, or you can use your Email client. Here's an example from Firefox:

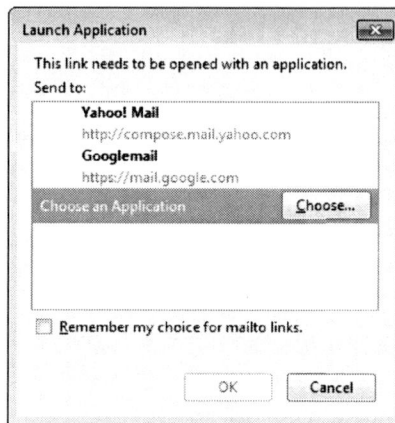

And that's how you add email links. As simple as that! Congratulations! Well done.

Insert drop-down menu using Spry

Imagine that you want to create an interactive drop-down menu on your website, that reveals submenu when the visitor clicks on one of the menu elements. To create this kind of menu, you would need HTML, CSS, and some JavaScript. If you were to create it from scratch, it would require a lot of knowledge of these technologies and the task would be very time consuming. Now, imagine creating it easily and effortlessly with just a few clicks within Dreamweaver. Wouldn't it be great? Now, it is possible within Adobe Dreamweaver as the Spry Menu Bar is a part of Dreamweaver.

Spry Menu Bar creates horizontal or vertical menu, using JavaScript and CSS, and it can be very easily added to your website in just a few steps. Because the Spry Menu Bar is based on JavaScript, it runs on all kinds of devices including mobile phones and tablets. And it runs on every computer of course.

What is Spry?

Spry is a JavaScript library for AJAX developed by Adobe. The **Spry** Framework offers easy to add and customise interface elements that can incorporate XML or HTML files. Now, you may be asking: What is AJAX. Let me explain.

AJAX (Asynchronous JavaScript and XML) is a combination of few technologies: JavaScript, XML, and DHTML. AJAX is used to develop Rich Internet Applications (RIAs), which create interactive content that can exchange data and update the page without reloading it. An example of AJAX technology that you definitely know is Google Mail, where you can update messages without reloading the page.

To find out more about Spry, go to Spry Framework for AJAX website:

http://labs.adobe.com/technologies/spry/

To create drop-down menu with the Spry Menu Bar, you will replace the existing menu in the sidebar.

52 Reopen **index.html** if you closed it.

53 Click and drag to highlight the entire menu in the sidebar.

54 Switch to **Split View** and check if the entire menu is highlighted:

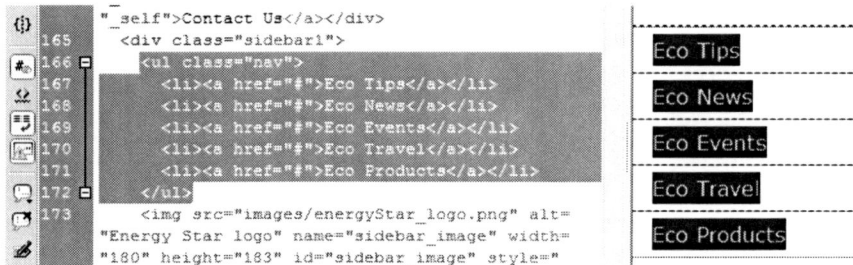

55 Press Delete key to remove the menu.

56 Insert the Spry Menu bar using the menu:

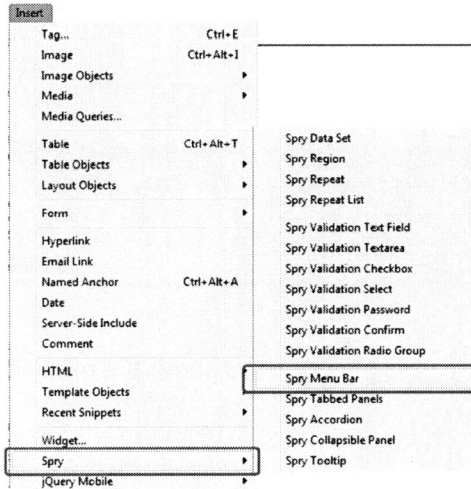

57 In the Spry Menu Bar dialogue box choose **Vertical** and press OK.

58 Switch back to **Design View**.

59 In the Properties panel you should now see the properties for the menu bar.

NOTE: If you don't see the properties for the menu bar, you need to select the Spry Menu bar on the page by clicking on its cyan tab.

60 Using the Properties panel change menu items (Item 1 to Item 4) by highlighting them one by one in thr first column and changing text in the Text area on the right as shown here:

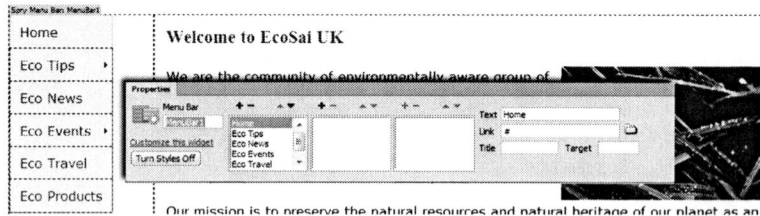

61 Add two more items using the plus sign (+) above the first column, so you end up with six menu elements.

62 Now start customising the submenus. Navigate to the Properties panel with the Spry Menu selected and highlight Home. You should see three submenu elements called Item 1.1, Item 1.2, and Item 1.3.

63 Delete them using minus sign (-) above the second column.

64 Customise the menu so that Eco Events has submenu with **Talks**, **Seminars**, and **Workshops** and Eco Products has submenu with **Food**, **Clothes**, **Cosmetics**, and **Home Products**.

65 Save the page and you should see this dialogue box:

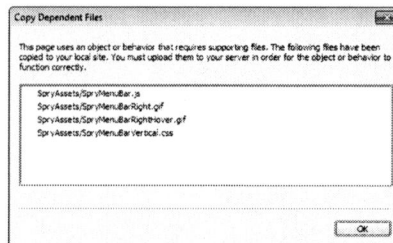

66 Click OK to accept, you need these files so that the Spry Menu Bar works properly.

67 Preview the page in a web browser. Roll over the menu items and notice how the submenus appear.

Notice that the menu items are not as wide as the sidebar and they have grey background. You're going to fix that in the next exercise.

Customise drop-down menu with CSS

You have inserted the Spry Menu, now it's time to customise it. Every Spry element in Dreamweaver includes its own stylesheet that you use to modify the look of the element. Because the stylesheet is being attached to the page, you can modify it using the CSS Styles panel.

68 Navigate to the CSS Styles panel and open **SpryMenuBarVertical.css** (you may need to scroll down to find it):

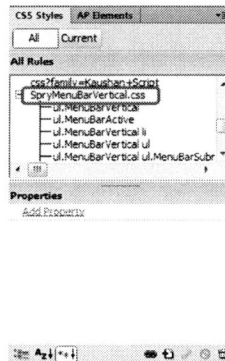

69 This is the stylesheet you're going to work with. Expand it if needed by clicking on plus sign on Windows, arrow on Mac.

First, you're going to resize the menu so it fits within the entire sidebar and then you're going to edit the colours.

70 Locate the rule **ul.MenuBarVertical** and change the width property to **180px**.

71 Locate the rule **ul.MenuBarVertical li** and change the width property to **180px**.

Now the menu is the same width as the sidebar (180px). If you prefer you can play with the values and adjust the width to your liking.

It's time to start changing colours. First, the default state colours – background and text. You're going to make the background white to match the background of the page and you 'll use black for text.

72 Locate the rule **ul.MenuBarVertical a** and click on the colour swatch next to the background-color property. Change it to **white**:

73 Still within the same rule change the text colour by clicking on the colour swatch next to color property and select **black**.

74 Press the **Live View** button on the top of the document window to preview the page in the Live View.

Notice that the background colour on rollover changes to blue. You're going to change it next. Just before you start changing the rollover effect, let's talk about Pseudoclasses.

PSEUDOCLASSES

The <a> element (for example a button) has four states, that can be customised with CSS using what we call pseudoclasses.

Here are the four states (pseudoclasses):

a:link — *default display and behaviour of the hyperlink*

a:visited — *formatting after the link has been visited*

a:hover — *formatting while the cursor is over the link*

a:active — *formatting when the mouse clicked on link.*

NOTE: Pseudoclasses need to be declared in this order to be effective.

So to change the rollover effect you're going to look for a rule with hover state.

75 Locate the rule **ul.MenuBarVertical a:hover, ul.MenuBarVertical a:focus** and click on the colour swatch next to the **background-color** property. When the colour picker appears choose green.

76 Repeat the last step for the next rule (very long rule that starts with **ul.MenuBarVertical a:MenuBarItemHover...**).

77 Press the **Live View** button to preview the page in the Live View.

Two more changes to make the menu look more interesting.

78 Find the rule **ul.MenuBarVertical li** and edit it. Give it a border like this:

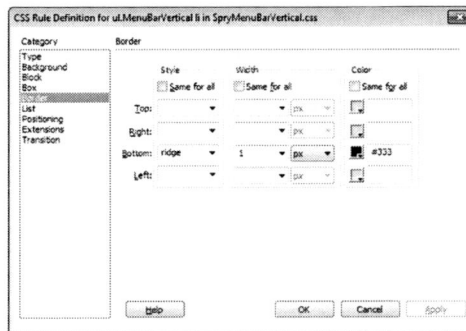

79 Finally find a rule **ul.MenuBarVertical** and delete border property.

Now there is no border around the menu, just the horizontal line below each menu element.

Congratulations! You have successfully made changes to the Spry Menu bar.

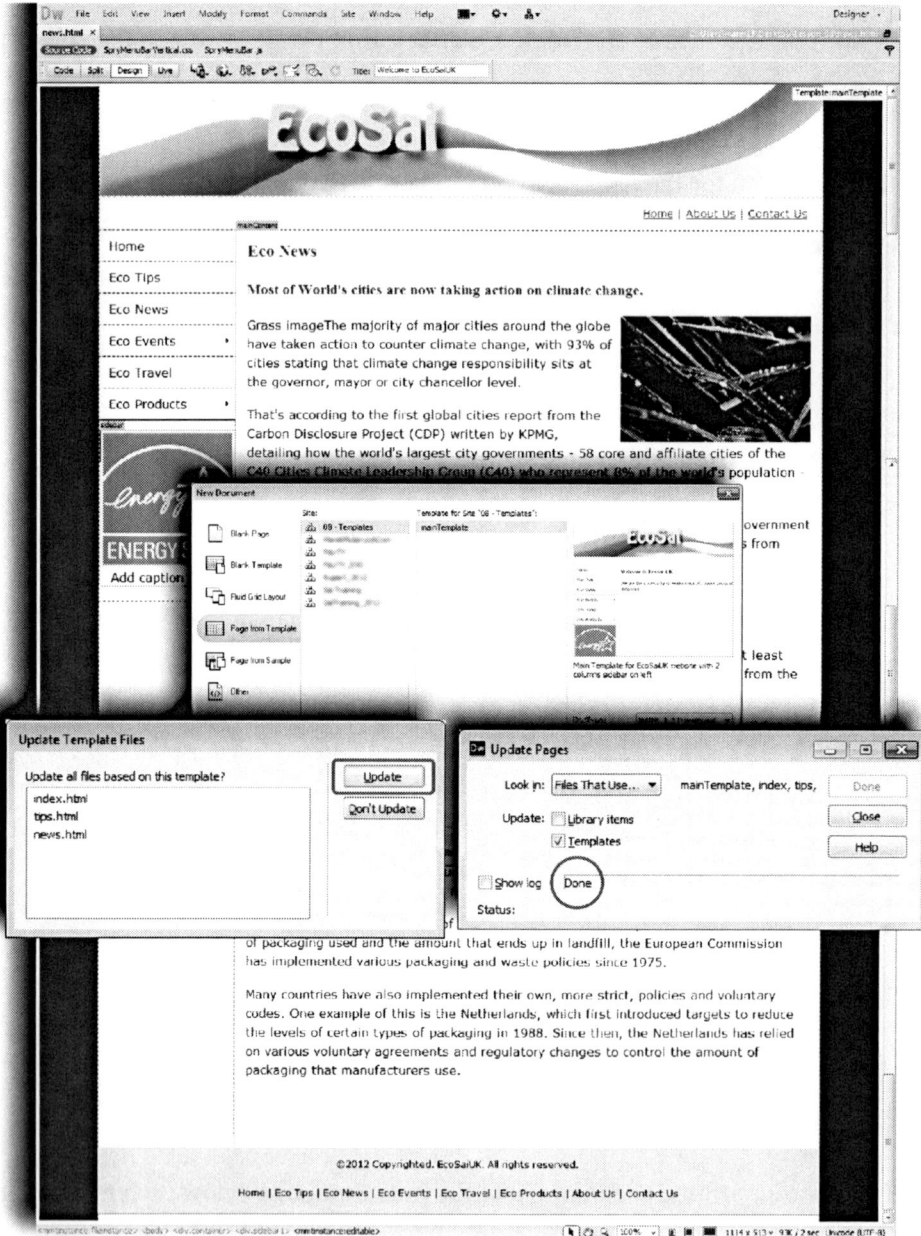

Lesson 8

Dreamweaver Templates

In this lesson you're going to learn how to be more productive and how to:

- create Dreamweaver templates

- create editable regions in templates

- create new pages from a template

- update templates

This lesson will take about 1 hour to complete.

Dreamweaver templates

What are Templates? Templates are like master pages that are used to produce child pages. Templates are great for quickly creating web pages within a site. A template has editable and non-editable regions within a page. The usual workflow for designing web pages is to start by creating the first page and then converting it into a template. Then, you create all pages from a template.

You could create a template starting with a blank page, but it is better to take an existing page and convert it into a template. And that is what you are going to do here.

1 Launch Adobe Dreamweaver CS6, if it is not already open.

2 Define a new Dreamweaver Site and call it **08 – Templates**.

3   In the Local Site Folder field, click on the folder icon to the right and navigate to the Lesson_08 folder containing the files for this lesson.

4 Select Lesson_08 folder, and click Open (Windows) or Choose (Mac). Then, click Select (Windows) or Choose (Mac) to choose this folder as your local root folder.

5 Go to Advanced Settings tab and define the images folder that can be found inside Lesson_08 folder.

6 In the Site Setup dialogue box click Save.

7 Open **index.html**.

The first step is going to be converting an existing page into a template and then defining editable regions within a page.

When the page opens, notice the structure of the page. This page is going to have two main editable regions: sidebar below the Spry Menu and the right column with a class .content.

8 Choose **File > Save as Template...**

9 In the **Save as Template** dialogue box check if the name of your site – 08 - Templates - appears in the Site drop-down menu.

10 In the Save as field type **mainTemplate**.

11 In the Description field type **Main Template for EcoSaiUK website with 2 columns sidebar on left**. Click Save.

12 A dialogue box asking whether you want to update links appears. Click Yes to update links.

Templates are stored in a seperate folder within your site. When you create a template, Dreamweaver creates a new folder called Templates and inserts the newly created template into this folder. That's why you see the dialogue box asking whether you want to update links. Now, to link to another page, Dreamweaver will point from the template folder up one level to the main root level and then to a page. That's why Dreamweaver needs to update links.

Notice how the name of the file has changed - the page is now called **mainTemplate.dwt**. Notice the file extension - **.dwt** - for Dreamweaver templates.

Template creates a dynamic link to the pages that you're about to create. When the template changes, Dreamweaver will update all the pages that were created from a template dynamically. This is one of the amazing features of Dreamweaver templates, a great time saver. Now it is time to create editable regions within the template.

Create editable regions

As you converted a page into a template, Dreamweaver started treating all the content within the template as part of the master design. As you start creating new pages form a template, all elements from the template will appear automatically on the pages (by default). Some page elements need to change from page to page and that's why you're going to create editable regions within the template now. Which page elements should become editable regions?

If you look at the design you'll notice that elements like header and footer are not going to change between the pages, so if these elements are locked on the new pages, then it's fine. But what about the rest of the content? You don't want to have the same content in the right column on every single page, do you? That's where you'll create editable regions to define which areas of the template are going to be editable and are going to change from page to page.

Before you start inserting editable regions, plan it and decide how many you're going to create and where will they be created. In this case, you're going to create two editable regions: one in the sidebar (div.sidebar1) and one in the content area (div.content). However, because there is a drop-down menu in the sidebar and it will appear on every single page, you need to exclude it from the editable region.

13 Place your cursor inside the sidebar and highlight all the content below the menu.

14 Use the Split view to check the code. Make sure all required code is highlighted (including opening and closing tags):

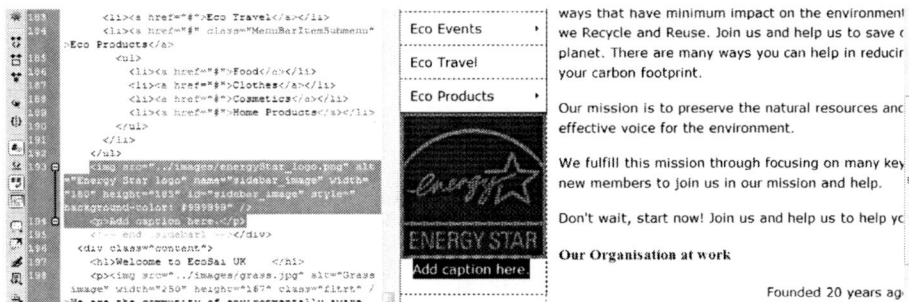

15 Choose **Insert > Template Objects > Editable Region**.

16 When **New Editable Region** dialogue box appears, type **sidebar** and press OK.

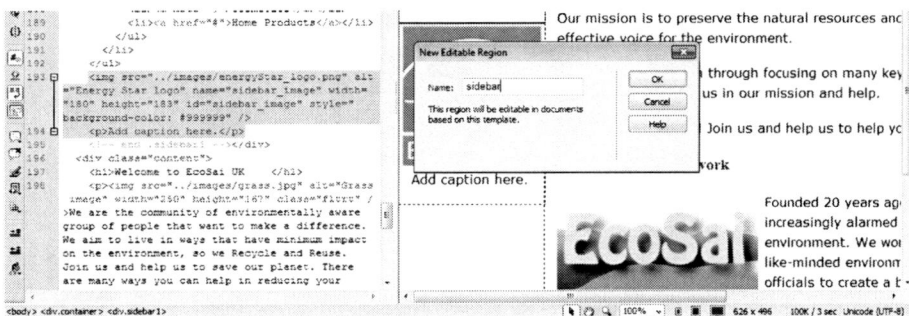

17 Navigate back to the Design view and notice the cyan tab with the name appear in the sidebar. That's the indication of the editable region.

18 Just before you create the second editable region, highlight all the content except the main heading and one sentence in the right column and delete it.

19 Delete the image as well, so all that is left is main heading and one sentence.

You don't need more as you're going to add content on all the pages when you start creating them from a template.

This time, when you create the second editable region, you're going to make the entire column editable. This is going to be easy.

20 Place your cursor in the right column and then using the tag inspector click on **<div. content>**. The entire column will now be highlighted.

21 Navigate to the Split view and check if the entire column is highlighted in the code as indicated on the screenshot here:

22 If the entire right column code is highlighted, choose **Insert > Template Objects > Editable Region** once again.

23 Name the editable region **mainContent** and press OK.

24 Navigate back to the Design view and notice the cyan tab with the name appear in the right column. That's your second editable region.

Congratulations! You have successfully created two editable regions within the template. Now it's time to save it and start creating pages from the template.

25 Save the template (**File > Save**) and close it.

Create new pages from Template

A few words of explanation before you start creating new pages. Before you start creating new pages, you need to understand that the process of creating new pages is very important. Here's why on the next page:

A PROPER WAY OF USING TEMPLATES

In the years that I have been training Dreamweaver and designing websites I have met so many people who make the same mistake and I want to warn you here so that you don't do the same. Here's what many people do:

- *one creates a template,*

- *he/she starts editing it by adding new content*

- *he/she saves it as a new page.*

This is a big mistake because this breaks the link between the template and the new page that's being created. Once you've created a template and defined editable regions, save it and close it. Do not open it unless you want to make some changes to the locked regions. The right way of creating pages from a template is to use New document dialogue box. That's what you're going to do now.

26 Choose **File > New** or press **Ctrl+N** on Windows, **Cmd+N** on Mac.

27 In the New Document dialogue box select **Page from Template** in the first column and you should see the preview of your template as shown here:

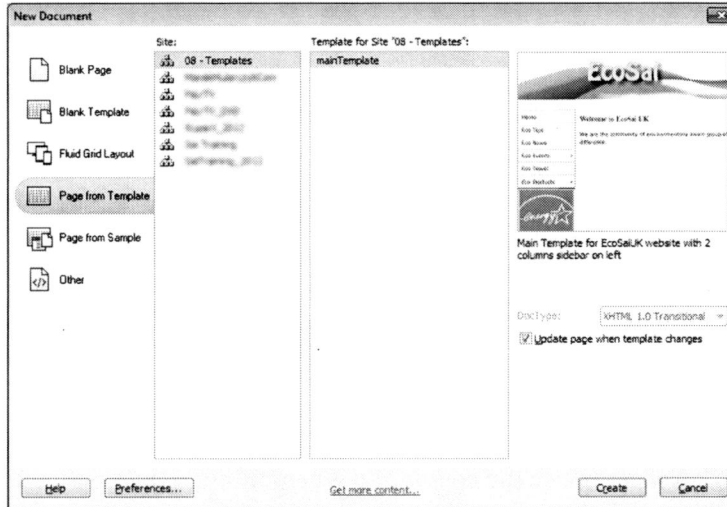

28 Make sure **Update page when template changes** is checked and click **Create**.

29 Dreamweaver opens a new page that's ready to start editing.

Notice the name of the template in the top right corner of the page. Sometimes you may be working with more than one template. That's how you would know which template was used for creating the page.

Now you're going to start adding content and creating pages. First, you're going to recreate home page.

30 Navigate to the Files panel and find file **textIndex.txt** in text folder.

31 Double-click on the file and it will open inside Dreamweaver.

32 Highlight all the text and copy it to the clipboard (**Edit > Copy** or **Ctrl+C/Cmd+C**).

33 Back to the page, highlight the paragraph below the main heading and paste the text (**Edit > Paste** or **Ctrl+V/Cmd+V**).

34 Save the page as **index.html**. Because the news page already exists, Dreamweaver will prompt you if you want to overwrite the file. Click Yes.

35 Preview the page in the web browser of your choice.

36 Back in Dreamweaver, place the cursor at the beginning of the first paragraph and insert an image – **grass.jpg**.

37 For Alternative text type **Grass image**.

38 Float the image to the right by selecting it and choosing **fltrt** class in the Properties panel.

39 Repeat the steps 36 to 38 for another image in the bottom section of the page – Our Organisation at work – image **header_cropped.jpg**. Float the image to the left.

40 Save and close the page.

Now you're going to create another page from a template – Eco Tips.

41 Choose **File > New** or press **Ctrl+N** on Windows, **Cmd+N** on Mac.

42 In the New Document dialogue box select **Page from Template** in the left column. Click **Create**.

43 In the Files panel, double-click on **ecoTips.txt** in the Text folder to open the file. The file opens in Dreamweaver. Copy all the text.

44 Back to the new page, highlight all the content in the right column and paste the text from the clipboard using **Edit > Paste** or **Ctrl+V** on Windows, **Cmd+V** on Mac.

45 Save the page as **tips.html**. Because the tips page already exists, Dreamweaver will prompt you if you want to overwrite the file. Click Yes.

46 Highlight the line that reads **Eco Tips** and format it as **Heading 1**:

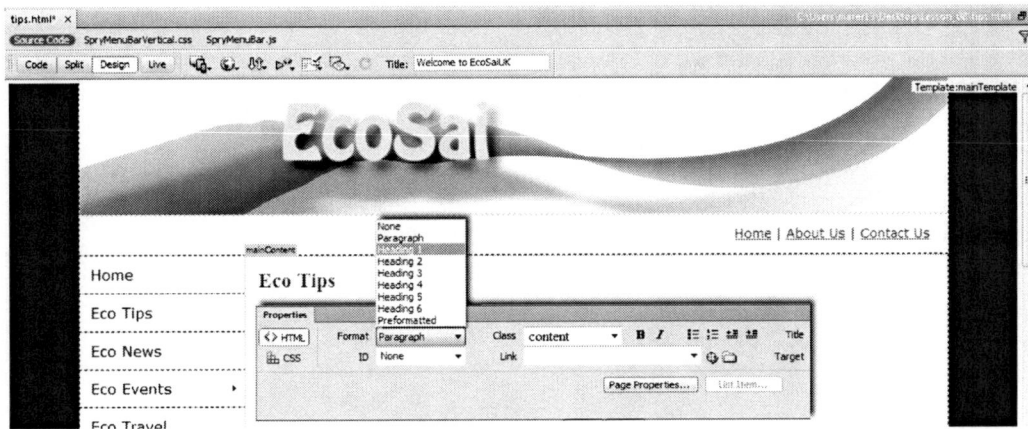

47 Highlight the line that reads **Eco Living at home** and format it as **Heading 2**. It turns green.

48 Scroll down the page, highlight the line that reads **Eco Living at work** and format it as **Heading 2** as well.

49 In the Title field, add – **Eco Tips** after Welcome to EcoSaiUK.

50 Now quickly turn the text within these two sections to unordered lists. Highlight all the text under Eco Living at home and turn it into an unordered list.

51 Highlight all the text under Eco Living at work and turn it into an unordered list as well.

52 One more change on the page. Insert an image of batteries at the beginning of the first subheading EcoLiving at home.

53 Align it to the right by applying a class **fltrt**.

54 Save the page and preview it in Live View. When done, close the page to return to the Welcome screen.

55 Repeat the steps you learnt to create one more page – **Eco News**.

56 When you're done, the page should look like this:

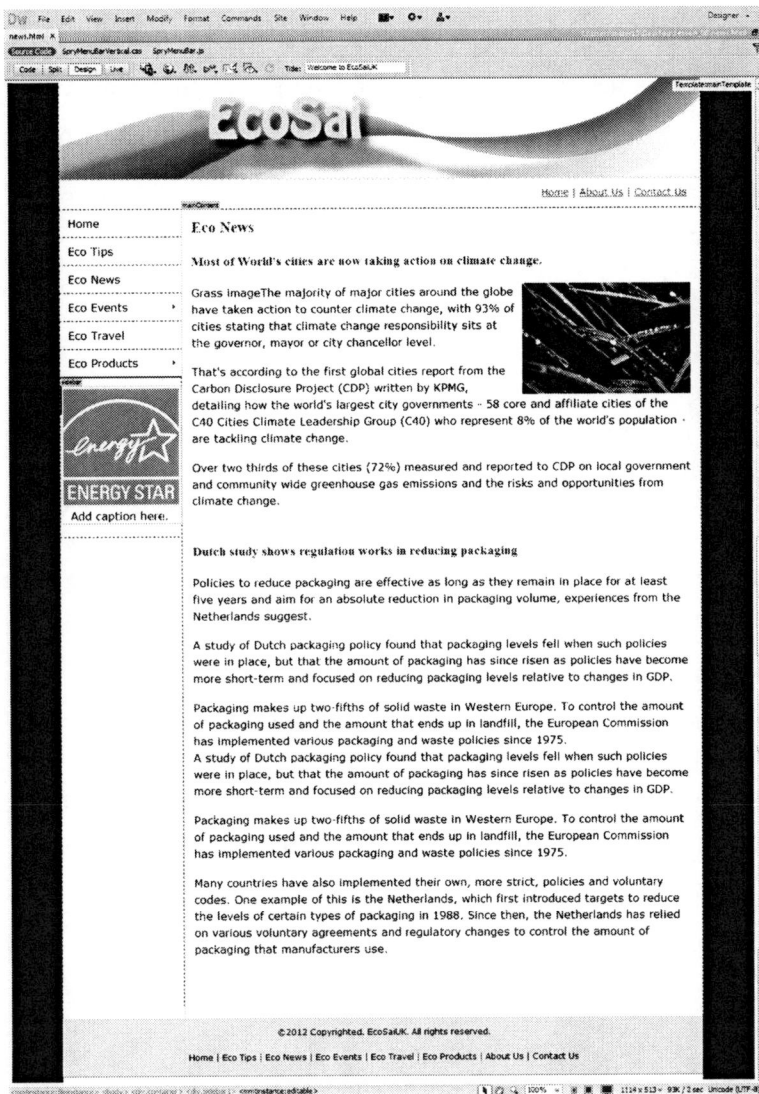

Congratulations! You have successfully created new pages from a template. Well done.

Update Dreamweaver Templates

Now you're going to introduce some changes to the template and you'll see how Dreamweaver will update all the pages for you as you change the template. A fantastic time saver!

57 Open the template (you can find it on the Welcome Screen or in the Files panel in the Templates folder).

58 When it opens, notice that you can click anywhere within the template without any restrictions. Place the cursor inside the menu in the sidebar.

59 Highlight the words **Home** and notice that the link in the Properties panel is set to #. Time to change it.

60 In the Properties panel click on the folder icon next to the Link box:

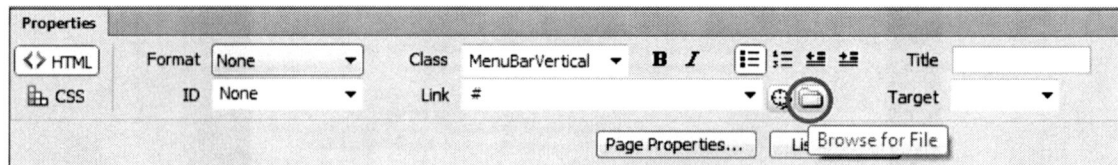

61 When the **Select File** dialogue box opens choose **index.html**.

62 Back in the Properties panel, in the Target field next to the link set it to **_self**. This way the link will open within the same web browser window.

63 Highlight **Eco Tips** in the sidebar and point it to **tips.html** using the same steps as above. Set the Target to **_self** as well.

64 Repeat the process for menu items **Eco News** and **Eco Events**.

65 Close and save the template.

66 **Update Template Files** dialogue box appears. Click **Update** and then **Close** when the message Done appears at the bottom of the Update Pages dialogue box appears:

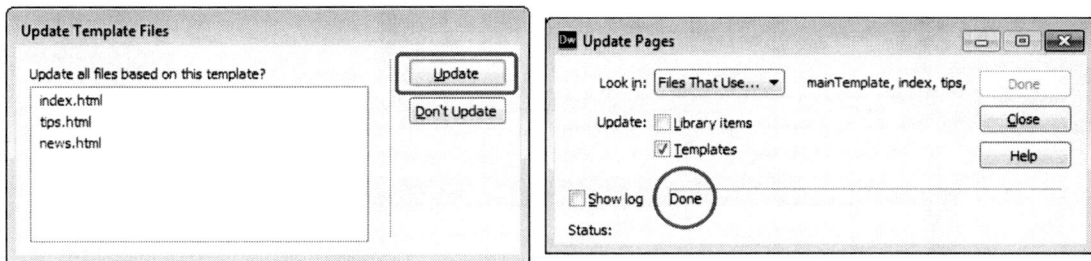

67 Open one of the pages you were working on recently and preview it in a web browser.

Now you can navigate between the pages within a site. Congratulations! You have successfully updated a template. Well done.

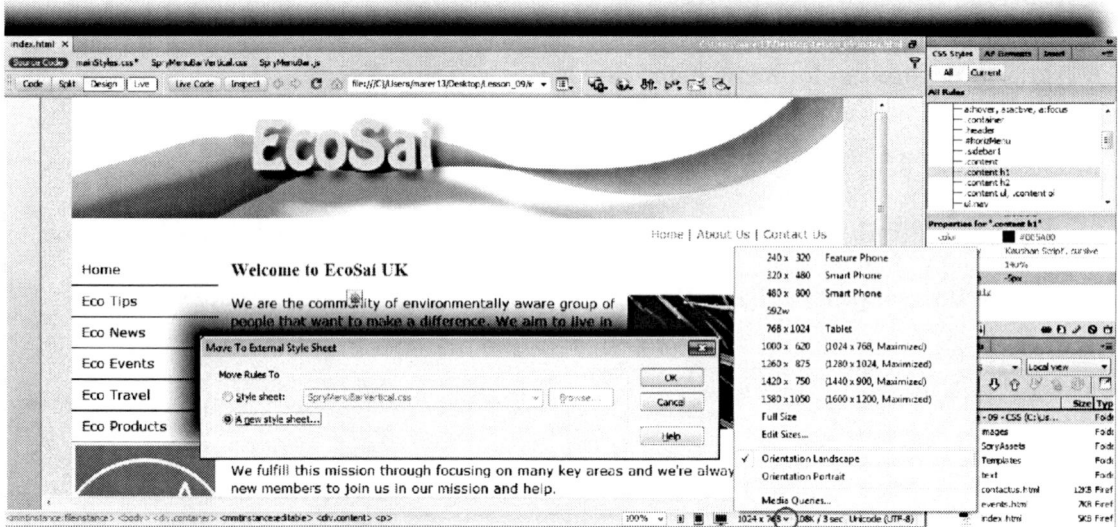

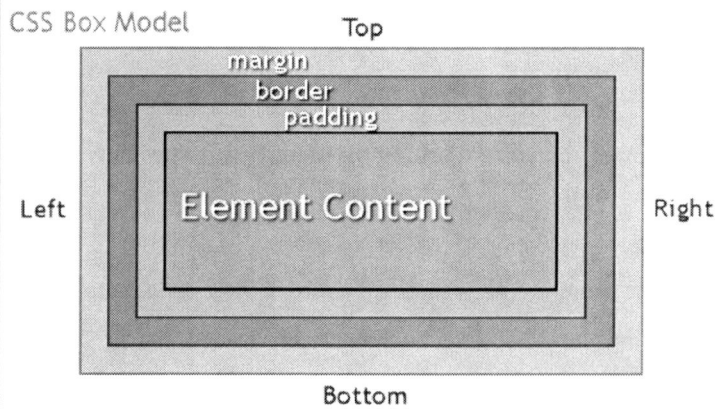

Lesson 9

Mastering CSS

In this lesson you're going to master CSS and learn how to:

- differentiate internal vs external CSS

- move CSS rules to external stylesheet

- create new external stylesheet

- customise links with Pseudo-classes

- use the CSS Box Model

- use Multiscreen Preview for Mobile Devices

This lesson will take about 1 hour 30 minutes to complete.

CSS Refresher

You already have some basics of Cascading Style Sheets (CSS) as you used some CSS in the other lesson and in the lessons that followed. As you have noticed, you will be using CSS all the time when designing websites. Every time you want to change the look of anything on the page, you will use CSS.

I would highly recommend using CSS Styles panel for all your CSS work - editing CSS rules as well as creating new ones and even creating stylesheets.

In this lesson, you're going to build on what you have already learned. You are also going to create an external stylesheet. So far you have been working with an internal stylesheet. But first, let me explain the differences between internal and external stylesheets.

Internal or External stylesheet?

When you work with an internal stylesheet, the rules are created directly within a document and they are contained within the <style> tag.

External stylesheet is a seperate document with all the rules and it has .css file extension.

One of the main differences between internal and external stylesheets is that the **internal stylesheet** only applies to one HTML document. If you had a website with six pages, you'd have six seperate stylesheets within all the pages. If you wanted to make some changes to the website, you'd need to make changes to every stylesheet seperately and you'd need to open every single page in Dreamweaver to make changes. With **external stylesheet** you'd have one stylesheet (one .css file) that would link to all the pages within the website and changing the stylesheet would update all the pages automatically. An external stylesheet can be attached to any number of HTML pages.

1 Launch Adobe Dreamweaver CS6, if it is not already open.

2 Define a new Dreamweaver Site and call it **09 – CSS**.

3 In the Local Site Folder field, click on the folder icon to the right and navigate to the Lesson_09 folder containing the files for this lesson.

4 Select Lesson_09 folder, and click Open (Windows) or Choose (Mac). Then, click Select (Windows) or Choose (Mac) to choose this folder as your local root folder.

5 Go to **Advanced Settings** tab and define the images folder that can be found inside Lesson_09 folder.

6 In the Site Setup dialogue box click Save.

7 Open the template.

Here's how you can tell if the web page is using an internal or external stylesheet:

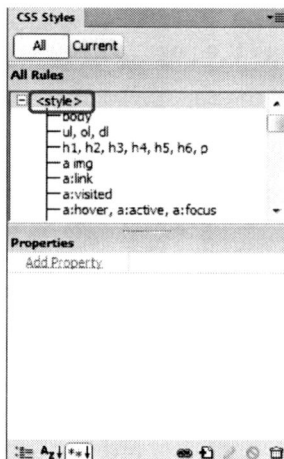

In **All Rules** section, the word **<style>** represents an internal stylesheet. If your web page relies on an external stylesheet, you'd see the name of the file, i.e. **styles.css** or **stylesheet. css**. So in this example you're dealing with an internal stylesheet.

Now, you're going to move all the CSS rules into an external stylesheet.

9 Resize the CSS Styles panel if needed, so that you can see many rules at one time.

10 Highlight all the rules within <style> header by clicking on the first rule, then holding the Shift key down and clicking on the last rule (holding the Shift key down will highlight all the rules in between).

NOTE: Do not highlight the rules inside the stylesheet for the Spry Menu bar – this is an external style sheet: SpryMenuBarVertical.css.

11 Go to the menu in the top right corner of the panel and choose **Move CSS Rules....**

12 In the **Move to External Style Sheet** dialogue box choose **A new style sheet** and click OK:

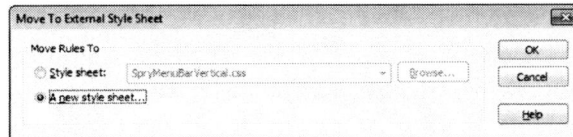

13 In the **Save Style Sheet File As** dialogue box, in the **File name** field type **mainStyles** and click Save.

14 Nothing's changed on the page, but the page is now linked to an external stylesheet. Notice in the CSS Styles panel a new stylesheet called mainStyles.css:

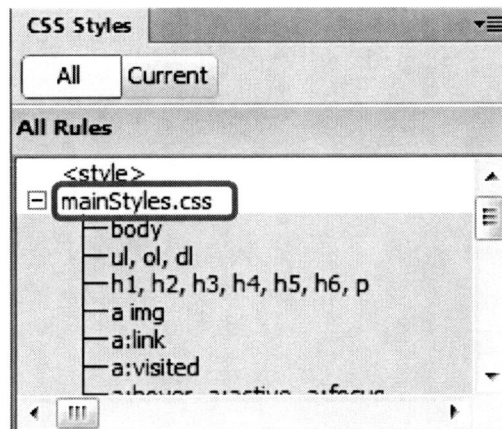

Now you need to tidy up a bit here. There are some remains of the old stylesheet as you can see from the <style> header at the top of the CSS Styles panel.

15 Highlight the **<style>** header in the CSS Styles panel and press Delete key on the keyboard to remove it.

Notice that the related documents toolbar at the top of the document window displays a new stylesheet:

mainTemplate.dwt* ✕

Source Code   mainStyles.css*   SpryMenuBarVertical.css   SpryMenuBar.js

Code | Split | Design | Live

16 Close and save the template and the stylesheet.

17 When **Update Template Files** dialogue box appears, click **Update** and then Close. All the pages created from a template update.

Congratulations! You have successfully updated a template and all the pages! Well done.

Customise links with Pseudo-classes

One of the great features of CSS is the ability to customise any page element. A concept you are going to get familiar with now is the concept of Pseudo-classes. In case of Pseudo-classes, they're used to customise the behaviour of different states of the links on web pages. The Pseudo-classes define how the link should appear, depending on which state it is in.

There are four different states of links and they must be defined in certain order to be effective:

- **a:link**

- **a:visited**

- **a:hover**

- **a:active**

Here's what all these states do:

a: link - default display and behaviour of the hyperlink

a: visited - formatting after the link has been visited

a: hover - formatting while the cursor is over the link

a: active - formatting when the mouse clicked on link

First, you will need to assign links to pages using the menu in the footer.

18 Open the template and add links to pages to the menu that appears in the footer. For the pages that don't exist yet, add a link **#**.

19 When done, save and close the template.

20 When prompted, update the pages from the template.

Now you can create rules for Pseudo-classes. Because changing the behaviour of the links requires changing CSS and all the pages are now linked to the same stylesheet, it doesn't matter which HTML page you have opened. Every HTML page points to the same stylesheet, so open one of the HTML pages and navigate to the CSS Styles panel.

21 Look into the CSS Styles panel and you're going to notice that Pseudo-classes are already there, so you will just need to edit them.

22 In the CSS Styles panel find the first Pseudo-class **a:link**. Edit the rule by clicking on the pencil icon at the bottom of the CSS Styles panel or by double-clicking on the rule.

23 Change the colour of the link to green and click Apply to notice how the links change.

24 Remove the underline by changing **text-decoration** to **none**:

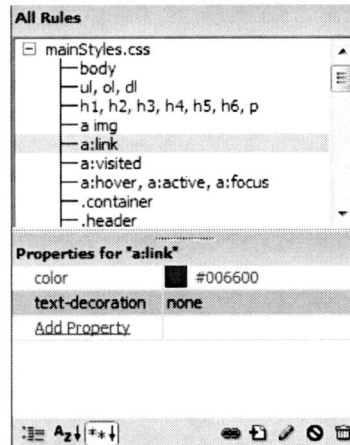

25 Preview the page in Live View.

26 Back to Design View, edit **a:visited** rule and set its properties to the same properties as a:link.

27 Now it's time for **a:hover, a:active, a:focus** rule. Edit the rule and add an underline as well as change the colour of the text:

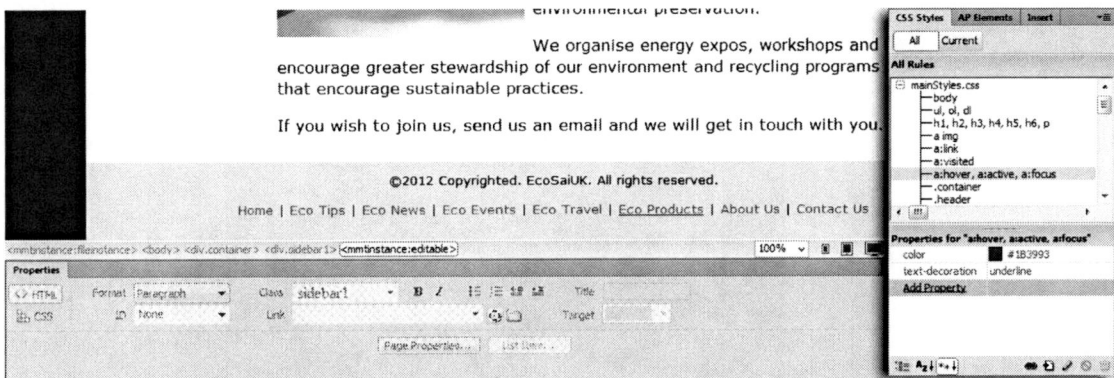

Well done! You are done with Pseudo-classes. Now it's time to move on to the CSS Box Model, another very important concept in Web Design.

28 Save any changes using **File > Save All**.

CSS Box Model

When designing web pages, consider all HTML elements as boxes on a page. Term "Box Model" is used when talking about the layout. The CSS Box Model is a box wrapping around each HTML element on a page.

It consists of four main elements:

- **margin**

- **border**

- **padding**

- **content**

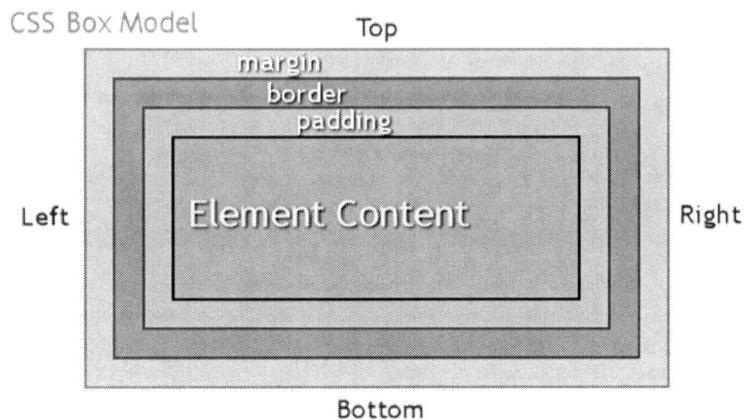

When you set the width or the height of the element, you just set the size of the content area. As you start adding margin or padding, you're expanding the "box". Let's work with an example.

29 Open one of the pages that were created from a template, i.e. index.html.

30 In this example, you're going to move the main heading down a bit. Place the cursor inside the main heading.

31 Check the Properties panel so you know which heading you're working with as shown:

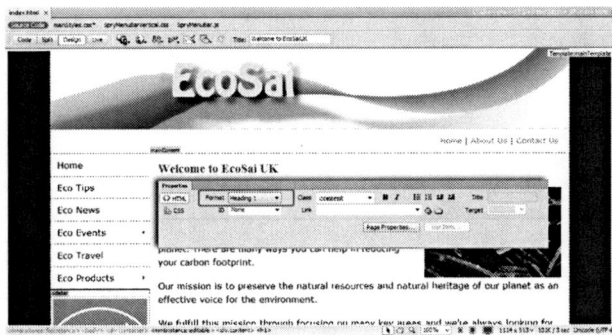

32 Now you're going to customise the CSS for the heading 1. Find **.content h1** rule and edit it, go to **Box** category:

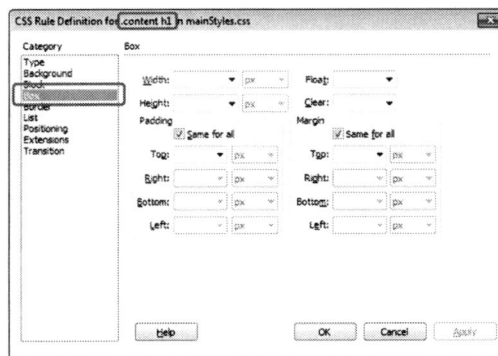

33 Your job now will be to align the main heading with the first line in the drop-down menu in the sidebar by adding extra margin to the main heading.

34 As you start adding margin (remember to uncheck Same for All), the heading starts moving down.

35 Add negative margin of **-10px** to move the heading up and you're done!

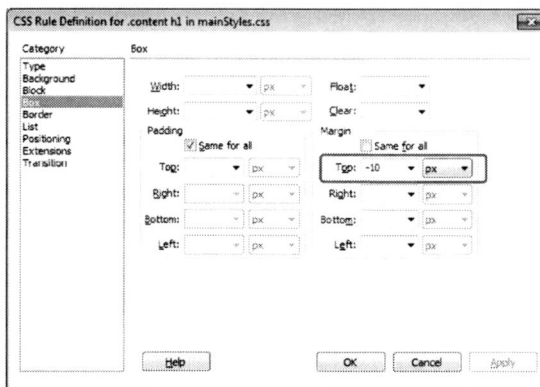

36 Save all the changes using **File > Save All** and preview the page in the Live View:

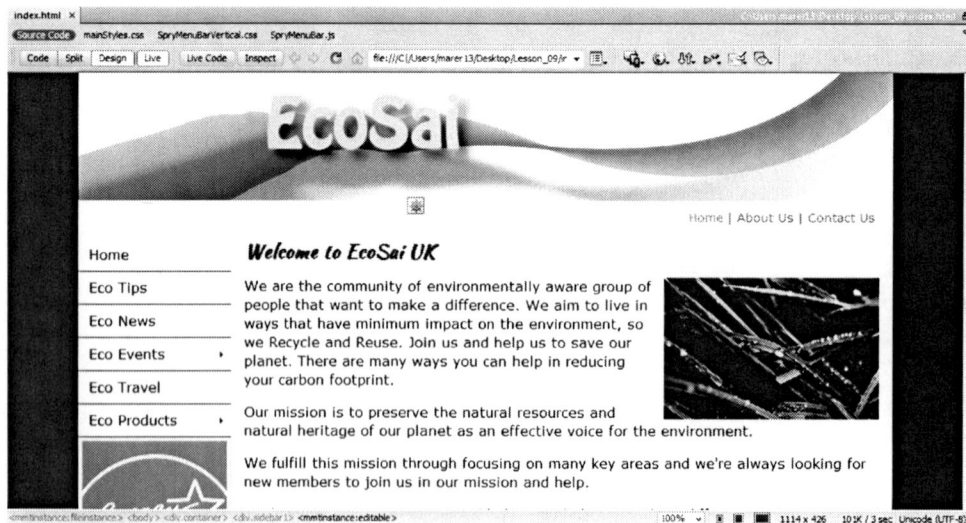

The main heading should now be aligned with the menu in the sidebar and because you changed the stylesheet, the heading will look the same on every page.

Congratulations! Well done! Now the spacing below the main heading. Let's align it with the second item in the menu in the sidebar.

37 Edit **.content h1** rule once again and this time add some margin on the bottom.

Experiment and make sure the text aligns nicely:

38 Now add more spacing at the bottom of the page, just before the footer. Edit **.content** rule and add some **padding-bottom**.

39 While you're still working with CSS change the colour of the text in the footer to green (the same as links) by editing **footer** rule:

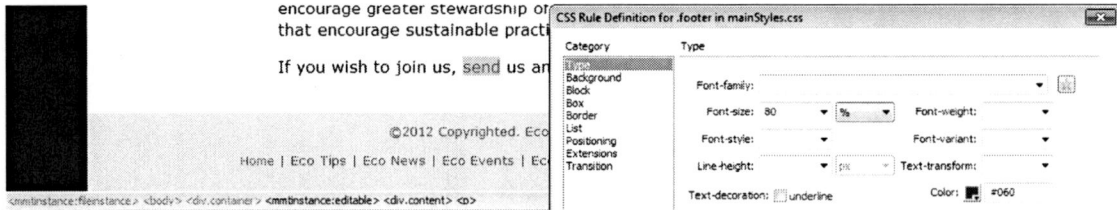

encourage greater stewardship of
that encourage sustainable practi

If you wish to join us, send us an

©2012 Copyrighted. Eco

Home | Eco Tips | Eco News | Eco Events | Ec

`<mmtinstance:fileinstance> <body> <div.container> <mmtinstance:editable> <div.content> <p>`

CSS Rule Definition for .footer in mainStyles.css

Category	Type
Background	
Block	Font-family:
Box	Font-size: 80 % Font-weight:
Border	Font-style: Font-variant:
List	
Positioning	Line-height: px Text-transform:
Extensions	
Transition	Text-decoration: underline Color: #060

Just a bit more CSS. I think it's time to change the background behind the web pages. Because you're going to change the CSS, it doesn't matter which page you have opened.

40 Navigate to the CSS Styles panel and edit **body** rule.

41 Switch to **Background** category and remove background colour.

42 Click on Browse button next to **Background-image** and select **background.jpg**:

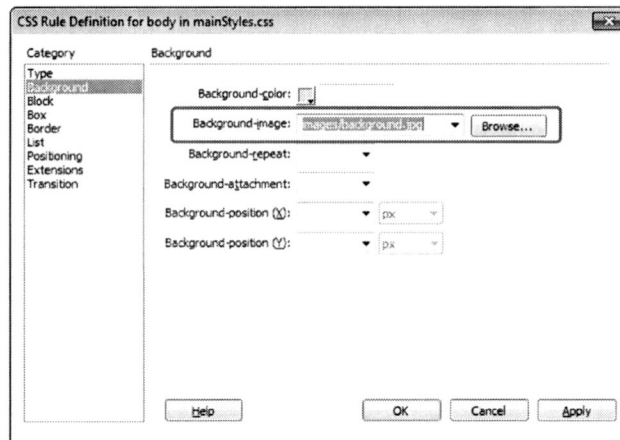

CSS Rule Definition for body in mainStyles.css

Category	Background
Type	
Background	Background-color:
Block	
Box	Background-image: Browse...
Border	
List	Background-repeat:
Positioning	
Extensions	Background-attachment:
Transition	
	Background-position (X): px
	Background-position (Y): px

Help   OK   Cancel   Apply

43 Click OK to accept the change and preview the page in Live View:

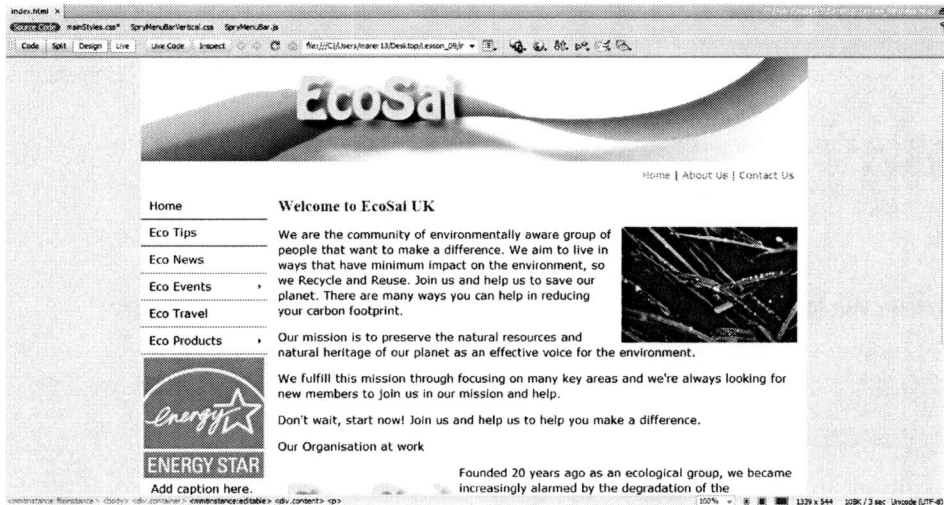

Multiscreen Preview for Mobile Devices

In Dreamweaver CS6 you can now simulate your web pages on mobile devices as well. At the bottom of your document window is a series of these icons:

You can use them to simulate the look of the website on different devices.

44 Click on the first icon to simulate the display of the page on a mobile phone with screen resolution of 480 x 800px:

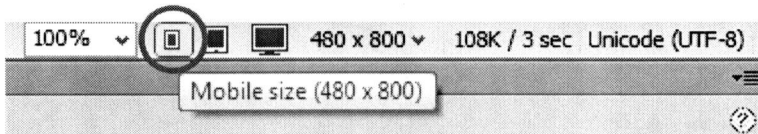

45 Click on the arrow next to the size and choose **Orientation Landscape**:

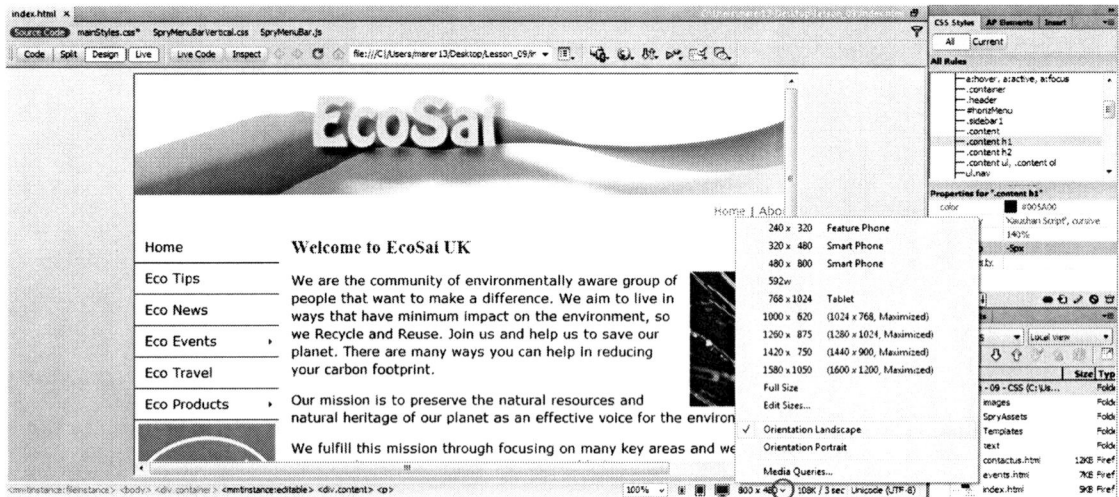

This is a better preview as most users would hold their mobile phone in landscape mode when browsing the internet.

46 Click on the second icon at the bottom of your document window to simulate the

preview on a tablet (like Acer Iconia or Samsung Galaxy Tab or Apple iPad):

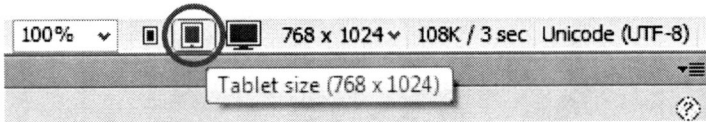

47 Click on the arrow next to the size and choose **Orientation Landscape**:

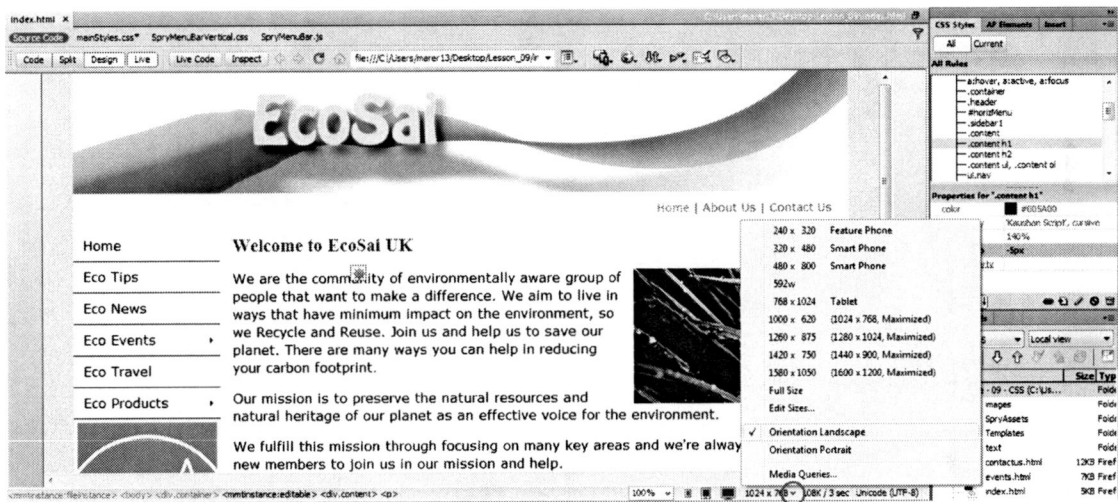

Again, most users would hold their tablet in landscape mode when browsing through the
internet.

Congratulations! Well done! Lesson 9 finished.

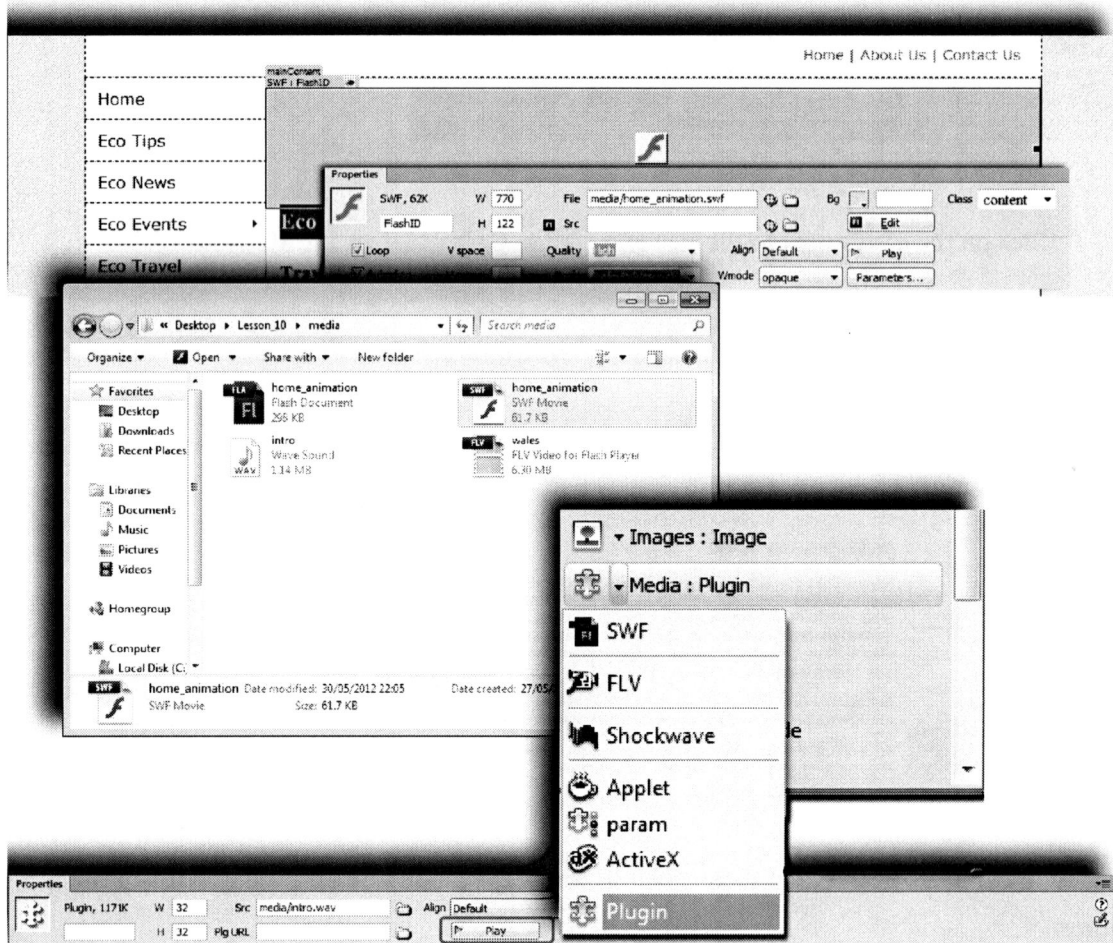

Lesson 10

Sound and Video

In this lesson you're going to learn how to incorporate media into your website and how to:

- add sounds

- add Flash animations

- add videos

- embed videos from YouTube

This lesson will take about 45 minutes to complete.

Media on web pages

Media are getting more and more common on most websites nowadays.

Adding audio and video on your pages is quite easy and you're going to learn it in just a moment. Adobe has been trying to make adding media to web pages easier and easier, and every new version of Dreamweaver brings improvements in the way we insert media on pages.

Before starting inserting media on your pages, there are a few things you need to be aware of. First of all, media files can be very large, especially videos so you need to plan a bit and decide on how you're going to incorporate your videos on the pages. And you will need to decide what file formats to use for your sounds/videos. We're going to discuss it more later in the lesson.

1 Launch Adobe Dreamweaver CS6, if it is not already open.

2 Define a new Dreamweaver Site and call it **10 – Sound and Video**.

3 In the Local Site Folder field, click on the folder icon to the right and navigate to the Lesson_10 folder containing the files for this lesson.

4 Select Lesson_10 folder, and click Open (Windows) or Choose (Mac). Then, click Select (Windows) or Choose (Mac) to choose this folder as your local root folder.

5 Go to Advanced Settings tab and define the images folder that can be found inside Lesson_10 folder.

6 In the Site Setup dialogue box click Save.

Adding Sounds

Let's start this chapter with sounds on web pages. Internet would be a different place without sounds. Some say that it would be a boring place and they may be right. On the other hand, some people don't like sounds on web pages, especially if the sounds keep on looping or play for a very long time. That's why, for this exercise, you're going to use a sound that is less than a minute long and it is not going to loop.

Before you add a sound to your web pages, you should also be aware that your sound will serve a purpose and will add value to the page. Using a short, smooth sound, that doesn't annoy the visitors to your website, may sound like a good idea. Of course, sound makes a lot of sense for websites for musicians, games, and websites aimed at children.

First, you're going to add a sound that will play in the background as the home page loads.

7 Open **index.html**.

8 Place your cursor at the end of the first paragraph in the content area.

9   Navigate to the Insert panel (Common category) and choose **Media > Plugin** as shown

on the screenshot here:

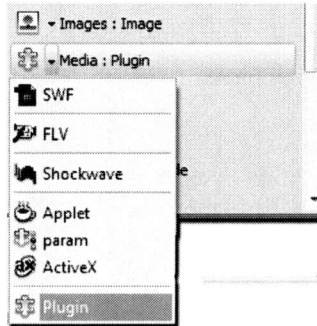

If you are wondering why you need to choose Plugin and why there is no Sound option in the Insert panel under Media, it is because Dreamweaver doesn't have a specific option for inserting sound files. Adding sound to web pages is a bit confusing as it will require the user to have a plugin installed within their web browser.

In this lesson, you are inserting a .wav file, because it is a short sound and this file format is widely supported in web browsers. Other file format commonly used on web pages is mp3.

10   Select File dialogue box is going to open, so you can select the file that will play. Navigate to the media folder and choose **intro.wav**. Click OK.

11   Plugin icon appears on the page and your Properties panel should read **Plugin, 1171K** in the top right corner as shown here:

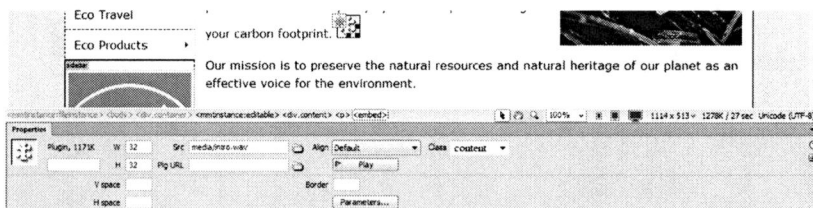

12 Select the plugin object on the page if it's not still selected and change its size using the Properties panel. Set it to **0px** for Width (W) and **0px** for Height (H).

13 Press Enter on your keyboard to accept the settings.

14 Click Play button in the Properties panel and you will hear the sound playing for a few seconds:

Even though you won't see the plugin on a web page, it will play anyway. Test it.

15 Preview the page in a web browser of your choice and listen to the sound playing.

NOTE: If the sound doesn't play then your web browser doesn't have the required codecs installed.

In the next few steps you're going to insert a sound on a page in a form of a music player. This time, the visitor will be able to pause the music as well as change the volume and mute it if needed. This option gives the visitor more control over the music playing, they can decide whether they want to listen to the sound or not. Also, this option gives you the opportunity to display information about the music track on the page by adding a description. And that's what you're going to do now.

16 Save and close the page.

In this section of the lesson you're going to work on Eco Travel page. You're going to add a sound as well as a video to this page.

17 Create new page from a template using **File > New** and then **Page from Template** as shown here:

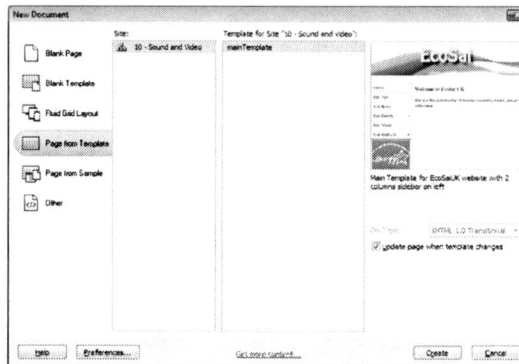

18 Rename main heading on a page to **Eco Travel**.

19 Highlight the paragraph below the main heading and delete it.

20 Open **ecoTravel.txt** from the text folder.

21 Highlight all the text and copy it to the clipboard. Close the text file.

22 Back to the Eco Travel page, paste the text below the main heading on the page.

23 Format the line that reads **Traveling Eco-Friendly** to **Heading 2**.

24 Format the line that reads **So, where do you start?** to **Heading 2** as well.

25 As in other pages, insert an image at the beginning of the first paragraph. This time insert **travel.jpg**.

26 As alternative text type **Eco Travel** and press OK.

27 Float the image to the right using a class **fltrt**.

28 Save the page as **travel.html** and preview it in a web browser.

29 Place the cursor inside the sidebar at the beginning of the line that reads **Add caption here**.

30 Highlight this line and instead of this text type in **Listen to our Soundtrack** as shown here:

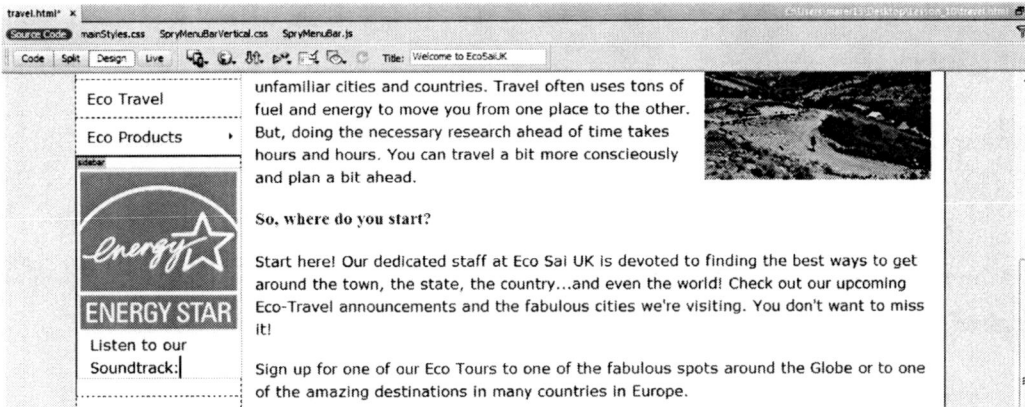

31 Press Enter to move cursor to a new line and insert a sound using the Insert panel and

Media : Plugin as shown here:

32 Navigate to the media folder and choose **intro.wav**.

33 The sound player is initially quite small, so resize it so that it fits into the sidebar by making it **150px** wide.

34 Preview the page in the web browser.

NOTE: If the sound player doesn't appear and the sound doesn't play it means that you don't have required codecs installed.

Adding Flash animations

Flash has been a standard in animations and web banners for a long time. Flash is well known for its multimedia functionality. Dreamweaver easily integrates with Flash and Flash files – SWF – can be easily inserted on web pages. And, if the source file is available (you have access to the original file), you can edit a SWF file in Flash and export it back to Dreamweaver.

You can test the Swf file that you are going to insert on a page by going to the Lesson 10 folder, inside media folder and double-clicking on **home_animation.swf** :

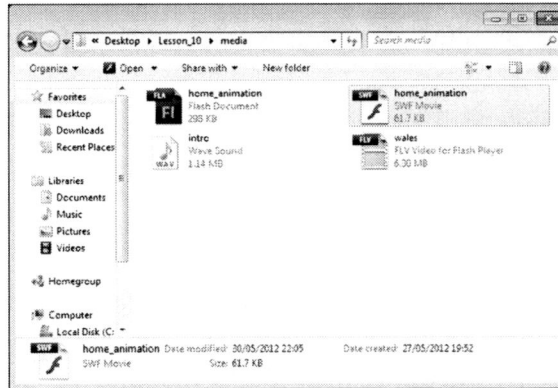

The animation launches in Adobe Flash Player and plays for a few seconds and then it stops.

35 Close Flash Player and go back to Dreamweaver.

36 Open **travel.html** and place the cursor in front of the main heading.

37 Choose **Insert > Media > SWF**.

38 When the **Select SWF** dialogue box opens, navigate to the media folder and choose **home_animation.swf**.

39 **Object Tag Accessibility Attributes** dialogue box opens.

40 In the Title field type **Eco Sai UK animation** and press OK:

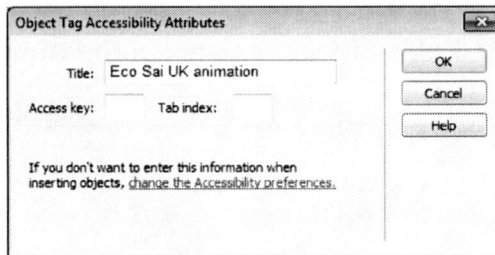

41 Preview the page in the web browser and save all the changes.

42 When **Copy Dependent Files** dialogue box opens, click OK.

43 If the image appears to be slightly indented, that's because the image ended up being inside the main heading. If this is the case, go to Split View.

44 In Split View find the code for the animation:

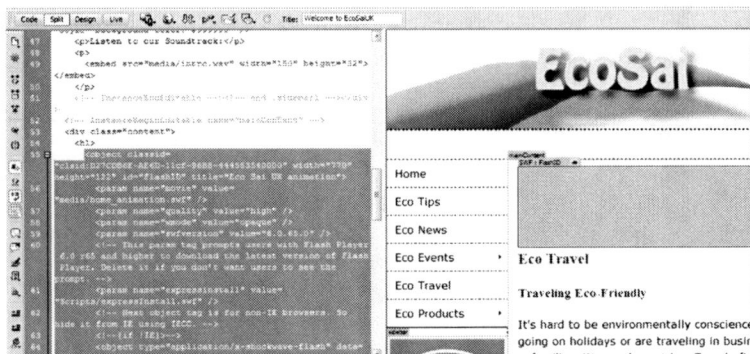

45 Opening **<h1>** tag should go after the animation, so cut it to the clipboard and past it after the animation code:

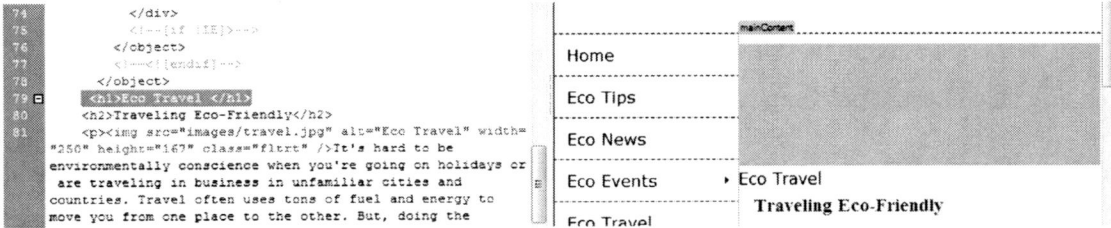

46 Preview the page in the web browser and save all the changes. Now the animation looks good.

47 Back to Dreamweaver select the animation on a page and look into the Properties panel:

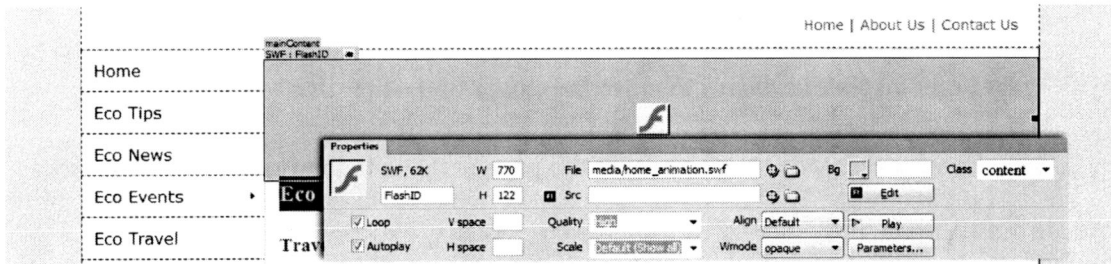

48 In the Properties panel you can click Play button to preview the animation in Design View in Dreamweaver.

Now, it's time to add a Flash Video on a page.

Adding Flash Videos

When considering adding video to pages, there are a number of file formats that come to mind, but none of them had such a dramatic impact as Flash. The FLV file format is the leading video format on computers and majority of mobile devices.

Videos that you may have from your camera or mobile phone can easily be converted to Flash video using Adobe Media Converter CS6. A native Flash video has a file extension **.flv** or **.f4v**.

In this part of the lesson, you're going to add to a web page a video called wales.flv.

49 Still on **travel.html**, scroll to the bottom of the page and place your cursor under the last paragraph.

50 Press Enter on your keyboard to move the cursor to the new line.

51 With the cursor placed at the bottom of the page navigate to the Insert panel and choose **Media > FLV**:

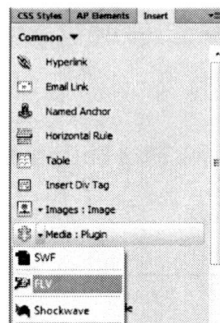

52 When the Insert FLV dialogue box appears, leave Video type set as **Progressive Download Video** and next to URL click on **Browse**.

PROGRESSIVE DOWNLOAD vs STREAMING

Progressive download – *with progressive download video will start playing after the first part of the video is received by the web browser. Video will continue downloading as it's playing. Progressive video can be hosted on any web server without any extra costs.*

Streaming video – *with streaming video will start playing immediately and the playhead can be moved to any position without waiting for the part to be downloaded, so it offers advantages over progressive download. However, streaming video needs to be hosted on a web server using Flash Media Server.*

53 Choose **wales.flv** from media folder and click OK/Choose.

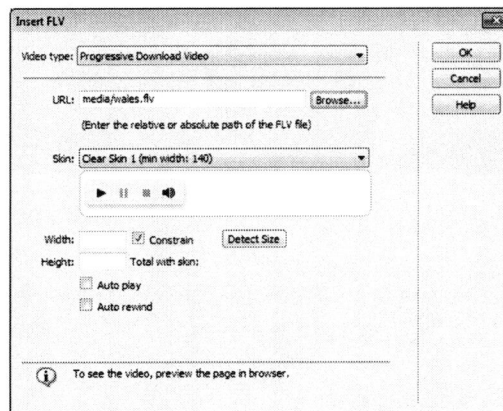

54 From the **Skin** drop-down menu choose any skin you like.

55 Click **Detect Size** button to display the width and height of the video. Constrain should be checked.

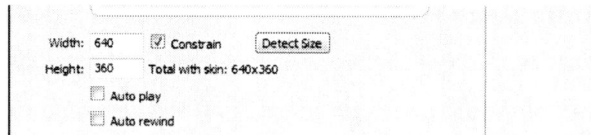

56 Check **Auto rewind**. Click OK.

Dreamweaver inserts the video placeholder and the Properties panel displays properties of the video that can be changed:

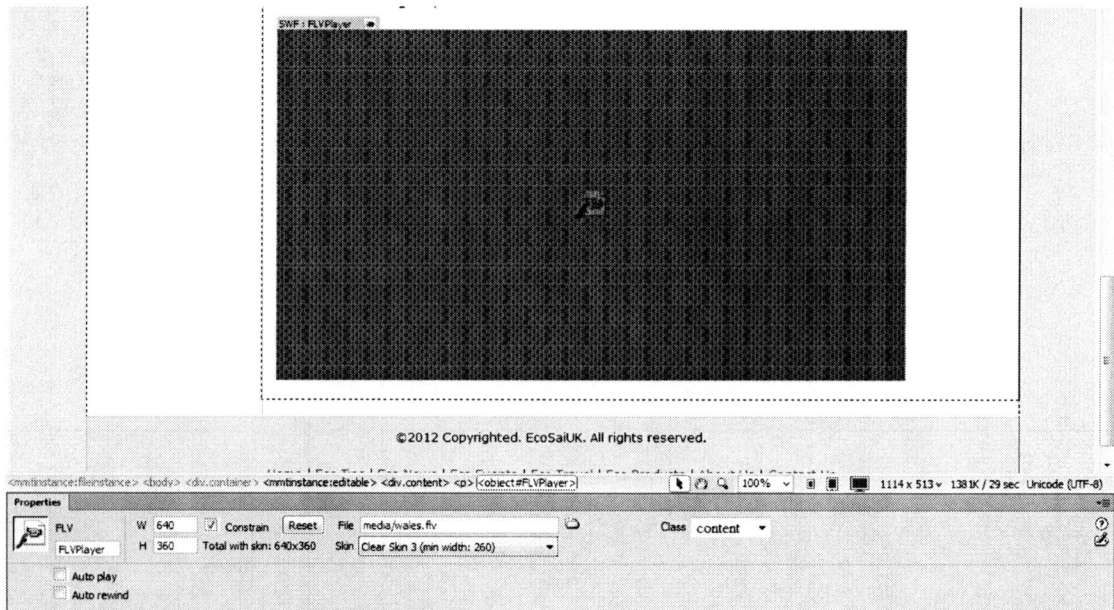

Videos cannot be played in Design view unlike SWF files and need to be previewed in a web browser or in Live View.

57 Preview the page in Live View and play the video. Well done.

Embed videos from YouTube

Embedding videos from YouTube is a simple process despite the fact that it requires for you to work in the Code View.

58 Open YouTube website and find the video that you want to use.

59 When the page with the video opens, click on **Share** button below the video as shown here:

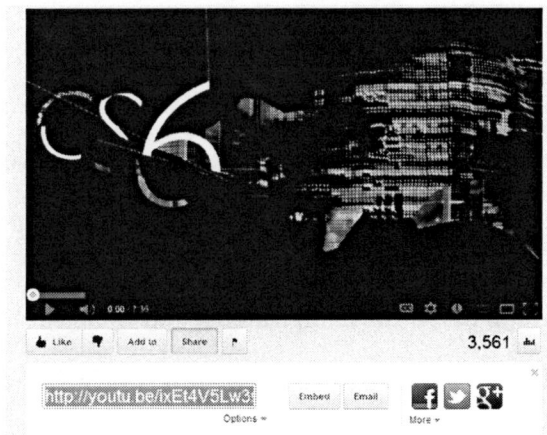

60 Next, click on **Embed** button next to the link that appears below the video:

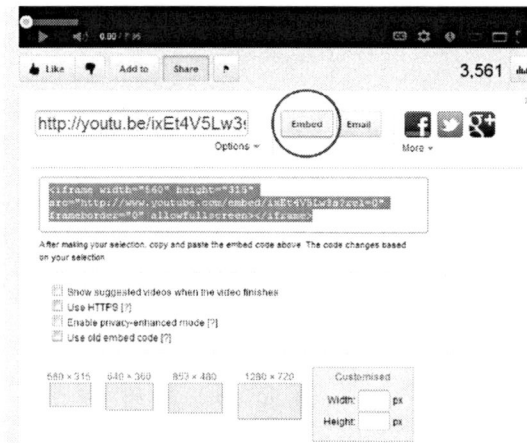

61 Now the code will appear below the Embed button and it will be highlighted, as shown in the previous screenshot. Copy it to the clipboard.

NOTE: You can change the dimensions of the video that will appear on your page by clicking on one of the boxes below:

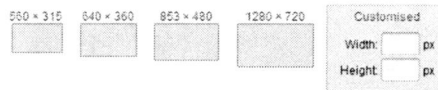

62 Back to Dreamweaver, create new page from a template and save it as **products.html**.

63 Replace main heading with **Eco Products**.

64 Highlight the paragraph below the main heading and change it to **Watch our video of the our products showcasing what we manufacture and how our products change people's lives.**

65 Go to Split View and place the cursor after the paragraph you have just typed as shown here:

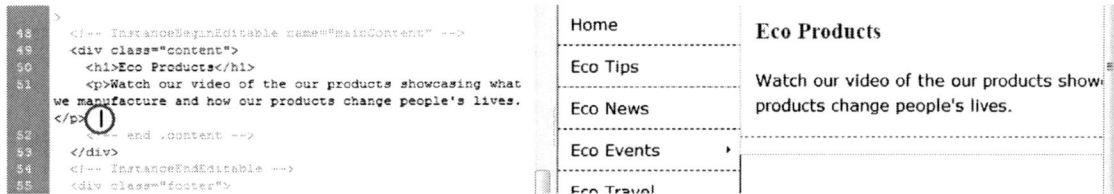

66 Paste the code for the video from the clipboard (you can use **Edit > Paste** or **Ctrl+V/ Cmd+V**)

67 Navigate back to Design View and you will now see the placeholder for video on the page.

NOTE: If the video doesn't align with the rest of the page on the left, put the video inside a paragraph.

68 Preview the page in a web browser and enjoy watching the video!

69 Close the page.

Congratulations! You have successfully finished the next lesson.

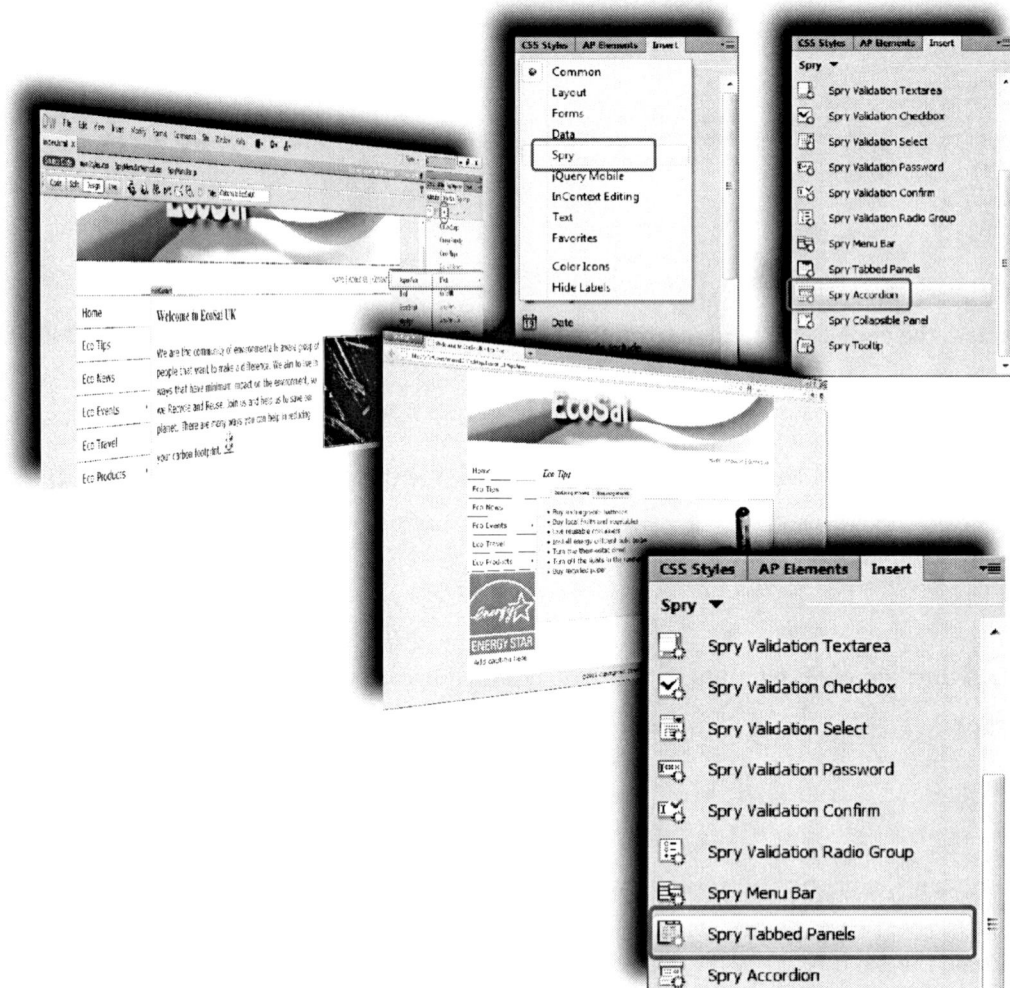

Lesson 11

Spry

In this lesson you're going to learn how to implement Spry into your website and how to:

- add Spry Accordion

- customise Spry Accordion with CSS

- add Spry tabbed panels

- add Spry Effects

This lesson will take about 1 hour 15 minutes to complete.

What is Spry?

The **Spry** (Spry Framework) is an open source Ajax framework developed by Adobe, and it is used in creating Rich Internet Applications. Spry is a JavaScript framework. What differs Spry from other JavaScript frameworks is that it has been developed with web designers, not web developers in mind. Adobe developed Spry because other Ajax frameworks were quite complex and hard to understand.

Because Spry was designed with web designers in mind, anyone with a bit of experience with Dreamweaver can create Rich Internet Applications. Spry uses what you already know: HTML and CSS, maybe a bit of JavaScript as well. Spry is a set of JavaScript libraries, that need to be included when testing and exporting to the web server.

There are three main Spry categories:

- **Spry Effects, i.e. Slide, Fade**

- **Spry Widgets, i.e. Accordion, Tabbed panels**

- **Spry Data, using data to populate the page, i.e. XML**

In this lesson, you will learn how to use the first two Spry categories. The good news is, when adding Spry elements to your pages, no plug-ins are required because it's JavaScript and HTML/CSS.

1 Launch Adobe Dreamweaver CS6, if it is not already open.

2 Define a new Dreamweaver Site and call it **11 – Spry**.

3 In the Local Site Folder field, click on the folder icon to the right and navigate to the Lesson_11 folder containing the files for this lesson.

4 Select Lesson_11 folder, and click Open (Windows) or Choose (Mac). Then, click Select (Windows) or Choose (Mac) to choose this folder as your local root folder.

5 Go to Advanced Settings tab and define the images folder that can be found inside Lesson_11 folder.

6 In the Site Setup dialogue box click Save.

7 Choose **File > Open** and open the template. You're going to insert a drop-down menu into the sidebar.

Spry Accordion

Spry Accordion is a widget (a part of Dreamweaver, you will find it in the Insert panel, or under Insert menu), and it is a page element combining HTML, CSS, and JavaScript.

Spry Accordion is a set of panels that collapse with the content of one of the panels visible at one time. Thanks to that, you can store a lot of content in a small amount of space. The content in the accordion is revealed or hidden by clicking on the tab of the panel.

The panels of the accordion expand and collapse in an animated fashion to reveal the content. The example here shows the Accordion widget with one of the panels expanded:

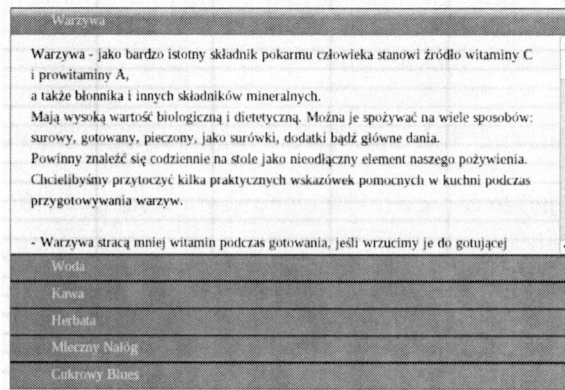

For a Spry Accordion to work you need two files (copied for you automatically by Dreamweaver, when you save and preview the page):

- **SpryAccordion.js (JavaScript file),**

- **SpryAccordion.css (CSS file).**

8 Open **news.html** if it's not already open. That's the page you're going to work with.

9 Insert the cursor into the heading **Most of World's cities...** and highlight it. Cut it to the clipboard (Ctrl+X on Windows, Cmd+X on Mac).

NOTE: Cut the heading to the clipboard instead of copying it because you're going to move it into the Accordion.

10 With your cursor blinking in the line, insert the Spry Accordion by clicking on Spry Accordion button in the Insert panel (Spry category):

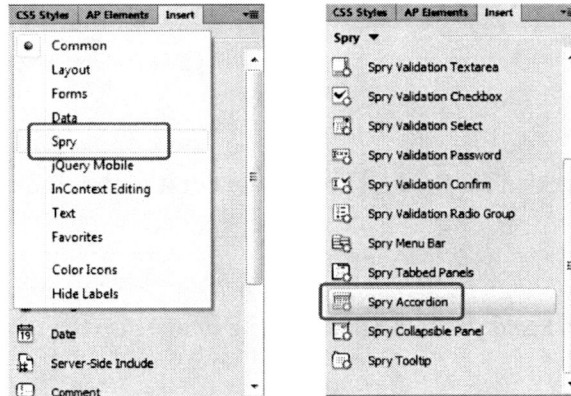

11 Dreamweaver inserts the Accordion on the page that looks initially like this:

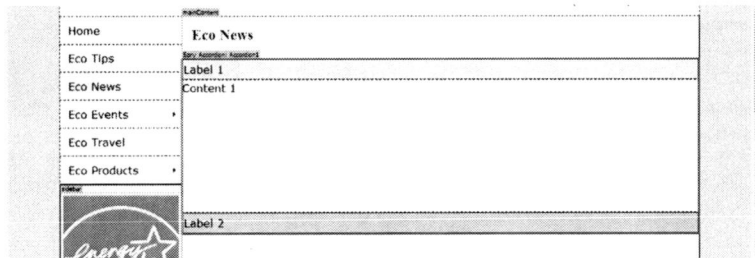

Initially, Spry Accordion has two panels and this will be fine in this situation as you have two articles on the page. The Accordion has two main parts:

- **Spry Accordion Tab**

- **Spry Accordion Content**

12 Highlight **Label 1** and paste the text from the clipboard:

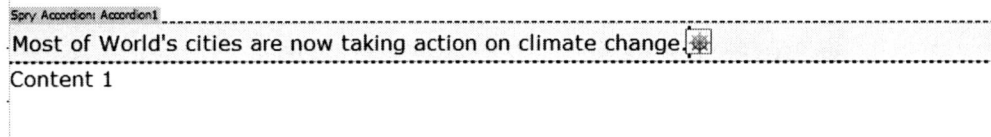

Spry Accordion: Accordion1

Most of World's cities are now taking action on climate change.

Content 1

13 Select the entire section for the first article and cut it to the clipboard as well, include the image.

14 Highlight **Content 1** and paste the text and the image into the Accordion:

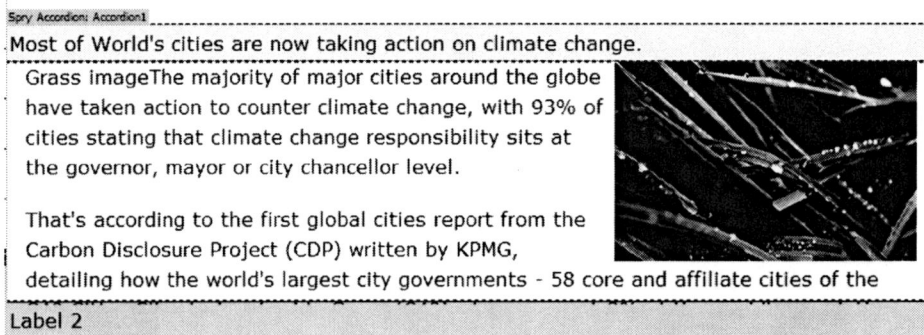

Spry Accordion: Accordion1

Most of World's cities are now taking action on climate change.

Grass imageThe majority of major cities around the globe have taken action to counter climate change, with 93% of cities stating that climate change responsibility sits at the governor, mayor or city chancellor level.

That's according to the first global cities report from the Carbon Disclosure Project (CDP) written by KPMG, detailing how the world's largest city governments - 58 core and affiliate cities of the

Label 2

15 If you get the text Grass image appear inside the Accordion, you'll need to remove it.

16 Go to the Code View and remove Grass image text:

```
53     <div id="Accordion1" class="Accordion" tabindex="0">
54       <div class="AccordionPanel">
55         <div class="AccordionPanelTab">Most of World's cities are now taking action on climate change.</div>
56         <div class="AccordionPanelContent">
57           <p><img src="images/grass.jpg" alt="Grass image" width="250" height="167" class="fltrt" >Grass imagee majority of
       major cities around the globe have taken action to counter climate change, with 93% of cities stating that climate change
       responsibility sits at the governor, mayor or city chancellor level.</p>
```

17 Go back to Design View and the text will disappear.

18 Save and preview the page in your web browser of choice.

19 You will see a dialogue box displaying files that Dreamweaver is going to copy into your site for the accordion to work properly. The screenshot here shows the dialogue box:

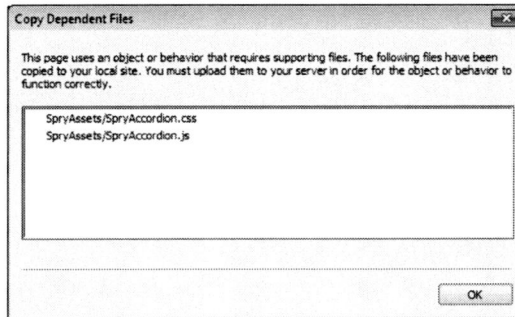

20 Just accept it and Dreamweaver will copy the files into the **SpryAssets** folder (if the folder doesn't exist, Dreamweaver will create it).

21 Back in Dreamweaver, select the accordion by clicking on the cyan tab with the name **Spry Accordion: Accordion1**.

22 In the Properties panel, click on **Label 2** as shown here, to display the second accordion:

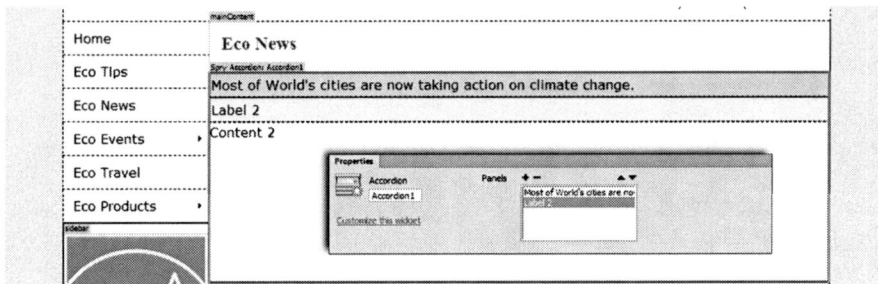

23 Repeat the steps to add content to the second accordion.

24 Save the page and preview it in a web browser.

You have completed both panels, now it's time to customise the accordion with CSS. Remember that the Accordion has its own stylesheet, so you're going to work with **SpryAccordion. css**.

Customise Spry Accordion with CSS

Now that the accordion is inserted on the page, it is time to start customising it.

25 Open the page in **Split View**.

26 Look at the top of the document window to see what file displays in the Code. It needs to be **SpryAccordion.css**:

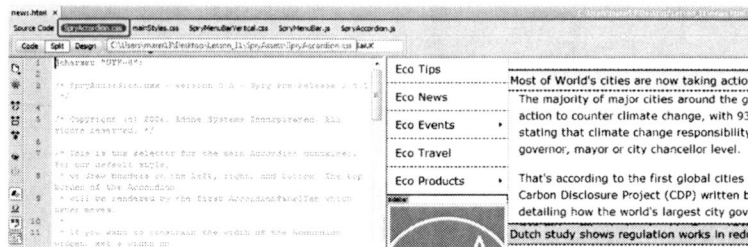

Every Spry stylesheet is heavily commented by Adobe so you will find it easier to start customising it. You're going to do most of the work in Split View in this exercise.

27 Start with the tabs. Find **.AccordionPanelTab** rule and change the background colour:

```
.AccordionPanelTab {
    background-color: #09C;
```

28 This changes the colour of the tab that's closed. Now change the background colour of the open tab by changing this rule:

```
.AccordionPanelOpen .AccordionPanelTab {
    background-color: #09C;
}
```

29 Now both tabs will have the same blue background.

30 Navigate back to .AccordionPanelTab rule and add a new line that reads:

```
color: #FF0;
```

31 This changes the colour of the text to yellow and your rule should now look like this:

```
.AccordionPanelTab {
    background-color: #09C;
    color: #FF0;
```

32 It's time to make the accordion narrower. Edit .Accordion rule and add this line:

```
.Accordion {
    width: 90%;
```

33 Now give it 20px padding on the left to align it with the rest of the content by adding this line below:

```
margin-left:20px;
```

34 For rollover effect, you'll make the text bold. Edit **.AccordionPanelTabHover** rule:

```
.AccordionPanelTabHover {
    font-weight: bold;
    color: #FF0;
}
```

35 Add the same properties to the next rule, so the open and closed tabs will get bold when you place the cursor over the tab:

```
.AccordionPanelOpen .AccordionPanelTabHover {
    font-weight: bold;
    color: #FF0;
}
```

Well done! Now the tabs are blue with yellow text and the text on the tab goes bold when the cursor goes over it. Just a bit more CSS.

36 Move the text in the tab 20px to the left by adding padding on the left. You can now use the CSS Styles panel, go back to Design View and edit .AccordionPanelTab rule:

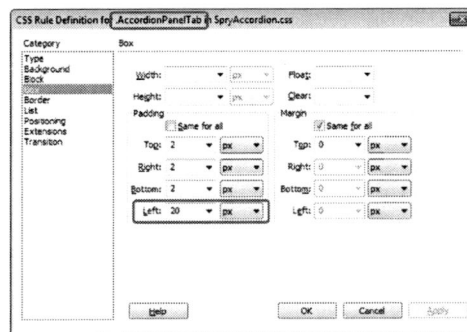

Congratulations! You have performed some customisation of the accordion. If you have more time, you can explore some additional options for customising the accordion.

Spry tabbed panels

Spry tabbed panels are another example of a space-saving element or widget placed on a web page. It is a widget with a series of tabs at the top of the widget and when you click on one of the tabs, the content appears. In a Spry tabbed panel widget, only one panel opens at a time.

In this part of the lesson, you're going to add a Spry tabbed panel to EcoTips page.

37 Start by opening **tips.html**. Place your cursor at the beginning of the line that reads **Eco Living at home** and press Enter to move it to the next line.

38 Navigate to the Insert panel and choose **Spry Tabbed Panels**:

39 The Spry tabbed panels widget appears on the page with two tabs.

40 Highlight the first tab and change it to **EcoLiving at home** (you can cut and paste from the heading).

41 Repeat the last step for the second tab so it reads **EcoLiving at work**:

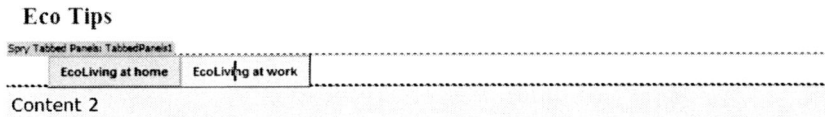

Eco Tips

Spry Tabbed Panels: TabbedPanels1

| EcoLiving at home | EcoLiving at work |

Content 2

42 Highlight the entire section for the first panel (the entire first list) and cut it to the clipboard.

43 Place your cursor over the first tab and when you see the eye icon, click on it to see the content for the panel - it should read **Content 1**.

44 Back in the panel, highlight the text that reads Content 1 and replace it with the list from the clipboard:

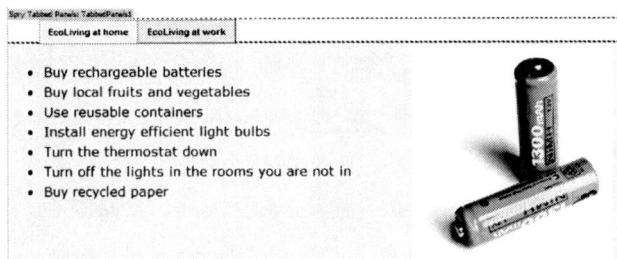

Spry Tabbed Panels: TabbedPanels1

| EcoLiving at home | EcoLiving at work |

- Buy rechargeable batteries
- Buy local fruits and vegetables
- Use reusable containers
- Install energy efficient light bulbs
- Turn the thermostat down
- Turn off the lights in the rooms you are not in
- Buy recycled paper

45 Repeat the same steps for the second panel.

46 Save and preview the page in a web browser.

47 When prompted to copy dependent files, click OK:

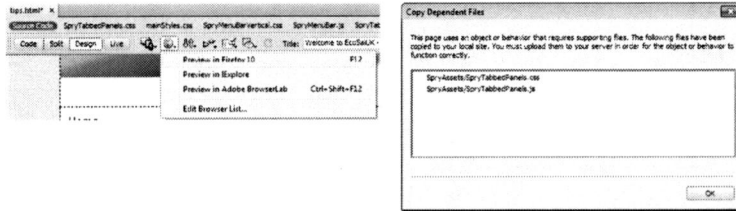

48 Now you can see beautiful tabbed panels in a web browser:

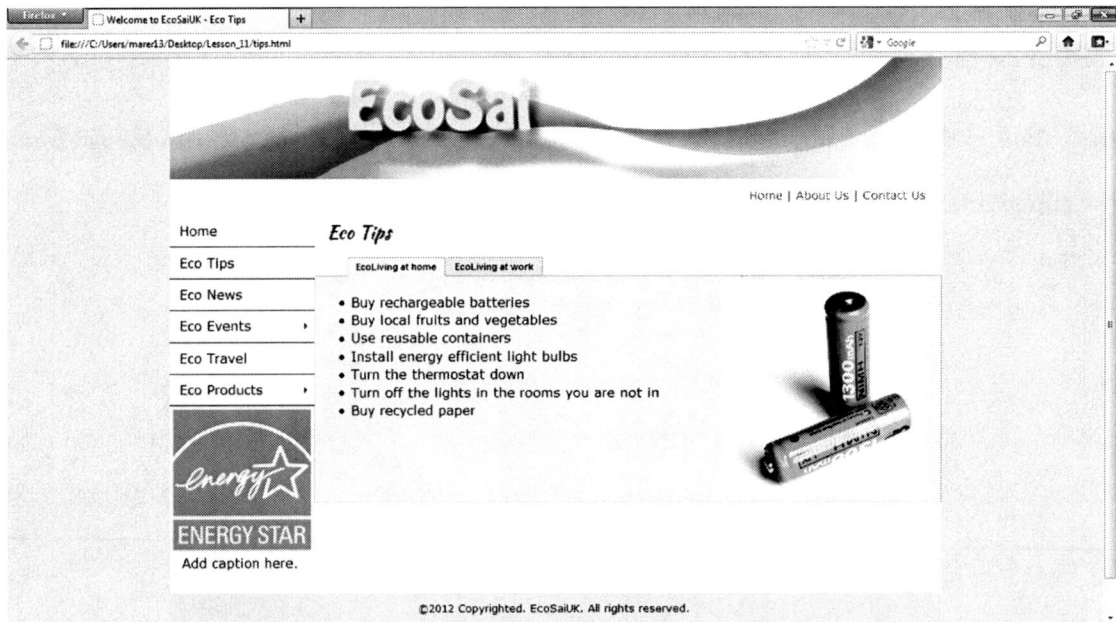

49 Test the panels and notice how the panel expands to fit all the content. Spry tabbed panels widget doesn't have width defined, it expands to fit the content.

50 If you want to customise the widget, edit **SpryTabbedPanels.css**:

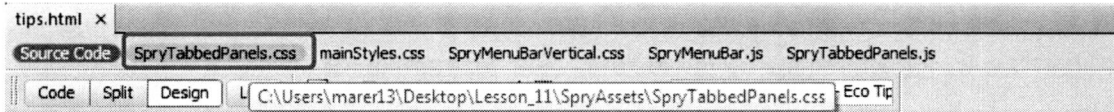

51 If you want to add additional tabs, highlight the widget by clicking on the cyan tab that reads **Spry Tabbed Panels: TabbedPanels1** and use the plus sign (+) in the Properties panel to add any extra tabs:

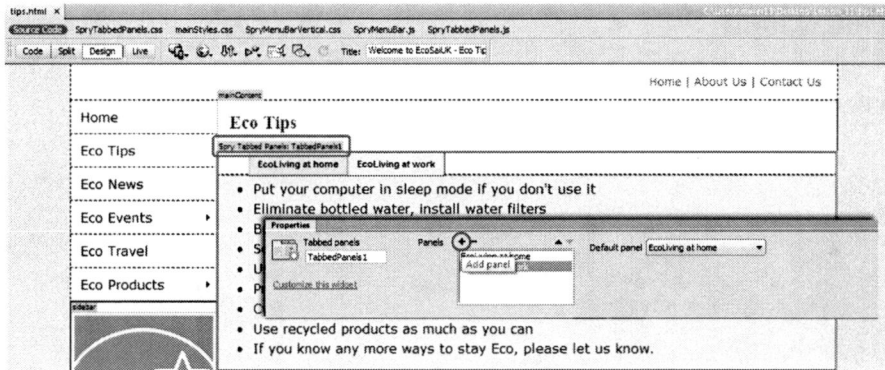

Spry effects

Here's what you're going to do now. You're going to add one of the Spry effects to animate an image so that it fades in when the page loads. And you're going to achieve that without Flash as Spry effects use JavaScript, and you don't need to know any JavaScript for that! How great is that? The image will require no interaction, it will load automatically and it will nicely fade in on a page.

To add Spry effects, you'll need to open a new panel called Behaviors because the Spry effects are basically JavaScript behaviours built into Dreamweaver. For a nice visual effect, you're going to animate an image on a home page.

52 Open **index.html**.

53 Open Behaviors panel by choosing **Window > Behaviors**:

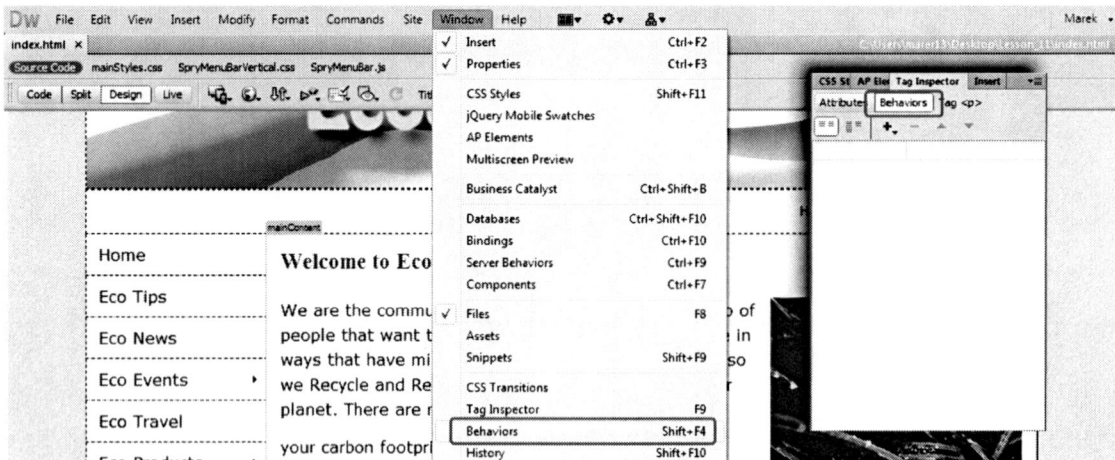

54 After the Behaviors panel opens, select the image on the page, the image of the grass on the right side of the page.

55 In Behaviors panel click the plus sign and choose **Effects > Appear/Fade** as shown here:

56 In the **Appear/Fade** dialogue box change the effect to **Fade** and click OK:

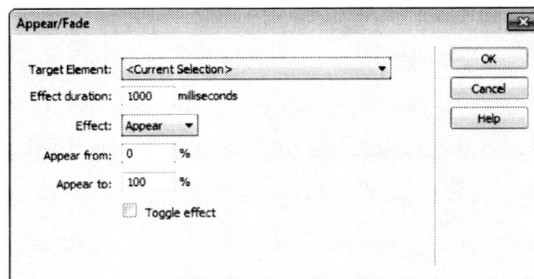

57 Look in the Behaviors panel and notice the effect that appeared. The default behaviour is **onClick**, so you need to click on the image to animate it.

58 Save the page. Accept **Copy Dependant files** dialogue box.

59 Test it in the Live view. As you click on the image, it fades in.

Looks great, but how about changing it so that the image fades in automatically as the page loads? This would look much better. And it's actually really simple.

60 Navigate to the Behaviors panel and click on **onClick**.

61 From the drop-down menu choose **onLoad**:

62 Save and test the page in Live View or a web browser.

Now it looks great. I think the animation is a bit too fast. If you think so too, let's change it.

63 Back to Behaviors panel, double click on the behaviour to edit it.

64 Change Effect duration to **4000 milliseconds**. This will be 4 seconds.

65 Save and test the page.

66 If required, change the effect duration again. Play with it.

This is just one example of using **Spry Effects** on web pages. Explore some additional effects if you wish.

Congratulations! You have successfully accomplished another lesson! Now it's time to create an online form.

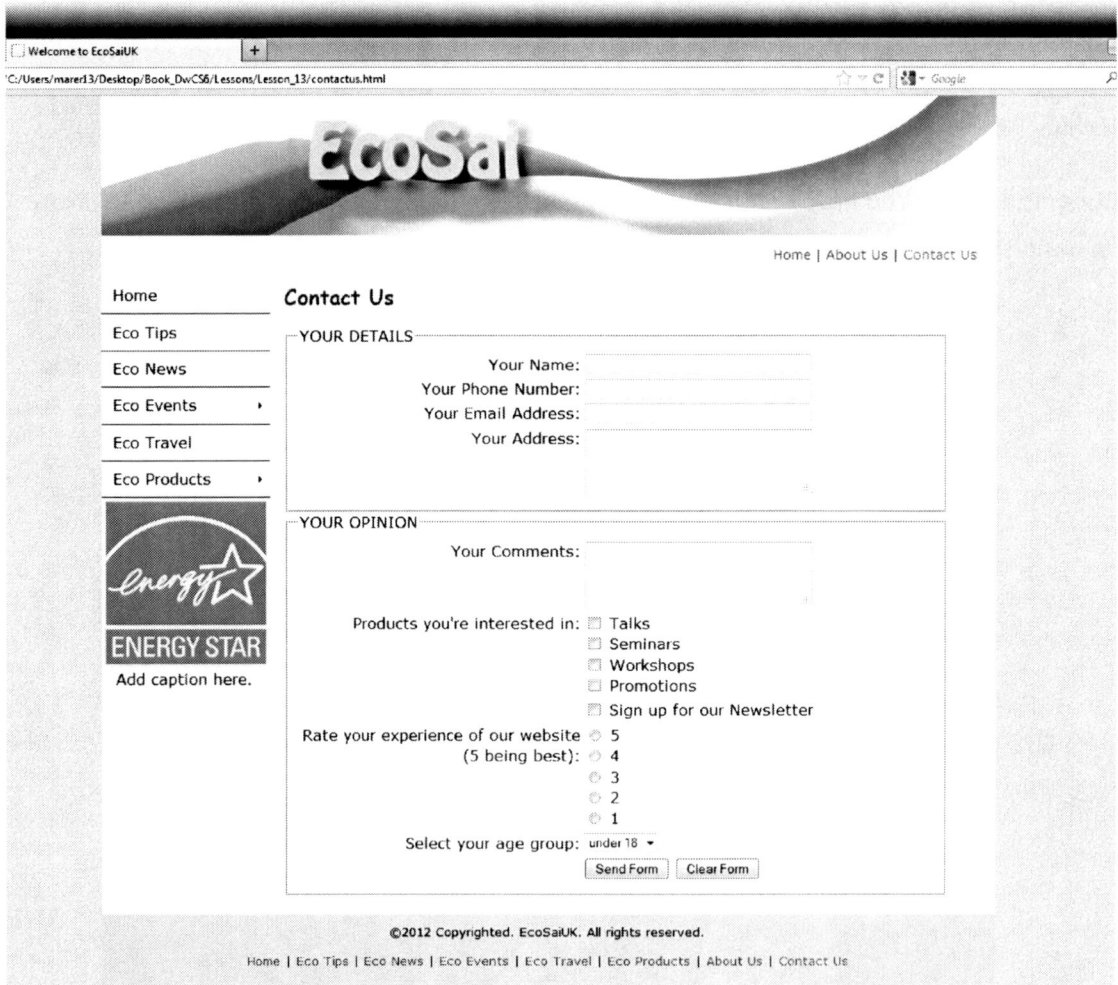

Lesson 12

Forms

In this lesson you're going to learn how to be more productive and how to:

- insert a Form

- insert text fields, radio buttons, check boxes

- insert drop-down menus

- insert buttons

- process form with PHP

This lesson will take about 1 hour 15 minutes to complete.

Online Forms

You may have come across the forms online before. Forms are interactive elements online that are usually used to gather some information from the visitors. It is like a form on paper, where you fill in some information about yourself, i.e. your details, comments etc. The form elements, fields, are used to gather the information from your visitors. Unlike with the paper forms, online forms can be easily changed/updated before the visitor sends it by simply resetting/clearing the form.

You can create a web form in Dreamweaver very easily by simply inserting form elements within the form element. The harder part is developing mechanism to handle the data when the visitor submits the form. Typically, web forms would be handled by web technologies like ColdFusion or PHP, and in this lesson you are going to use PHP to handle the form you are about to create.

There are a number of form elements and you are going to get to know them as you start inserting elements one by one. But first, you're going to define a new Dreamweaver site and create a new page.

1 Launch Adobe Dreamweaver CS6, if it is not already open.

2 Define a new Dreamweaver Site and call it **12 – Forms**.

3 In the Local Site Folder field, click on the folder icon to the right and navigate to the Lesson_12 folder containing the files for this lesson.

4 Select Lesson_12 folder, and click Open (Windows) or Choose (Mac). Then, click Select (Windows) or Choose (Mac) to choose this folder as your local root folder.

5 Go to Advanced Settings tab and define the images folder that can be found inside Lesson_12 folder.

6 In the Site Setup dialogue box click Save.

7 Open **contactus.html**.

All the form elements need to be contained within the form element, so you are going to insert the form element first. If you insert one of the fields outside the form element, the field will not be submitted with the form.

8 Place the cursor below the main heading.

9 Navigate to the Insert panel and change the category to **Forms**.

10 In the Insert panel click on the **Form** icon to insert the form element:

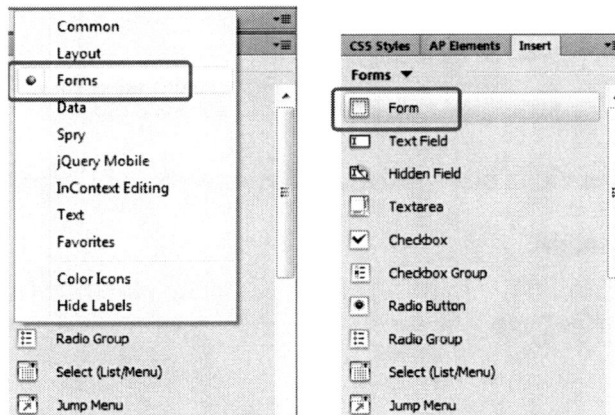

The form element is indicated by the red dashed line on the page. You are going to style the form a bit with some CSS, so now you're going to give the form element its own unique ID.

11 In the Properties panel you should find the **Form ID** in the top left corner. Type in **ecoForm**.

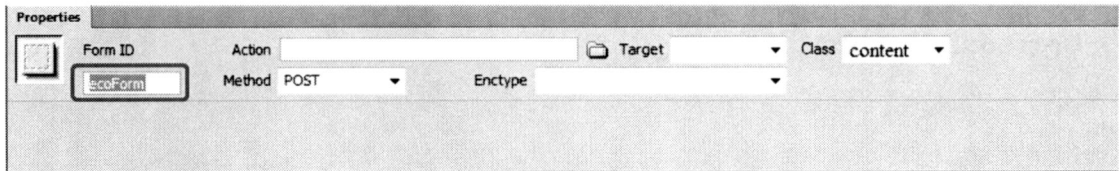

12 Let's add some margin to the form. You're going to align it with the heading. Create new CSS Rule:

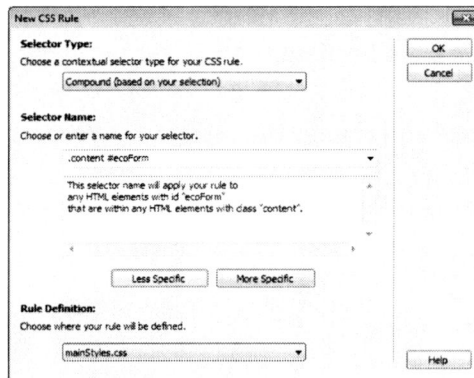

13 In the CSS Rule Definition dialogue box, in Box category, add **15px margin on left** and **50px margin on right**.

14 Click OK and save the page.

Text Form elements

Now it's time to start adding text form elements, i.e. text fields, text areas etc. Text fields are basic elements used to gather information from the visitors to your website. It is hard to imagine a form without any text form elements. You're going to start with text fields and then text areas.

Text fields are basically fields that accept letters and numbers and you can limit the number of characters. But just before you insert the text field, you're going to insert a Fieldset first to create a logical group of form elements. After the Fieldset has been inserted, you're going to see a border around the elements that will go inside the Fieldset and the Fieldset also has a Legend that will display on the top.

15 Place the cursor inside the form element and insert a **Fieldset** from the Insert panel:

16 When prompted for **Legend**, type **YOUR DETAILS** and press OK.

Now you are going to insert a table inside the Fieldset. It's going to be easier to use Code View first.

17 Navigate to the Code View and place the cursor after closing tag for Legend.

18 Back to Design View, insert a table using **Insert > Table** menu.

19 Set the Table to **3 rows**, **2 columns**, Table width **90%**, Border **0**, and Header **None**. Press OK.

20 Place the cursor in the first row in the right column and insert a Text Field. Set ID to **name** and Label to **Your name:**. Press OK:

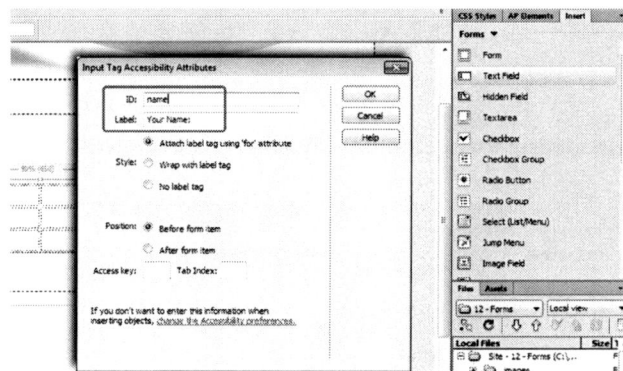

NOTE: ID field will be used to process the form, hence no spaces and all lowercase. Label will appear on the page so you can use any characters you want.

NOTE: When inserting a Text Field, leave Style set to Attach label tag using 'for' attribute, as this allows you to move the two elements and keep them linked together.

21 Highlight the label on the page and drag it to the left column as shown here:

Contact Us

YOUR DETAILS
Your Name:

22 Repeat the steps for the next row inserting another **Text Field,** but this time set ID to

phone and Label to **Your phone number:**.

23 Once again drag and drop the label to the left column.

24 Select the first text field and using the Properties panel set the element's width using

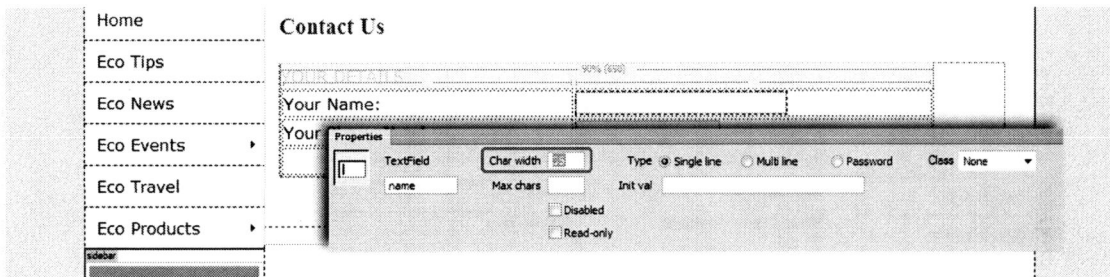

Char width to **35**:

Home	Contact Us
Eco Tips	
Eco News	Your Name:
Eco Events ▸	Your
Eco Travel	
Eco Products ▸	

Properties

TextField Char width 35 Type ⦿ Single line ○ Multi line ○ Password Class None ▾

name Max chars Init val

☐ Disabled

☐ Read-only

25 Apply the same to the second text field, so that they have the same width.

26 Limit number of characters that can be entered into Phone Number text field by setting

Max chars, i.e. in Britain all phone numbers are 11 digits long, so I'm setting it to 11:

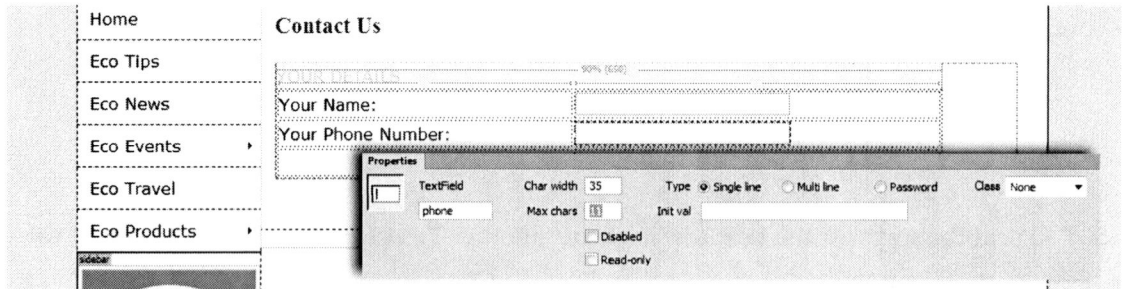

27 Save the page and preview it in Live View:

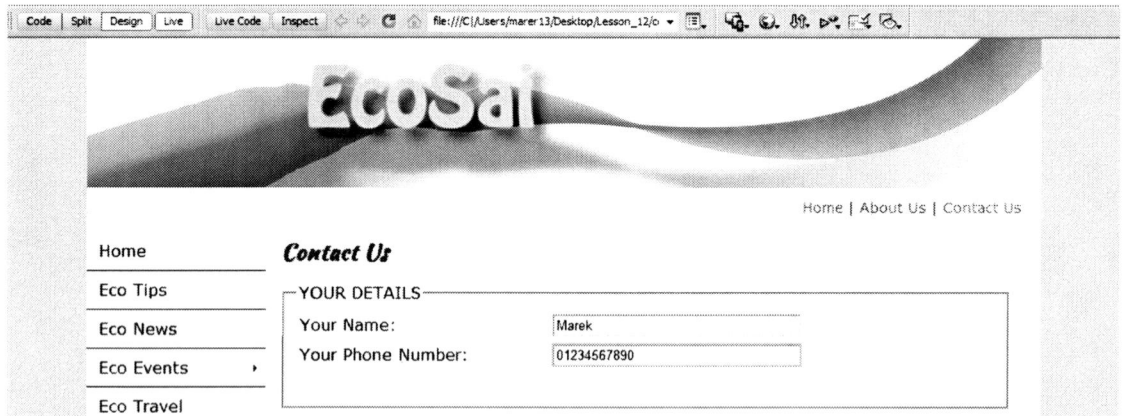

Notice that as you type numbers into Your Phone Number text field, only a limited number of digits appears. Well done! One more text field here.

28 Exit the Live View and insert one more **Text field** in the row below.

29 Set ID to **email** and Label to **Your Email Address:**. Press OK.

30 Repeat previous steps to move the label to the left column and set the width of the Text Field to **35 characters**.

Now you're going to customise the table with some CSS. You're going to create two new CSS classes for both columns inside the table.

31 In the CSS Styles panel create a new CSS class and call it **leftColumn**.

32 Give it a **Width of 50%** and set **Text-align** to **right**. Set **Vertical-align** to **top**. Press OK.

33 Select the left column and apply **leftColumn** class to it as shown here:

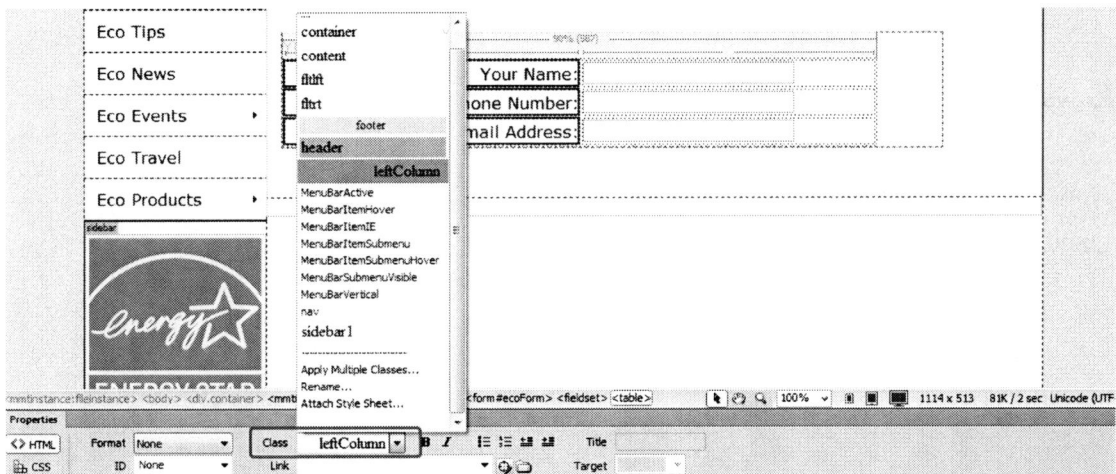

34 Create one more CSS class and call it **rightColumn**.

35 Give it a **Width of 50%** and set **Text-align to left**. Set **Vertical-align to top**. Press OK.

36 Apply the newly created class to the right column.

37 Save the changes and preview the page (you can use Live View):

Contact Us

```
┌─YOUR DETAILS──────────────────────────────────────────┐
│              Your Name: [                            ] │
│      Your Phone Number: [                            ] │
│      Your Email Address: [                           ] │
│                                                        │
└────────────────────────────────────────────────────────┘
```

One more form element will go into this Fieldset – a Text Area element for address.

38 Place the cursor inside the last row in the table, right-click and choose **Table > Insert Rows or Columns...**

39 In the **Insert Rows or Columns** dialogue box set Insert to **Rows**, Number of rows to 1, and Where to **Below the Selection**. Press OK.

40 In the new row that appears below the existing rows insert a **Text Area**:

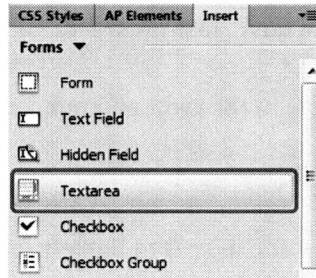

41 Give it an ID of **address** and Label **Your Address:**. Press OK.

42 Drag and drop the label to the left column.

43 Select the Text Field and set its height – **Num lines to 3** and **Char width to 30** or something around it.

44 Save and test.

The first section of the form, the first Fieldset is done. Now the second Fieldset, where you will ask your visitors about their comments and opinions.

45 Place your cursor before the closing tag for the first Fieldset (you may want to use Split view/Code view) and press Enter on the keyboard in Design view to add some space.

46 Insert another Fieldset and set the Legend to **YOUR OPINION**.

47 Go to the Split view and find the code for the Legend.

48 Place your cursor after closing tag for Legend, go back to Design view and insert a Table.

49 Accept the last settings for the table, just press OK.

50 Place the cursor in the first row in the right column and insert a **Text Area**. For ID type **comments**, for Label **Your comments:**.

51 Highlight the label on the page and drag it to the left column.

52 Assign classes **leftColumn** and **rightColumn** to the columns inside the table like you did earlier.

53 Select the Text Field and set its height – **Num lines to 3** and **Char width to 30** or something around it.

Now you're going to add a Radio Group and a Checkbox Group. The main difference between the Checkbox Group and Radio Group is that with Radio Group the visitors will only be able to select one of the options, whereas with Checkbox Group they can select as many as they want. You are going to insert both elements.

54 In the next row, in the right column as usual, insert a **Checkbox Group**:

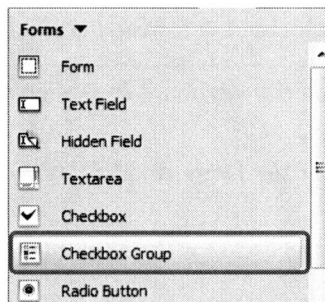

55 You're going to use the Checkbox Group for products/services your visitor may be interested in. Add the following values:

Label	Value
Talks	**talks**
Seminars	**seminars**
Workshops	**workshops**
Promotions	**promotions**

56 Rename the Checkbox Group to **CheckboxGroupProducts** and press OK.

57 In the left column type **Select products you're interested in:**.

58 Save and test the page in either Live view or in a web browser.

What you may have now is a slight indent in the right column before the checkbox group. If you do, we'll fix it now. It looks like the checkbox group ended up being inside the paragraph, so your job will be now to remove the paragraph.

59 Go to Split View or Code View and find the code for the checkbox group:

```
<tr>
          <td class="leftColumn">Products you're interested
in:</td>
          <td class="rightColumn"><p>
        <label>
          <input type="checkbox"
name="CheckboxGroupProducts" value="talks"
id="CheckboxGroupProducts_0" />
          Talks</label>
        <br />
        <label>
          <input type="checkbox"
name="CheckboxGroupProducts" value="seminars"
id="CheckboxGroupProducts_1" />
          Seminars</label>
        <br />
        <label>
          <input type="checkbox"
name="CheckboxGroupProducts" value="workshops"
id="CheckboxGroupProducts_2" />
          Workshops</label>
        <br />
        <label>
          <input type="checkbox"
name="CheckboxGroupProducts" value="promotions"
id="CheckboxGroupProducts_3" />
          Promotions</label>
        <br />
      </p></td>
    </tr>
```

60 Notice the opening and closing **<p>** tag in the code. That's what needs to be removed. Remove opening and closing **<p>** tag in the code.

61 Save and preview the page. It should look fine now.

Now you're going to add another form element - a checkbox to let people sign up for your newsletter.

62 In the next row, insert a Checkbox:

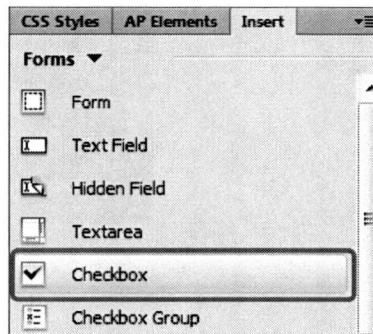

CSS Styles	AP Elements	Insert	▾≡

Forms ▾

☐ Form

☑ Text Field

☒ Hidden Field

☐ Textarea

☑ **Checkbox**

☷ Checkbox Group

63 Set ID to **signup** and Label to **Sign up for our Newsletter**.

64 Select the Checkbox on the page and make sure that Initial state is set to **Unchecked** (in Properties panel).

You shouldn't force users to sign up for newsletter (or similar offers) automatically, they should make informed decision and check the box if they want to sign up. Unfortunately many websites fail at this, maybe on purpose, and force users to uncheck it if they don't want to receive any newsletters/emails.

Now, you're going to add a radio group element to ask your visitor to rate their experience on the website. The reason why you're inserting a radio group is because with the radio group your visitor will only be able to choose one option. Selecting another option will deselect the previous selection.

65 Add another row using the method you learnt earlier and insert a **Radio Group**:

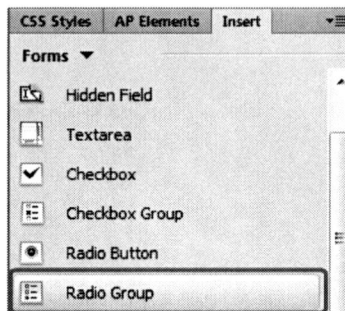

66 In the **Radio Group** dialogue box change the name to **RadioGroupRating**. Set Labels and Values to **5, 4, 3, 2**, and **1**.

67 Press OK to insert the Radio Group.

68 In the left column type **Rate your experience of our website (5 being best)**.

69 If once again the group of buttons appears to be indented, repeat earlier steps to remove the <p> tag.

70 Save and preview the page.

71 Place your cursor in the last cell in the table and press the Tab key on your keyboard to add another row.

Now you're going to add a drop-down menu to the form. The element you're going to add is **Select (List/Menu)** element. **Select (List/Menu)** element displays entries in a drop-down menu format. Where Lists differ from Menus is that with the Lists you can allow users to select multiple items instead of just a single one as is the case with the Menu.

72 Place your cursor in the right column in the last row of the table and insert **Select (List/Menu)** element using the Insert panel:

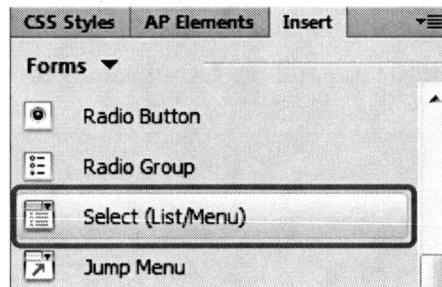

73 In the **Input Tag Accessibility Attributes** dialogue box type **ageGroup** in ID field, leave the Label field empty, and set Style to **No label tag**. Click OK.

An empty menu appears on the page. Now you're going to add entries through the Properties panel.

Rate your experience of our website ○ 5
(5 being best): ○ 4
○ 3
○ 2
○ 1

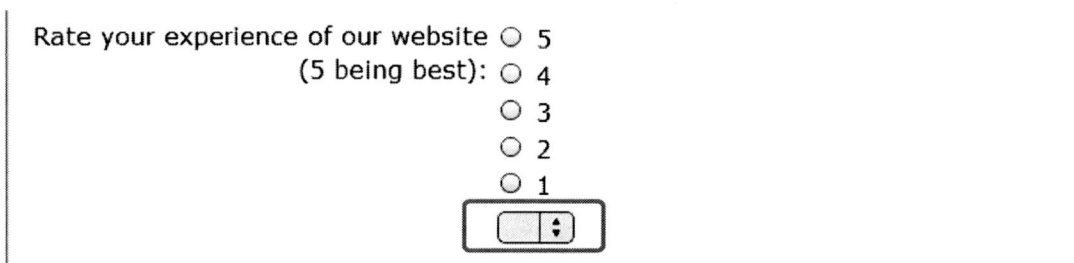

74 Highlight the menu element on the page.

75 In the Properties panel click on **List Values** button:

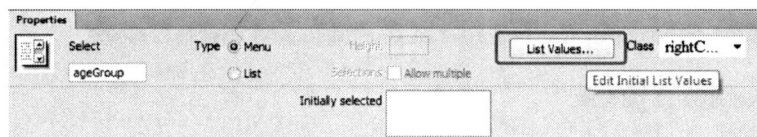

76 In the **List Values** dialogue box add the **Labels** and **Values** as shown here:

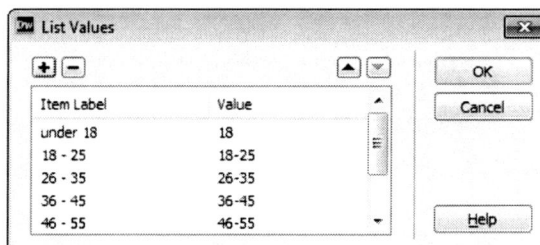

77 In the column next to the Menu type **Select your age group:**.

78 In the Properties panel you can choose what's going to initially display in the menu by highlighting it in the options next to Initially Selected. Highlight **under 18**.

It is time to add a button that will submit the form. Place the cursor in the last row and add another one by pressing the Tab key on your keyboard.

79 In the Insert panel click on the **Button** icon:

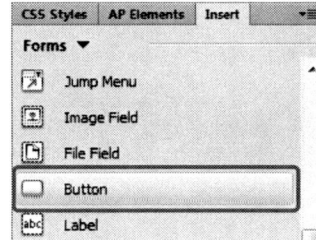

80 Type **submit** for ID and click OK.

The Submit button appears at the bottom of the form and the Properties panel displays the properties of the button. Button's Value is set to Submit and that's what displays on the button on the page. You're going to change it now.

81 Change the Value field in the Properties panel to **Send Form**:

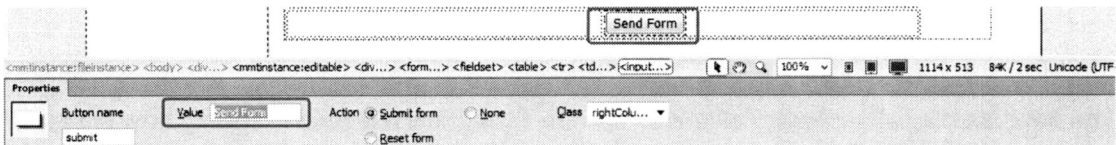

You need another button here, one that resets the form so that a visitor could start over if they make a mistake.

82 Insert space after the Submit button and then insert another button, this time giving it an ID of **reset**.

83 Change the Value field in the Properties panel to **Clear Form**.

84 Set the Action in the Properties panel to **Reset form**:

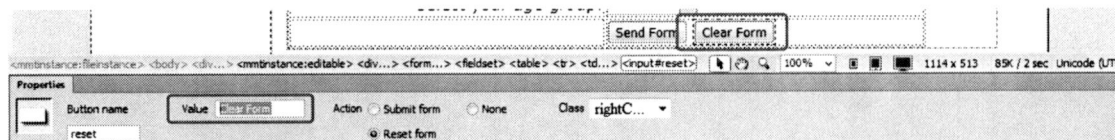

85 Save the page and preview it.

You're almost done. Now it's time to make the form work. Now you're going to specify the action for the form to be processed.

Process form with PHP

You have inserted all necessary elements into the form, now it is time to specify how the form is going to be processed. A typical example, and easy to accomplish, would be to send the form data by email and that's what you're going to do now.

By now you may be thinking about typing mailto command into the Action field (with the entire form selected).

However, you need to keep in mind that many people won't have email clients installed on the machines they use to access your website, so you're going to use PHP to process the form and have it sent by email to you. And the visitor won't even know that! Pretty clever.

Inside the folder containing this lesson you have got included a file **sendresults.php**. You're going to use it in this exercise. This is the file that is going to process the form and send it via email.

86 Back to the page in Dreamweaver, highlight the entire form and in the Properties panel you will see the **Action** field. Next to it, you'll find a folder icon:

87 Click on the folder icon and in the Select File dialogue box select **sendresults.php**. Click OK.

88 Save and close contact page.

Now you're going to edit the sendresults.php for form processing. There are only a few things to change, so don't be scared. You can do it even if you have no experience in programming.

89 Choose **File > Open**, and open **sendresults.php**.

90 If the file opens in Design View, you won't see anything. Switch to **Code View**.

There are only four lines of code that need to changed, actually just three near the top of the page.

91 To make this work, you need to upload your website to the server, so I'll just show you what to change (highlighted in bold and underlined):

```php
<?php
//-------------------------Set these
paramaters-------------------------

// Subject of email sent to you.
$subject = 'Insert a subject here';


// Your email address. This is where the form information will be
sent.
$emailadd = 'info@web.com';


// Where to redirect after form is processed.
$url = 'http://www.web.com/formsent.html';


// Makes all fields required. If set to '1' no field can not be
empty. If set to '0' any or all fields can be empty.
$req = '0';


// -------------------------Do not edit below this line---------
-----------------
```

NOTE: Email needs to be on the same server as the website, i.e. if you have a website www. ecosaiuk.com, the email will need to be info@ecosaiuk.com or contact@ecosaiuk.com.

92 To finish the lesson you can create a "Thank you" page and point the PHP file to the page, so it opens when the visitor clicks Submit button.

93 Since you are not uploading the website to the server in this lesson, when the "Thank you" page was created, change the Action for the form to this page.

94 Save the page and preview it.

Congratulations! You have successfully completed another lesson. Well done.

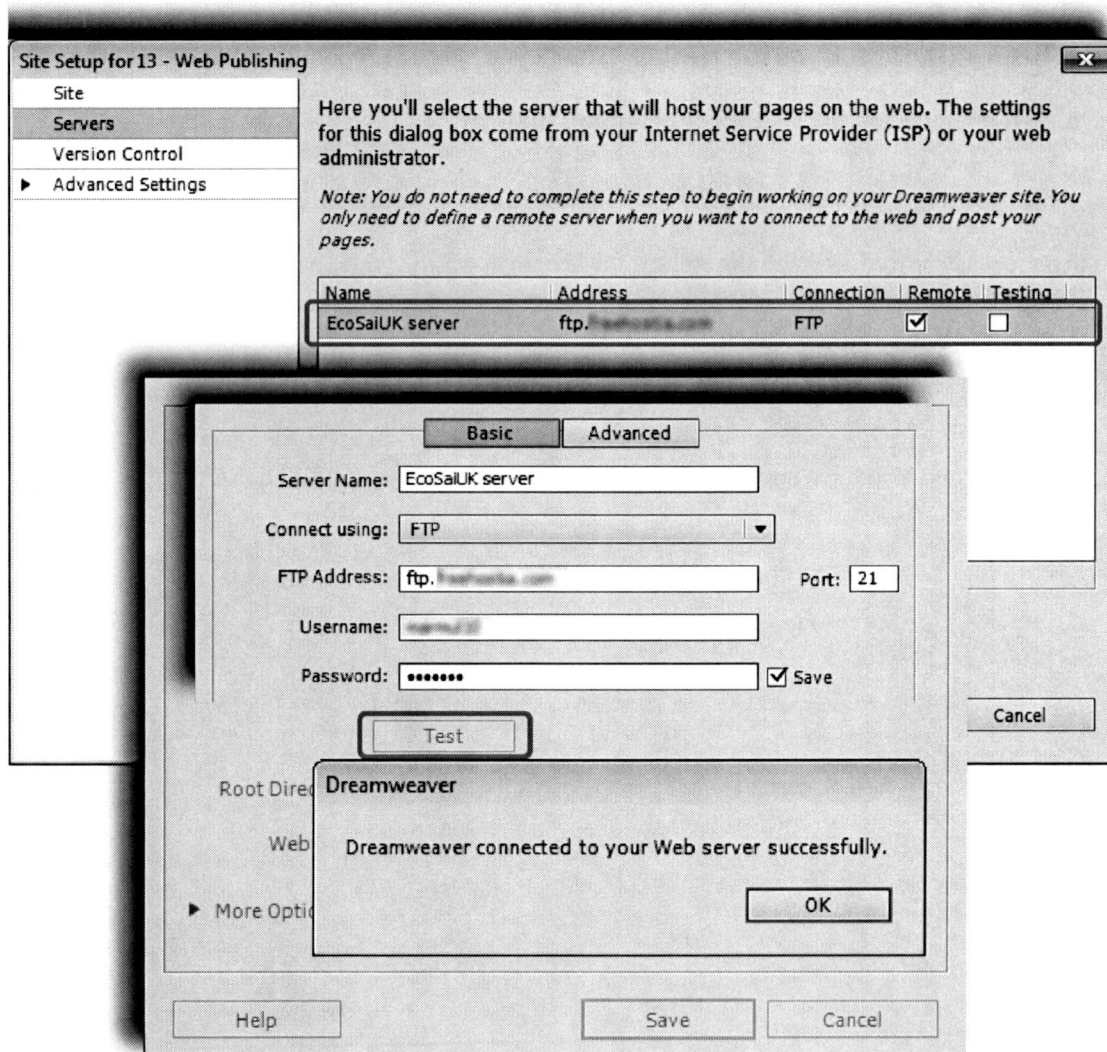

Lesson 13

Publish your website

In this lesson you're going to learn how to be more productive and how to:

- define a remote site

- upload files to the server

This lesson will take about 30 minutes to complete.

Define a remote site

So far you have been working locally on your machine, a local site as it is called in Dreamweaver - a local version of the website. Now, it is time for a remote site - a remote/live version of the website on server, server being another computer connected to the internet.

1 Launch Adobe Dreamweaver CS6, if it is not already open.

2 Define a new Dreamweaver Site and call it **13 – Web Publishing**.

3 In the Local Site Folder field, click on the folder icon to the right and navigate to the Lesson_13 folder containing the files for this lesson.

4 Select Lesson_13 folder, and click Open (Windows) or Choose (Mac). Then, click Select (Windows) or Choose (Mac) to choose this folder as your local root folder.

5 Go to Advanced Settings tab and define the images folder that can be found inside Lesson_13 folder.

6 In the Site Setup dialogue box click Save.

Now, you're going to add a server connection. To do that, you need to edit your site definition.

7 Navigate to the Files panel and double-click on the name of the site to open **Site Setup** dialogue box.

NOTE: Alternatively you can use the menu **Site > Manage Sites**, and then double-click on the site.

8 In the Site Setup dialogue box click **Servers** category as shown here:

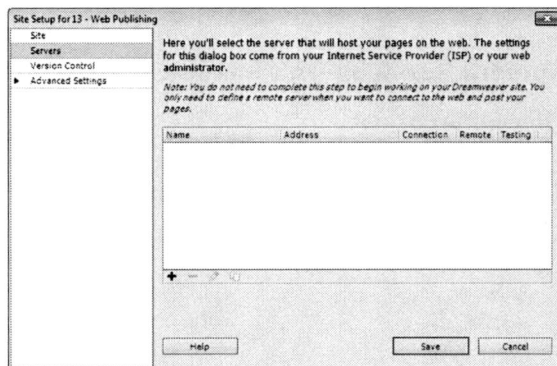

9 Click the **Add New Server icon** (plus symbol) and in the **Server Name** field type **EcoSaiUK** server.

To connect to the server, Dreamweaver allows you to use one of the many methods:

FTP - File Transfer Protocol - this is the most popular, standard method for connecting to the web server.

SFTP - Secure File Transfer Protocol - this is a newer method for connecting in a more secure manner.

Local/Network - this is usually used when the web pages are first uploaded to a local server, and then upload to the web server online. This kind of connection can be used to use a testing server without uploading files to the web.

RDS - Remote Development Services - this was developed by Adobe for ColdFusion and is used to work with ColdFusion websites.

WebDav - Web Distributed Authoring and Versioning - this is a web based system known as Web Folders or iDisk.

10 From the **Connect** using drop-down menu choose **FTP**:

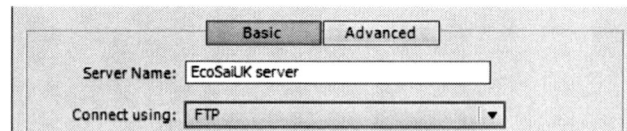

11 In the **FTP Address** field type the URL of your FTP server.

NOTE: If you use a hosting provider, most of us do, you will be provided with an FTP address. Enter the address as it was provided to you. Usually it is something like: ftp.ecosaiuk.org with the name of your site. Check with your hosting provider.

12 In the **Username** field type your FTP username.

13 In the **Password** field type your FTP password.

NOTE: Make sure you type the username and password exactly as they were provided to you as these are case-sensitive.

14 In the **Root Directory** field, type the name of the folder that contains your website - all the files that are made public on the web.

15 If you don't want to type your password every time you try to connect to the server, check Save option on the right.

NOTE: Don't do it if other people have access to your computer as this would allow them to upload/download anything to/from your web server.

16 Now you can click **Test** to see if Dreamweaver can connect to your server:

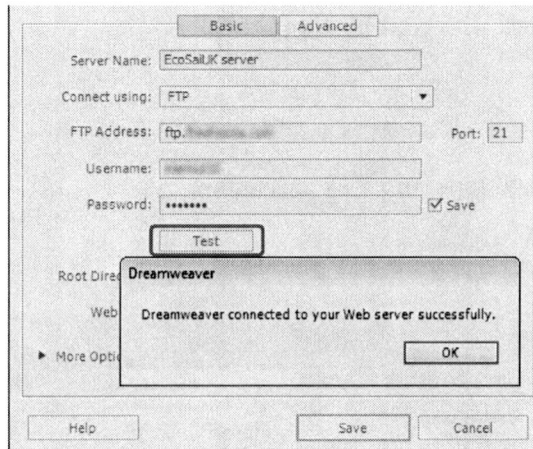

17 If Dreamweaver manages to connect successfully to your server you should see the message as on the last screenshot. Click OK.

18 Click Save to save all the server settings.

19 Now you will see your server in **Site Setup** dialogue box as shown here:

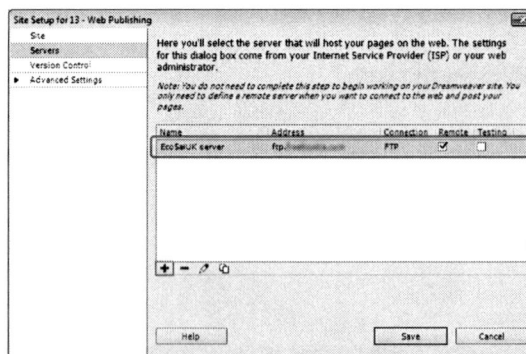

20 Click Save once again to save all the site settings and exit the Site Setup dialogue box.

21 If you see the dialogue box informing you that the cache will be recreated because of the change in the settings, click OK:

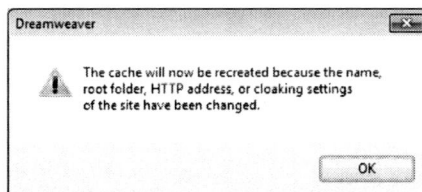

Dreamweaver

> The cache will now be recreated because the name, root folder, HTTP address, or cloaking settings of the site have been changed.

OK

Congratulations! You have successfully established a connection to your remote server.

Uploading your site

Now it is time for you to upload the files to the remote server to put them online. When you transfer files from your local site to remote site, you're putting files in Dreamweaver terms. Dreamweaver will put files into the equivalent folder on your remote site.

What's great about Dreamweaver is that you can upload one file as easily as the entire website in one session. I love this feature in Dreamweaver. When uploading the website to the remote site, Dreamweaver may ask you if you want to upload the dependant files - these will be files like images, CSS, scripting files, flash content etc.

NEW IN DREAMWEAVER CS6!

Now in Dreamweaver CS6 you can save time uploading larger files with the re engineered multithreaded FTP transfer tool. You can now upload site files faster and more efficiently to speed production time.

22 Navigate to the Files panel and click the **Expand** icon to activate Expanded panel mode:

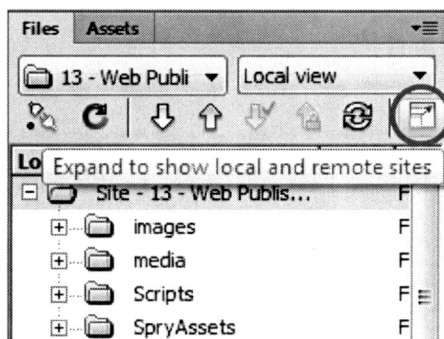

In the Expanded panel mode you will see the Files panel take over your entire screen and there will be two main columns: one for local site (Local Files) and one for remote site (Remote Server) as shown on the screenshot here:

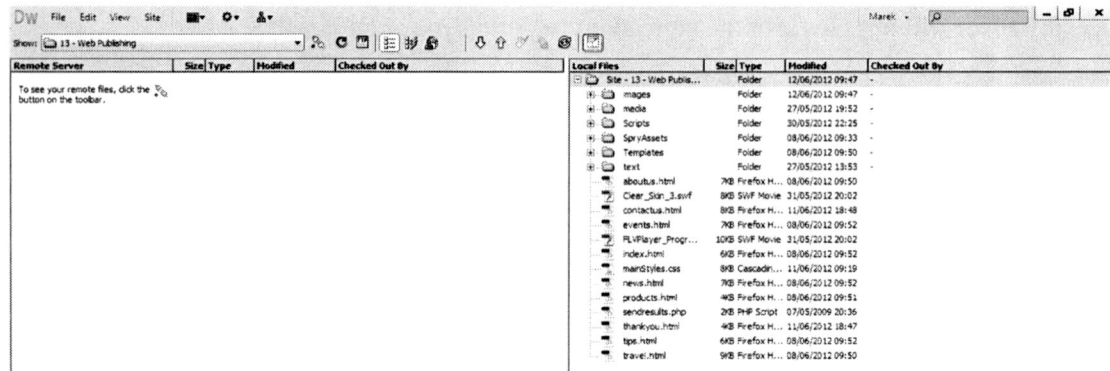

23 To connect to your server click on **Connects to Remote Host** icon:

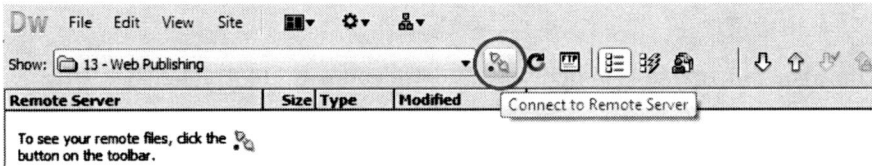

In just a moment you should be connected to your web server.

You can now start uploading the files. Here's what I normally do:

24 Close the Expanded view by clicking on the same icon you used to open it (you'll find it at the end of the bar with icons).

25 Back in document view in Dreamweaver, select one of the files in your site and click the **Put** icon:

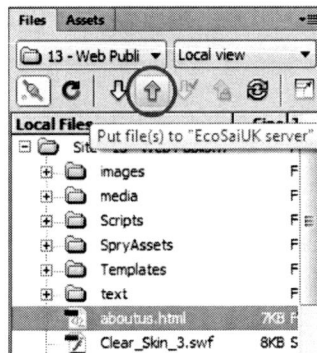

Because you are working with a fresh website, it is time for uploading the entire website.

293

25 In the Files panel, select the site folder, right-click on it and from the context menu choose **Put.**

26 The following dialogue box opens asking if you are sure you want to upload the entire site:

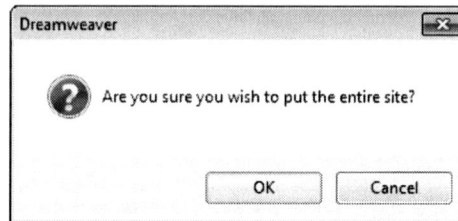

27 Click OK and Dreamweaver will start uploading the entire site.

Dreamweaver is now uploading all the files within your local site to the remote site (to the web server). Depending on how many files you have it may take just a few seconds or maybe a minute (or longer).

28 When Dreamweaver is finished uploading the files, open your web browser and test the website by typing the URL of your website.

Congratulations! You have designed and built an entire website and successfully uploaded your website to the web server. Well done!

Now you are ready to put your knowledge to practise and start creating websites for others.

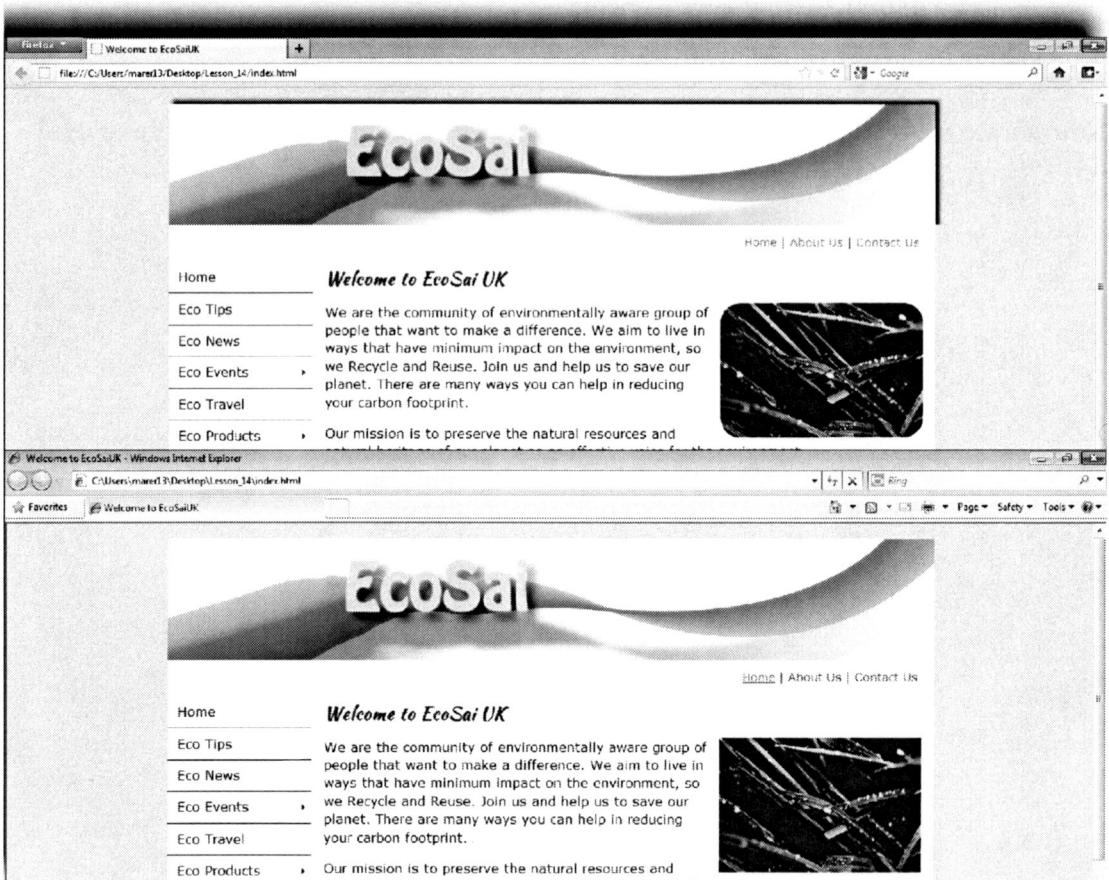

BONUS

Lesson 14

The Future of the Web - CSS 3

In this lesson you're going to learn the new features in the latest incarnation of Cascading Style Sheets - CSS3:

- CSS3 Borders with shadows

- CSS3 Multiple Backgrounds

- CSS3 Text Effects

This lesson will take about 1 hour to complete.

1 Launch Adobe Dreamweaver CS6, if it is not already open.

2 Define a new Dreamweaver Site and call it **14 – CSS 3**.

3 In the Local Site Folder field, click on the folder icon to the right and navigate to the Lesson_14 folder containing the files for this lesson.

4 Select Lesson_14 folder, and click Open (Windows) or Choose (Mac). Then, click Select (Windows) or Choose (Mac) to choose this folder as your local root folder.

5 Go to Advanced Settings tab and define the images folder that can be found inside Lesson_14 folder.

6 In the Site Setup dialogue box click Save.

As I was finishing this book, I thought it would be great to share with you the future of web design that is coming with the latest version of Cascading Style Sheets – CSS3. And I got so excited that I decided to add another chapter to the book! And here we go.

CSS3 specification is still under development by **W3C**, so many of the new features I am about to share with you won't work in every browser yet (actually they will work in all browsers but one, if you know what I mean...).

Many of the new CSS3 properties have already been implemented in modern web browsers like Firefox, Chrome and Safari.

So, let's get started!

CSS3 Borders

Now with CSS3 you can create borders with rounded corners and add shadows to boxes, without using images designed in Photoshop or Fireworks.

In this part of the lesson you're going to learn how to add rounded corners and shadows to the page using these two properties:

- **border-radius**

- **box-shadow**

Here's the browser support:

Firefox	**Chrome**	**Safari**	**Opera**	**IE**
4+	All	5+	10.5+	9

7 Open any of the pages within the website to get access to the stylesheet.

8 When the page opens, navigate to Split View or Code View.

9 First, you're going to move the website down a bit by adding some margin to the browser window.

10 Change the body rule so that it says:

```
body {
    margin: 20px 0;
```

11 Save and preview the page.

Now you will have 20px space between the top of the page and the browser window. Now it's time for rounded corners. You're going to add rounded corners to images.

13 Back in Dreamweaver, scroll to the bottom of the stylesheet and add a new CSS rule:

```
img {
```

14 After the curly brace, press Enter to move to the new line and start typing — and when the drop-down menu appears, choose **-moz-** :

```
161    font-size: 1px;
162    1  ◈ moz-
163    }     ◈ ms-
164    img {  ◈ o-
165          ◈ webkit-
              -
```

15 When the next drop-down menu appears, choose **border-radius** :

```
162    line-  ◈ border-end-width
163    }       ◈ border-image
164    img {   ◈ border-radius
165           ◈ border-radius-bottomleft   ▾
       -moz-|
```

This is the code for Mozilla Firefox. You need extra code for other browsers.

16 Add the following code below for WebKit and other browsers:

```
-webkit-border-radius: 25px;
border-radius: 25px;
```

17 Close the curly brace and test your page in one of the browsers that support this feature. Enjoy!

Notice the difference between Firefox 10 and Internet Explorer 8:

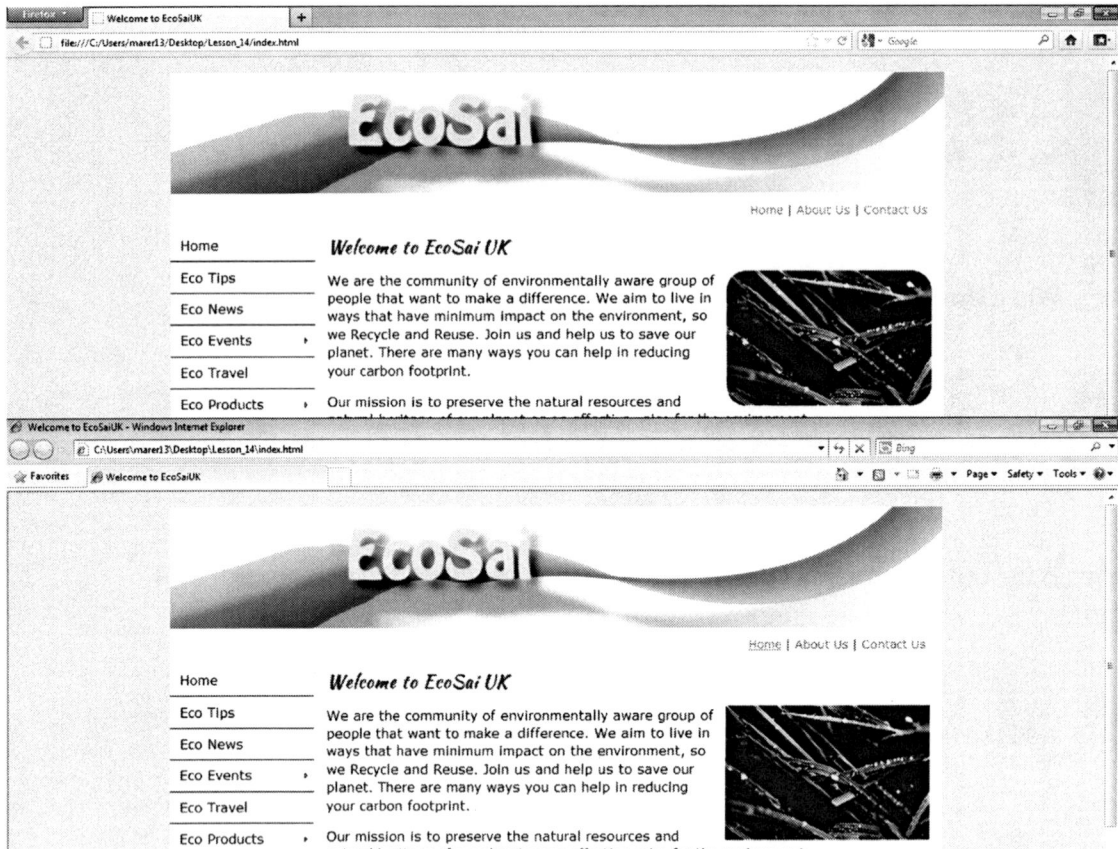

Now you're going to add a shadow behind the website.

18 Back to Dreamweaver, still in code, find the **.container** rule and add the following code:

```
-moz-box-shadow: 5px -5px 4px #333;
-webkit-box-shadow: 5px -5px 4px #333;
box-shadow: 5px -5px 4px #333;
```

Here are the four values for shadow:

offset-x   offset-y   blur-radius   colour

NOTE: Offset-y with a negative value creates a shadow on the top instead of the bottom

19 Save and test the page and enjoy the beautiful shadow behind your web page!

CSS3 Backgrounds

CSS3 has many new background properties that give you more control of the background. In this lesson, you're going to learn about one of the properties:

background-size

The background-size property specifies the size of the background image. In the past, the size of the background image was defined by the actual size of the image, but now in CSS3 you can specify the size of the background image in pixels or percentages.

NOTE: If you specify the size of the background image in percentages, the size of the image will be relative to the dimensions of the parent element.

Here's the browser support:

Firefox	**Chrome**	**Safari**	**Opera**	**IE**
4+	*All*	*5+*	*10.5+*	*9*

20 Back in code, in Dreamweaver, find the **body** rule.

You're going to modify it so that you will have two background images (the flower and the pattern you had so far), but only one of them will repeat (the pattern). Very impressive!

21 Change the background section of the **.body** rule so that it reads:

```
background-image: url(images/background.jpg);
background:url(images/flower.png), url(images/background.jpg);
-moz-background-size: 300px 268px, 104px 104px;
background-size: 300px 268px, 104px 104px;
background-repeat: no-repeat, repeat;
```

NOTE: Unfortunately you need to leave the first line for Internet Explorer, otherwise you won't see background in IE at all (unless IE 9).

Also, **-moz** prefix is used here for Firefox 3.6 and earlier. Later versions of Firefox as well as Chrome and Safari 5+ don't need prefixes.

CSS3 Text Effects

CSS3 has several new text features, you're going to focus on one of them:

text-shadow

As you may have guessed, text-shadow property applies shadow to the text.

Text-shadow property takes following values:

offset-x offset-y blur-radius colour

Text-shadow browser support:

Firefox	**Chrome**	**Safari**	**Opera**	**IE**
Yes	Yes	Yes	Yes	No

22 Back in Dreamweaver, find the **.footer** rule and add the following code:

```
text-shadow: 1px 1px 2px #333;
```

23 Save and preview the page in a web browser that supports CSS3.

That's it! As simple as that.

That's just a bit of CSS3 for you to get you hungry for more. There are many books on just CSS3 alone, so this is just an example of what you can accomplish with CSS3. Explore.

Congratulations! You have successfully finished the book. Well done.

Index

A

Adobe Bridge 144
AJAX 179
Assets panel 140

B

Behaviors 256
Browser List 48
Button 279

C

Checkbox 275
Checkbox Group 273
Code Navigator 92
Code View 28
CSS 50
CSS3 Backgrounds 304
CSS3 Borders 299
CSS3 Text Effects 306
CSS Box Model 214
CSS Starter pages 63
CSS Styles panel 53

D

Description tag 73
Design View 29
DocType 66
Domain Names 34
Dreamweaver interface 19
Dreamweaver templates 190
Drop-down menu 179

E

Editable regions 192
Edit images 154
Email links 176
Embed videos 237
External links 168
External stylesheet 206

F

Fieldset 265
File Formats 131
Flash animations 231
Flash Videos 234
Fonts 111
Form elements 265
Forms 262
FTP 288
FTP Address 288

G

GIF 131

H

Headings 106
HTML 38
HTML Structure 39
Hyperlinks 162

I

Internal links 165

J

JPEG 131

K

Keywords tag 74

L

Live Google Map 170
Local/Network 288

M

Media 224
Metadata 72
Mobile Devices 219
Multiscreen Preview 219

N

Naming conventions 68

O

Online Forms 262
Ordered/Unordered Lists 119

P

Page from Template 197
panels 20
Paragraphs 106
Photoshop 147
Photoshop Smart Objects 149
Plugin 226
PNG 132
Process form 280
Progressive download 235
Pseudoclasses 186

R

Radio Group 276
Raster graphics 128
RDS 288
Remote site 286
Responsive web design 64

S

Select (List/Menu) 277
Server 287
Servers 34
SFTP 288
Sounds 225
Split View 29
Spry 179, 242
Spry Accordion 243
Spry Accordion with CSS 248
Spry effects 256
Spry tabbed panels 252
Streaming video 235

T

Tables 121
Templates 190
Text Area 271
Text Field 266

U

Update Dreamweaver Templates 202
Uploading site 291

V

Vector graphics 128

W

WebDav 288
Web Fonts 112
Welcome screen 30
Widget Browser 170
Wireframing 84
workspaces 23

Lightning Source UK Ltd.
Milton Keynes UK
UKOW021129231112

202631UK00003B/20/P

9 780957 121454